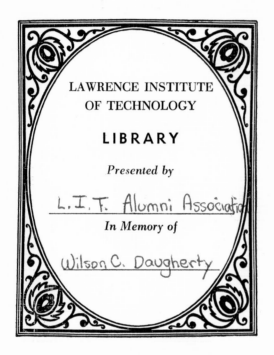

Crime, Detective, Espionage, Mystery, and Thriller FICTION & FILM

Crime, Detective, Espionage, Mystery, and Thriller FICTION & FILM

A COMPREHENSIVE BIBLIOGRAPHY OF CRITICAL WRITING THROUGH 1979

Compiled by
David Skene Melvin and Ann Skene Melvin

GREENWOOD PRESS
Westport, Connecticut •
London, England

Library of Congress Cataloging in Publication Data

Skene Melvin, David, 1936-
    Crime, detective, espionage, mystery, and thriller
fiction and film.

    Includes indexes.
    1.   Detective and mystery stories—History and
criticism—Indexes.   2.   Detective and mystery films—
History and criticism—Indexes.   3.   Spy stories—
History and criticism—Indexes.   4.   Spy films—History
and criticism—Indexes.   I.   Skene Melvin, Ann, joint
author.   II.   Title.
Z5917.D5S55   [PN3448.D4]   016.809'916   80-1194
ISBN 0-313-22062-X (lib. bdg.)

Library of Congress Catalog Card Number: 80-1194
ISBN: 0-313-22062-X

First published in 1980

Greenwood Press
A division of Congressional Information Service, Inc.
88 Post Road West, Westport, Connecticut 06881

Printed in the United States of America

10 9 8 7 6 5 4 3 2 1

Dedicated to
Joanne Harack Hayne
whose course at the University of Toronto
on "The Detective in Literature" led us
from merely reading crime literature for
enjoyment to studying the field and
whose name we hope may soon be
included in subsequent editions
of this bibliography,

and to
Terence Bishop
whose infectious enthusiasm for the
genre kept us buoyed up during its
compilation.

CONTENTS

ACKNOWLEDGMENTS

The compilers are thankful for and gratefully acknowledge the assistance of their onetime colleagues at both the University of Waikato Library and the Hamilton Public Library, both in Hamilton, New Zealand, and also wish to thank the staff of the Metropolitan Toronto Library, Toronto, Ontario, Canada, who cheerfully answered esoteric questions and uncomplainingly toiled back and forth between the enquiry desks and the stacks. The compilers also give their thanks and appreciation to all those correspondents around the world who gave so freely of their time replying to the compilers' questions and who provided the compilers with actual copies of material for inclusion. In addition, the compilers are grateful for the support of all kinds given by the family Simms. Last, but not least, the compilers also say thank you for your typing to Liz Conroy, Pam Edwards, and the people at Telephone Dictation Services Ltd.

INTRODUCTION

As to the future of the detective story . . . its acceptance as a dynamic literary form by scholars and historians cannot be much longer delayed . . . without doubt the laurels, and the professional chairs, will be accorded in equal strength to the leading exponents of detective fiction before the 21st century is far advanced. Scholars prefer historical perspectives to be undistorted, but always seem to take an unconscionable time to persuade themselves that what the common man enjoys may be intrinsically worthwhile and intellectually praiseworthy.

Eric Quayle. *The Collector's Book of Detective Fiction*. (London: Studio Vista, 1972), p. 121.

More reference books devoted to the mystery have been published in the past decade than in all the years before. At last, it seems, critics and scholars are abandoning the simplistic snobbishness of Edmund Wilson and similar critics who denigrated the genre. Almost every great writer of the past century has turned his hand to novels and stories of mystery, crime, suspense, espionage, or detection. It is arguably the most important literary development of the twentieth century, and has attracted many of the best writers at one time or another. It is serious literature, and it is about time that it be treated with the respect and dignity it deserves.

The editors (1975): "Introduction," *The Encyclopedia of Mystery and Detection*, 1976.

Crime in literature: the savagery of Medea, the villainy of Iago, the depravity of Moll Flanders, and its detection: the perception of Holmes, the doggedness of Inspector French, the psychological insight of Maigret, has always exercised a strange fascination upon readers.

There are only two kinds of writing: factual and imaginative. All imaginative writing is fiction and the question "When does fiction become literature?" is as unanswerable as "What is truth?" The cynical answer to the latter query is: "What the majority of the populace believe," and this reply can be paraphrased to answer the first question: "Literature is that fiction that the majority of the populace choose to accept as such." The term literature is one of those loaded words and connotes excellence, whereas fiction has pejorative overtones and often denotes second-class as intellectually snobbish librarians who separate their collections of imaginative writing into "Literature" and "Fiction" sections demonstrate. Literature in the classic definition of the word can be and has been written on the subject of crime and murder— witness Hugo's *Les Miserables*, Dicken's *Bleak House*, Dostoevsky's *Crime and Punishment*, Dreiser's *An American Tragedy*, Faulkner's *Sanctuary*. The theme runs through even Durrell's *Alexandra Quartet*. The fact that a novel's subject is crime, or specifically murder, does not necessarily mean that it is second-rate, that somehow it is "fiction" as opposed to "literature." Literature is merely fiction that has become immortal. Unfortunately, at the price of their own deprivation of pleasure and learning, too many intelligentsia and artsy-crafty *litterateurs*, and the gullible who allow themselves to be taken in by these intellectual snobs, cavalierly slough off crime literature. Granted that more second-rate, or worse, novels about crime tend to be published than about other aspects of society, this does not negate the fact that some excellent writing has been and is produced about this left-handed side of human endeavor.

In its broadest definition, literature can encompass all forms of imaginative writing (in fact, it may and sometimes does include factual writing as well), and it is with that meaning that we use it here. We are concerned with imaginative writing that deals with crime and, in a broader sense, with the traditions of human violence: crime literature. Consequently, we include criticism not only of novels, novellas, and short stories, but also of plays, poetry, comics, and film.

Acts against God are sinful, acts against society are immoral, and acts against the State are criminal. We have not been interested in true accounts of malefactors: brigands, robbers, bushrangers, dacoits, outlaws, thieves, thugs, hoodlums, gangsters, and other assorted rogues and scoundrels. As well, there are two areas of crime in literature we deliberately ignored: first, the outlaw as defined as a "badman" of the American West, i.e., the literary genre of the "Western"; and second, the medieval outlaw, e.g., Robin Hood. Temporally, we are post-picaresque and have endeavored not to detour into picaresque literature.

The word *criminal* is defined loosely to mean the professional violator of the law who practises his or her art regularly and who has certain skills and attitudes toward his or her work, though occasionally the amateur, especially in regard to murder, is recognized. The word *detective* is used to identify the person who in either a professional or an amateur capacity endeavors to bring law-breakers to justice.

Our definition of crime literature as a specific class is equally broad. The crime story, detective novel, espionage tale, murder mystery, thriller, call it what you will, is a legitimate mode for social comment and quite often an excellent source for social history.

Some purists will deplore a reference to comic books, but they are a form of writing and as such are a subspecies of literature, and some are concerned with crime; besides, the comics are the form in which appeared Dashiell Hammett's 'Secret Agent X-9,' and no study of the genre would be complete if it ignored that gentleman. His absence would be a serious lacuna in a study of his creator. This is not even to mention the cultural influence of comics. Anyway, we have a nostalgic fondness for the comics: our interest in heroes representing justice in pursuit of villians began with comics (we preferred Captain Marvel to Superman and liked Submariner; our favorite was The Phantom), progressed to the Hardy Boys, graduated to the pulps (we were fortunate to be around in their twilight, though we must confess that our primary interest at that time was science fiction—but that, as Kipling was wont to say, is another story), blossomed into a wholesale delight in detection, and has settled down into a true appreciation of this form of literary endeavor.

Broadly speaking, there are three basic categories of crime literature: the thriller, or suspense adventure; espionage; and the crime/detective/mystery novel. This last category breaks down into three more divisions: the classic tradition, the private eye, and the police procedural.

To start with what the British call the "thriller"—this is a tale of adventure and suspense that, though it may not pertain specifically to a crime or to espionage, certainly has crimes in a generic sense invariably committed throughout. It is most often the preserve of the amateur, who is more than likely to be an enmeshed innocent, and has a long tradition. Its origins go back to the picaresque novel. It grew up as the Victorian "penny dreadful and shilling shocker," and by this century it had become respectable. There are two distinct schools of thriller: the realistic and the fantastic; and the quality descends from the former to the latter. The realistic school of thrillers evolved from John Buchan to the best contemporary exponents: Hammond Innes, Desmond Bagley, Berkeley Mather, Gavin Lyall, and Geoffrey Jenkins. The heyday of the fantastic thriller is the period spanning from E. Phillips Oppenheim, Bulldog Drummond, and the jejune and puerile Sexton Blake, through Sam Rohmer's Fu Manchu to Ian Fleming's James Bond novels.

The second class is espionage. Often it blends with the thriller, but in its purest form its exemplars are Eric Ambler's novels of the late 1930s and Len Deighton's chronicles of his unnamed narrator. The proto-spy novel is Erskine Childer's *The Riddle of the Sands* and the bench mark is Somerset Maugham's fictionalized account of his work as a British agent during World War I: *Ashenden*.

Lastly, there is the crime novel, encompassing detection, crime and mystery. This began with Edgar Allan Poe's short stories about the Chevalier August Dupin, was kept alive by Wilkie Collins's *The Moonstone*, and burst into maturity with the entry of the Master—the immortal Sherlock Holmes. The stage was now set for the proliferation that flowered in the twentieth century.

Above, we mentioned three subdivisions of this third class: the classic tradition, the private eye, the police procedural. The classic tradition is the puzzle mystery, the "whodunit," the tale of pure detection and ratiocination, usually featuring a well-meaning amateur, and it flowered in full bloom in the 1920s. Of all the list perhaps the best known and best remembered are Dorothy L. Sayers's Lord Peter Wimsey, Dame Agatha Christie's Hercule Poirot and Miss Marple, Rex Stout's Nero Wolfe, and Ellery Queen's himself.

The private eye is an American invention. This subspecies grew out of the turn-of-the-century Nick Carter stories that in turn had grown out of the earlier dime novels and was nurtured and developed in Captain Shaw's *Black Mask Magazine* during the 1920s and 1930s. The hardboiled private eye variety followed two roads—one downhill to the excesses of Mickey Spillane, and the other upward to some of the finest writing in the whole genre: Dashiell Hammett, Raymond Chandler's saga of Philip Marlowe, and the superb contemporary work of Ross Macdonald.

Finally, we have the police procedural: this the form best known in Europe where as the *roman policier* it has always been more popular than the other types. These are the novels portraying the regular police and concentrating on police methods. In the United States there are the 87th Precinct novels of Ed McBain; in Britain the grotesqueries perpetrated by John Creasey; and on the Continent the outstanding *roman policiers* of psychological insight and humaneness of Georges Simenon presenting Inspector Jules Maigret, and of the husband and wife team of Per Wahloo and Maj Sjowall about Martin Beck of the Stockholm Police Homicide Bureau.

The genre has proliferated, and besides whodunits there are why-dunits, how-dunits, and novels written from every point of view from the detective to the murderer to the victim. It is to facilitate the study of the genre that we compiled this bibliography of material dealing with the history, background, and development of crime literature.

In keeping with the scope of our study, we cast our net equally as wide (and resultingly, brought in some very strange fish indeed) and caught over 1,600 items from 25 countries representing 16 national literatures in 18 languages (including English). The mesh was of a middling size and as many good-sized herrings, red and otherwise, swam safely through as were caught.

We might have subtitled this compilation: "Gaps, Ghosts, and Garbage." "Gaps" there most certainly are as there are a number of basic sources that have not yet been thoroughly surveyed. We hasten to point out one: this bibliography is *not* an index to *The Armchair Detective*. The omission was deliberate on our part. To have indexed *The Armchair Detective* would have stretched the bibliography beyond manageable proportions. *The Armchair Detective* requires an index of its own and we leave it to some enterprising person to produce one.* There are articles from *The Armchair Detective* listed but only when they have been cited elsewhere. We salve our conscience by recommending *The Armchair Detective* to all interested, for whatever reason, in crime, detective, espionage, mystery, and thriller literature. "Ghosts" there may possibly be since despite all attempts at verification some entries may be incorrect. "Garbage" there probably is in the sense that material is included that does not meet the criteria outlined below. We will greatly appreciate receiving contributions and corrections.

In 1940, Howard Haycraft wrote in the "Foreward" to his *Murder for Pleasure* that the critical material referring to detective and mystery fiction was represented by "a handful of prefaces and a larger but widely scattered and unco-ordinated body of magazine articles." At the start of the 1980s, although the body of material has grown, it is still widely scattered and uncoordinated. This bibliography is an attempt to remedy the situation by imposing some sort of control over the field. And control is necessary. It is best that this be done now as the subject increases in popularity and as more and more is published. If it is not done now, waiting for the floodgates of print to open will put it past any chance of reasonable management and order.

To define our terms, crime literature is defined herein as that body of imaginative writing encompassing all writing categorized separately or collectively as: crime, detective, espionage, mystery, and thriller fiction, literature, or novels. It excludes: gothic, horror, supernatural, and science fiction and fantasy.

The purpose is to provide an international and interdisciplinary source of works written on the topic. None such presently exists, and although it is not definitive, it is hoped that this bibliography will fill a need and be a valuable reference tool.

Although bibliography is considered objective it is actually subjective, governed by personal taste, and arbitrary decisions. There is no end to bibliography. No sooner has one published a bibliography than omissions turn up, and collectors, librarians, specialists, and other bookmen discover errata. This is, however, as it should be. Not only have we no objection, but we welcome addenda.

We have deliberately avoided any attempt to be comprehensive in respect of "mainstream" writers. Poe, of course, is here, for Poe IS the detective story; and Wilkie Collins cannot be ignored. We have, however, bypassed Dickens save for material relating specifically to *Bleak House* (Edwin Drood is quite another matter, being Dickensiana in the sense of Sherlockiana and afficionados thereof will find references conspicuous by their absence), and have excluded Dreiser, Faulkner, and others of their tribe save for a few

---

*Since completing compilation, we have learned that this has indeed been done. The reader is referred to: *'The Armchair Detective' Index (Volumes 1-10) 1967-1977*, comp. Steven A. Stilwell (New York: *The Armchair Detective*, 1979).

basic reference works in particular cases. It is not that the aforementioned and others of their calibre are undeserving of mention, but to include them would be to expand our parameters beyond anyone's capacity to achieve even relative completeness.

One problem facing the bibliographer in this field is the temptation to follow after the Friar Rush's lanthorn of violence in literature as it flickers through the thickets of literary exegesis, only to find one's self lost far from the path. Though a few commentators have crept in, we have tried to cull and prune until only those directly applicable to the main topic remained. Sometimes in the forest of popular culture it was difficult to see the path at all, and occasionally we may have gone around one side of the tree when we could have safely have gone around the other. But, a dead straight road is boring just as perfection is intolerable. As one follows the twists and turns of the trail of criminal literature one must watch for the potholes of crime in literature lest one trip while at the same time making sure one doesn't bump one's head on the low-hanging branches of picaresque literature. We fear we have often stumbled and knocked our heads about.

Material has been included when it seemed to be in direct association with our subject and when an article, essay, monograph, or thesis is or could be of scholarly interest. Some will disagree with various choices, but it is not the bibliographer's job to decide—his or her purpose is to make data available so scholars may best decide among themselves.

Just as Chandler compared novels published to mysteries published, so an awful lot of frivolous trivia masquerading as critical material has appeared in the form of periodical articles. We have tried to limit content to those with a scholarly approach and ignored the uncritical adulation of the fanzine. Crime literature has suffered jointly from the 'schtick response,' *cf.* Carolyn Wells's "What's in a name," and the 'good read syndrome,' symbolized by either a red-faced blimpish type, like the Walker's Uncle Jim, with a bushy white moustache, dressed in white ducks, a white shirt, and with a floppy white hat of the style of the U.S. Army in the Pacific in World War II called "farmer's hats", lounging in a deck chair, or by a sunburnt overweight middle-aged middle-class American in sports shirt and shorts relaxing in a hammock with a can of beer after mowing the lawn. Crime literature generally has not been critized in a mass media except for, first among equals, Anthony Boucher and Newgate Callendar in the *New York Times Book Review* and Derrick Murdoch in the Toronto *Globe and Mail* but "reviewed," thus perpetuating the conditions that Raymond Chandler deplored.

Regrettably, very little indeed of criminal literature receives even adequate critical treatment and analysis, and though more is "reviewed," such reviews are usually merely notices rather than proper comment. One gets heartily sick of the phrase "a good read" that for the discerning has become the kiss of death when applied to a book. Anything that is of interest is a "good read," no matter how scholarly or how popular, and the label has become further debased by being applied to everything from a scholarly, well-researched and documented study of the role of women in Celtic Europe to the latest yellow-jacketed thriller. If this sobriquet were applied to novels of real worth, it would have some value, but because it is applied wholesale to the most appalling trash, it has become cheapened and so cheapens all titles to which it is applied.

We have excluded the following:

1. Writers who deal with crime who are accepted *literati*. To include them would be to rival Besterman.
2. Holmesiana—for which SEE De Waal.
3. Buchan and Greene are limited to those items that discuss their thrillers and entertainments.
4. Articles dealing solely with techniques for writers. A few monographs have been included.
5. Picaresque literature is touched upon but not gone into deeply.
6. Pre-1841. For all intents and purposes we start with Edgar Allan Poe.
7. Macabre; Fantasy; Ghosts; Supernatural; Gothic; and Sci-fi.
8. Incidental or casual references.

We have included the following:

1. Doyle *per se*.
2. Biographies of practitioners.
3. Articles of lasting value; articles that make a contribution; articles of depth and substance; definitive and topical articles; and those that, although not of the foregoing quality, are indicative of their time.
4. Post-1841.
5. Shockers and thrillers.

Our biggest gap is books about individual authors. Except for checking against the name of every known writer in the field(s), it would be impossible to state with certainty that all pertinent autobiographies or biographies are listed. We welcome notification of omissions. There may well be buried like some Caesar's rose in the countless volumes of critical essays on literature as a whole or the literature of particular countries or in sundry literary journals many valuable articles on crime literature in general or specifically on an individual author or work. We will be gratefull to have any such drawn to our attention.

One great difficulty is in obtaining critical material for evaluation. Libraries don't buy because the genre is not respectable. Critical material is, or at least has been in the past, rarely reviewed. It is difficult to trace and hard to come by. Often it was published in limited press runs by small and obscure publishers.

All entries have been verified as far as possible so that "Skene-Melvin's" can stand as a source on its own for interlibrary loan. If we judge correctly the innate and entrenched conservatism of our compeers, they will insist on reverifying the entries in the standard and traditional sources. At least we can assure that they will not have to hunt far. The form of entry is primarily that of the Library of Congress with some leavening of contributions according to the British National Biography. As is sometimes the case with the National Union Catalog contributions, the vagaries of personal taste among cataloguers resulted in our having to choose between more than one discrete entry for the same item. Where neither the Library of Congress nor the British National Bibliography was helpful or where they conflicted too dramatically, commonsense has prevailed. We prefer authors' and editors' entries to the title entries of the International Standard Book Description, and we must confess a preference for the personal main entry, either individual or corporate. We hope our cross-references will alleviate some of any possible strain.

A word about the Subject Index: since the bibliography *per se* is concerned with the history and development of the genre, that particular subject heading has not been used; to have done so would have been to repeat the bibliography.

In conclusion, may we request those kind souls who wish to send us additions, to *please* give (1) for books: author, title, place of publication, publisher, date of publication, and pagination; and (2) for periodical articles: author of article, title of article, title of periodical, volume and number within volume of issue, date of issue (month and year), and pagination.

Better still, please send us a copy.

DAVID SKENE MELVIN
ANN SKENE MELVIN
THE HOLMESTEAD
398 St. Clair Ave. East
Moore Park
Toronto, Ontario
Canada
M4T 1P5

HOW TO USE THE BIBLIOGRAPHY

The main listing is alphabetical by either a personal or corporate author, or in a few instances by title. We decided that the most useful arrangement with the least duplication was to list the material in this manner and to provide both a title and a subject index.

Each discrete item is numbered; the numbering runs consecutively from A through Z.

Cross-references (SEE and SEE also) are designated by an asterisk and are interfiled in the numbered sequence. They are limited to joint authors or editors, pseudonyms, or from an editor to a title entry.

The form of entry chosen follows, whenever possible, the national bibliography of the country of origin.

In cases of conflict, the entry reflecting the editor's opinion of what represents commonsense has been used.

Monographs have been entered as catalogued at the time of publication regardless of subsequent changes in cataloguing rules.

The names of cities in the imprints of material in other languages have been given, for the most part, in the common English form.

The format of the listing for books is as follows: the main entry is given first, followed by the title (underlined). Next there is the imprint: place of publication, publisher, and date of publication. Pagination follows, and lastly there is a series notice, if applicable, in parentheses. Subsequent editions, if any, are listed next.

Where there is more than one item by the same author entered, repetition of the name is shown by ellipsis.

For periodical articles or essays in collections, first there is the name of the author of the piece, next the title of the piece in quotation marks, followed by the word IN in capitals, and then the source wherein the item can be found. If a periodical, there is the title of the periodical (underlined), occasionally the place of publication (in brackets), the volume and number of the issue concerned, the date of the issue (in parentheses), and last the page location. Books containing material are shown in the same manner as main entries with the addition of the page location of the article concerned.

Only anthologies that deal solely with some aspect of the overall subject have been listed. In such cases, not only is the anthology per se included but analytics have been made for each individual article therein as well. In other instances, only the pertinent article has been abstracted for inclusion.

To reiterate, the subject heading that is omitted is: "Detective and mystery stories—History and criticism". Since the bibliography is on this topic, to have used this heading would have been superfluous and would have resulted in practically every entry having been repeated. Consequently, the subject headings utilized have been limited to specific categories within the overall field.

Crime, Detective, Espionage, Mystery, and Thriller FICTION & FILM

A
_____

1. Abrahams, Etta Claire. Visions and values in the action
detective novel; a study of the works of Raymond Chandler,
Kenneth Millar and John D. MacDonald ... Ph.D. dissertation,
Michigan State University, 1973. 209p.

2. ... Where have all the values gone?; the private eye's
vision of America in the novels of Raymond Chandler and Ross
Macdonald. - excerpt from [her] Ph.D. dissertation,
Michigan State University, 1973; presented to Popular Culture
Association Conference, May 1974. (v. supra) [Cited IN
Weibel, Kay. "Mickey Spillane as a fifties phenomenon".
(q.v.)].

3. Achard, Marcel. Sophocle et Archimède; pères du roman
policier. Liège: Editions Dynamo; 1960. 15p. (Collections
Brimborions, 70).

4. Adams, Donald K. (1925-). "The first thin man". IN
The mystery and detection annual; 1972. pp.160-177.

5. ... "Recalled and awakened; the romantic fiction of
William Godwin, Jr.". IN The mystery and detection annual;
1973. pp.142-166.

* ... (ed.). SEE also The mystery and detection annual.

6. Adams, Elsie Bonita (1932-). Israel Zangwill. N.Y.:
Twayne; 1971. 177p. (Twayne's English Authors series
no.121).

7.   ...   "Israel Zangwill; an annotated bibliography of
writings about him." IN English Literature in Transition;
1880-1920. v.13 (1970) pp.209-244.

8.   ...   "Israel Zangwill; ghetto realist and romancer."
IN English Literature in Transition; 1880-1920. v.13
(1970) pp.203-209.

9.   Adams, John. "Mr. R. Austin Freeman." IN The Bookman
[London] v.44:no.259 (April 1913) pp.6-7. ("The Bookman
Gallery" column)

10.   Adams, Robert M. "Introduction" IN Hogg, James.
The private memoirs and confessions of a justified sinner.
N.Y.: W. W. Norton; 1970. xiv, 242p. (The Norton Library,
N515)

11.   Adcock, Arthur St. John. "Sir Arthur Conan Doyle." IN
The Bookman [London] v.43 (November 1912) pp.95-110.

   repr. abr. IN Adcock, Arthur St. John. Gods of modern
   Grub Street; impressions of contemporary authors. N.Y.:
   Frederick A. Stokes; 1923. pp.83-89.

12.   Adey, Robert C. S. "A brief history of the early
years of the locked room." IN Antiquarian Book Monthly
Review - not verified; cited IN Yates, D. A. Locked
rooms and puzzles. (q.v.)

13.   ...   Locked room murders; and other impossible crimes.
London: Ferret Fantasy; 1979. 190p.

*   Adley, Derek J. (jnt.auth.). SEE Lofts, William O. G.
The British bibliography of Edgar Wallace; The men behind
boy's fiction; The Saint and Leslie Charteris.

14.   Agatha Christie; first lady of crime. Ed. by H. R. F.
Keating. London: Weidenfeld & Nicolson; 1977. 224p.,
illus. - U.S. ed.: N.Y.: Holt Rinehart & Winston; 1977.

15.   "The Agatha Christie titles." IN Agatha Christie
(q.v.) pp.217-219.

16.   Alburquerque, Paulo de Medeiros e (1919-). Os maiores
detetives de todos os tempos; o heroi na evolução da estória

policial, ensaio. Rio de Janeiro: Civilização Brasileira;
1973. 191p.

17. Alewyn, Richard. "Anatomie des Detektivromans." IN
Vogt, Jochen (ed.) Der Kriminalroman. (q.v.) pp.372-404.

18. ... "Die Anfänge des Detektivromans." IN Žmegač, V.
(ed.) Der wohltemperierte Mord. (q.v.) pp.185-202.

19. Alexander, David. "Is television necessary?" IN
Gilbert, M. (ed.). Crime in good company. (q.v.)
pp.232-242.

20. Alexander, Jean (1926-). Affidavits of genius; Edgar
Allan Poe and the French critics, 1847-1924. Port Washington,
N.Y.: Kennikat Press; 1971. 246p. (Kennikat Press national
university publications. Series on literary criticism;
no.9015).

21. Alexandersson, Jan (1934-). (jnt.auth.). Leslie
Charteris och Helgonet, under 5 decennium: Biobibliografi.
By J. Alexandersson and Iwan Hedman. Strängnäs, Sweden:
Dast Magazine; 1972. 93p.

*   ... (jnt.auth.). SEE also Hedman, I. Fyra decennier
med Dennis Wheatley.

22. Alington, C. A. "A discussion of detectives." IN
Gold and Gaiters. No.28 pp.166-168.

*   Allen, Dick. SEE Allen, Richard Stanley.

23. Allen, R. C. "Traffic in souls." IN Sight and Sound.
v.44:no.1. (Winter 1974-1975) pp.50-52.

24. Allen, Richard Stanley. (jnt.comp.). Detective fiction;
crime and compromise. Ed. by Dick Allen and David Chacko.
N.Y.: Harcourt Brace Jovanovich; 1974. xiv, 481p.

25. Allen, [William] Hervey (1889-1949). Israfel; the life
and times of Edgar Allan Poe. N.Y.: George H. Doran; 1926.
2 vols. repr. - 1927 - U.K. ed. - London: Brentano's;
1927. 2 vols. (932p.) - repr. - N.Y.: Farrar & Rinehart;
1934. xix, 748p. (1 vol.) repr. - 1949. - Portuguese lang.
ed. - Rio de Janeiro: Livraria do Globo; 1945. 2 vols.

26. Allinson, A. A. (jnt.auth.). Mystery and crime.
By A. A. Allinson and F. E. Hotchin. Melbourne: Cheshire;
1968. 27p., illus. (14-16: a reading guide).

27. Allott, Kenneth. (jnt.auth.). The art of Graham
Greene. By K. Allott and Miriam Farris. London: Hamish
Hamilton; 1951. 253p.

28. Alloway, Lawrence (1926-). Violent America; the
movies 1946-1964. N.Y.: The Museum of Modern Art; 1971.
95p.

29. Allyn, John. "'Double Indemnity'; a policy that paid
off." IN Literature/Film Quarterly vol.6:no.2 (Spring 1978)
pp.116-124, illus.

30. Alter, Jean. "L'Enquête policière dans le nouveau roman."
IN Un nouveau roman?: recherches et tradition. Ed. by J. H.
Matthews. Paris: Minard; 1964. 256p.

31. Altick, Richard D. (jnt.auth.). Browning's Roman
murder story; a reading of "The Ring and the Book". By
R. D. Altick and James F. Loucks. Chicago: University
of Chicago Press; 1968. x, 376p.

32. ... The English common reader; a social history of
the mass reading public 1800-1900. Chicago: University of
Chicago Press; 1957. ix, 430p. repr. 1963ff.

33. ... Victorian studies in scarlet[; murders and manners
in the age of Victoria]. N.Y.: W. W. Norton; 1970. 336p.

34. Ambler, Eric. "Introduction." IN Ambler, Eric (ed.)
To catch a spy; an anthology of favourite spy stories edited
and introduced by Eric Ambler. London: The Bodley Head;
1964. - repr. London: Collins; 1974. 189p. (Fontana
Books) pp.7-19.

35. Ambrosetti, Ronald. "The world of Eric Ambler; from
detective to spy." IN Dimensions of detective fiction.
(q.v.) pp.102-109.

36. "American view of English detective fiction." IN
Bookman [London] v.82:no.490 (July 1932) pp.191.

37. Amis, Kingsley. The James Bond dossier. London:
Jonathan Cape; 1965. 159p. - U.S. ed.: N.Y.: New American
Library; 1966.

38. ... "My favourite sleuths; a highly personal dossier
on fiction's most famous detectives." IN Playboy
v.13:no.12 (December 1966) pp.145, 343-344, 346-349.

39. ... "Unreal policemen." IN Amis, Kingsley. What
became of Jane Austen?; and other questions. London:
Jonathan Cape; 1970. 223p. pp.108-125. U.S. ed.: N.Y.:
Harcourt Brace Jovanovich; 1971. 223p.

40. Anderson, Isaac. "The life of Riley." IN Haycraft,
H. The art of the mystery story. (q.v.) pp.363-366.

41. Andrews, R. V. Wilkie Collins; a critical survey of
his prose fiction with a bibliography. Potchefstroom,
South Africa: [s.n.]; 1959. 367p. - repr. - N.Y.: Garland;
1978.

*   Anker, Jens [pseud.] SEE Hansen, Robert.

42. Archer, Eugene. "John Huston; the Hemingway tradition
in American film." IN Film Culture No. 19 (1959)
pp.66-101.

43. Arlen, M. J. "Blood marks in the sylvan glade." IN
New Yorker. v.51. (13 October 1975) pp.142-151.

44. Arno Press, publishers, N.Y. Literature of mystery and
detection; 44 books. N.Y.: Arno Press; 1976. 20p.

45. Arnold, Armin. Friedrich Dürrenmatt. N.Y.: Frederick
Ungar; 1972. viii, 120p. (Modern Literature Monographs).

*   ... (jnt. ed.). SEE also Reclams Kriminalromanführer.

46. As her whimsey took her; critical essays on the work of
Dorothy L. Sayers. Ed. by Margaret P. Hannay. Kent, Ohio:
Kent State University Press; 1979. xviii, 301p.

47. Ashbrook, Bernard. "Dürrenmatt's detective stories."
IN The Philosophical Journal. v.4 (1967) pp.17-29.

48. Asheim, Lester. "Response to John Houseman: Today's
hero (Hollywood Quarterly, v.2:no. 2 (January 1947))." IN
Hollywood Quarterly. v.2:no.4 (July 1947) pp.414-416.

49. Ashley, Robert. Wilkie Collins. London: Arthur Barker;
1952. 144p. (English Novelists series).

*   Ashton, Winifred. SEE Dane, Clemence [pseud.].

50. Asselineau, Roger. Edgar Allan Poe. Minneapolis,
Minn.: University of Minnesota Press/London: OUP; 1970.
48p. (University of Minnesota Pamphlets on American Writers
No.89).

51. d'Astier de la Vigerie, Emmanuel. "Preface." IN
Simenon, Georges. Zelty pes; Cena golovy; Negritjanskij
kvartal; President. Moscow: Izd. inostr.; 1960. 480p.,
illus.

   repr. IN Lacassin, F. (jnt. ed.). Simenon. (q.v.)
   pp.264-267.

52. Atkins, John Alfred (1916-). Graham Greene. London:
Calder; 1957. 240p.

*   Atkins, Thomas R. (ed.). SEE Graphic violence on
the screen.

53. Auden, Wystan Hugh (1907-). "The guilty vicarage;
notes on the detective story, by an addict." IN Harper's
Magazine. v.196 (May 1948) pp.406-412.

   repr. IN Fiedler, Leslie Aaron (1917-) (ed.). The art
   of the essay. N.Y.: Thomas Y. Crowell; 1958. 640 p.
   pp.443-453.

   repr. IN Auden, Wystan Hugh (1907-). The dyer's hand;
   and other essays. N.Y.: Random House; 1948, repr. 1962.
   xv, 528p. pp.146-158. - U.K. ed. - London: Faber; 1963.
   xv, 528p. - repr. 1975 (Faber Paperbacks).

   repr. IN Allen, R. S. (jnt. ed.). Detective fiction.
   (q.v.) pp.400-410.

   repr. in German AS "Das verbrecherische Pfarrhaus."
   IN Žmegač, V. (ed.). Der wohltemperierte Mord. (q.v.).

54.   Austin, Richard.   "Maigret and Adler."   IN Adam
[University of Rochester, N.Y.]   No.340-342   (1970).

   repr. in Fr.   AS "Maigret et Adler" IN Lacassin, F.
   (jnt. ed.).   Simenon.   (q.v.)   pp.197-203.

55.   Aydelotte, William O.   "The detective story as a
historical source."   IN Yale Review   v.39:no.1 (September
1949)   pp.76-95.

   repr.   IN Deer, Irving (jnt. ed.).   The popular arts.
   Ed. by I. and Harriet A. Deer.   N.Y.: Scribner's; 1967.
   xi, 356p.   pp.132-153.

   repr.   IN Dimensions of detective fiction.   (q.v.)
   pp.68-82.

   rev. and repr.   IN Nevins, F. M. (comp.).   Mystery
   writer's art.   (q.v.)   pp.306-325.

B

56. Bagby, George [pseud.]. "Inspector Schmidt." IN
Penzler, O. M. The great detectives. (q.v.) pp.193-204.

57. Baker, Isadore Lewis. E. C. Bentley; 'Trent's last
case'. London: Brodie; 1956. 54p. (Notes on Chosen English
texts).

58. Bakerman, Jane S. "Patterns of guilt and isolation in
five novels by 'Tucker Coe'." IN Armchair Detective
vol.12:no.2 (Spring 1979) pp.118-121.

*   Baldick, Robert. SEE Goncourt, Edmond Louis Antoine de

59. Ball, John Dudley (1911-). "The ethnic detective."
IN The mystery story. (q.v.) pp.143-160.

60. ... "Murder at large." IN The mystery story. (q.v.)
pp.1-26.

61. ... "Virgil Tibbs." IN Penzler, O. M. The great
detectives. (q.v.) pp.227-234.

*   ... (ed.) SEE The mystery story; an appreciation.

62. Bandy, W. T. "Who was Monsieur Dupin?" IN PMLA
v.79:no.4 (September 1964) pp.509-510.

63. Banks, R. Jeff. "Anti-professionalism in the works of Mickey Spillane." IN Notes of Contemporary Literature. [Carrollton, Ga.] v.3:no.2 (1973) pp.6-8.

64. ... "Spillane's anti-establishmentarian heroes." IN Dimensions of detective fiction. (q.v.) pp.124-139.

65. Baring-Gould, William S. Nero Wolfe of West Thirty-fifth Street; the life and times of America's largest private detective. N.Y.:Viking Press; 1969. xviii, 203p.

66. Barker, Dudley. G. K. Chesterton; a biography. London: Constable; 1973. 304 [13]p., illus.

67. Barker, G. A. "Justice to Caleb Williams." IN Studies in the novel. v.6 (Winter 1974) pp.377-388.

68. Barnes, Daniel R. "I'm the eye"; Archer as narrator in the novels of Ross Macdonald." IN Mystery and detection annual; 1972. (q.v.) pp.178-190.

69. ... "A note on "The murder of Roger Ackroyd"." IN Mystery and detection annual; 1972. (q.v.) pp.254-255.

70. Barnes, Melvyn P. Best detective fiction; a guide from Godwin to the present. London: Clive Bingley; 1975. 121p. - U.S. ed.: Hamden, Conn.: Shoe String; 1975. (Linnet Books).

71. Barzun, Jacques Martin (1907-). A birthday tribute to Rex Stout, December 1, 1965. By J. Barzun and the Viking Press. N.Y.: Viking Press; 1965. 15 [1]p.

72. ... "The book, the bibliographer, and the absence of mind." IN American Scholar v.39 (Winter 1969) pp.138ff.

73. ... (jnt. auth.) A book of prefaces to fifty classics of crime fiction 1900-1950. By J. Barzun and Wendell Hertig Taylor. N.Y.: Garland; 1976. vii, 112p.

74. ... "A briefbag of felonies." IN American Scholar v.31:no.4 (Autumn 1962) pp.628, 630, 632, 634, 636 ("The Revolving Bookstand" column).

75. ... (jnt. comp.) A catalogue of crime; being a
reader's guide to the literature of mystery, detection, and
related genres. By J. Barzun and Wendell Hertig Taylor.
N.Y.: Harper & Row; 1971. xxxi, 831p. - 2d impression
corr.: N.Y.: Harper & Row; 1971. xxxi, 831p.

76. ... "Detection and the literary art." IN New Republic
v.144 (24 April 1961) pp.17-20.

   repr. AS "Introduction." IN Barzun, Jacques Martin
   (1907-). The delights of detection. N.Y.: Criterion
   Books; 1961. 381p.

   repr. IN Nevins, F. M. (comp.). Mystery writer's art.
   (q.v.) pp.248-262.

77. ... "Detection in extremis." IN Gilbert, Michael
(ed.). Crime in good company. (q.v.) pp.134-145.

78. ... "The detective story." IN Holiday. Party of
twenty; informal essays from Holiday magazine. Ed. and with
an intro. by Clifton Fadiman. N.Y.: Simon & Schuster; 1963.
252p.

79. ... "From 'Phèdre' to Sherlock Holmes." IN Barzun,
Jacques Martin, (1907-). The energies of art; studies of
authors, classic and modern. N.Y.: Harper; 1956. 355p. -
repr: N.Y.: Knopf; 1962. 355p. (Vintage Books) - repr.:
Westport, Conn.: Greenwood Press; [1956] 1975. 355p.

80. ... "The illusion of the real." IN Gross, M. (ed.).
The world of Raymond Chandler. (q.v.) pp.159-163.

81. ... "Meditations on the literature of spying." IN
American Scholar v.34:no.2 (Spring 1965) pp.167-178.

82. ... "Not 'whodunit' but 'how'?" IN Saturday Review
of Literature v.27 (4 November 1944) pp.9-11.

83. ... "A note on the inadequacy of Poe as a proofreader
and of his editors as French scholars." IN Romanic Review
v.61:no.1 (February 1970) pp.23-26.

84. ... "The novel turns tale." IN Mosaic [Winnipeg:
University of Manitoba Press] v.4:no.3 ([Spring] 1971)
pp.33-40.

85. ... "Suspense suspended." IN American Scholar v.27
(Fall 1958) pp.496ff.

86. Basney, Lionel. "'The nine tailors' and the complexity
of innocence." IN As her whimsey took her. (q.v.)
pp.23-35.

87. Basney, L. "Pornography of moral indignation." IN
Christianity Today v.20 (19 December 1975) pp.17-19.

88. Bates, George, bookseller, London. Catalogue the
seventh of rare and interesting books illustrating the
development of the detective and mystery story. London:
George Bates; [1935?] 16p.

89. Batten, Jack. "Who will wear the sacred trenchcoat for
Canada?; Who, in fact, will stand on guard?: a sour look at
what passes for crime fiction in our midst." IN Saturday
Night [Toronto] v.88:no.1 (whole no.3535) (January 1973)
pp.28-30.

90. Baxter, John. (1939-) The gangster film. London:
A. Zwemmer; 1970. 160p., illus. (Screen series) - U.S.
ed.: N.Y.: A. S. Barnes; 1970. 160p., illus. (screen
series).

91. Bazelon, David T. "Dashiell Hammett's 'Private Eye, no
loyalty beyond the job'." IN Commentary v.7:no.5 (May
1949) pp.467-472.

   repr. IN Brossard, Chandler (1922-). (ed.). The scene
   before you; a new approach to American culture. N.Y.:
   Rinehart; 1955. xii, 307p.

92. Beaumont, Charles. "The bloody pulps." IN Playboy
vol.9:no.9 (September 1962) pp.90-92, 182, 184-191.

   repr. IN The fantastic pulps. (q.v.) pp.397-414.

93. Becker, Jens-Peter (1943-). Der englische
Spionageroman; historische Entwicklung, Thematik,
literarische Form. Munich: Goldmann; 1973. 202p. (Das
wissenschaftliche Taschenbuch: Abt. Geisteswiss.; Ge 19).

94. ... "The mean streets of Europe; the influence of the
American 'hard-boiled school' on European detective
fiction." IN Bigsby, Christopher William Edward. ed.
Superculture; American popular culture and Europe. Bowling
Green, Ohio: Bowling Green University Popular Press; 1975.
225p., illus. pp.152-159 - U.K. ed.: London: Elek; 1975.
225p., illus.

95. ... Sherlock Holmes & Co.; Essays zu englische und
amerkanische Detektivliteratur. Munich: Goldman; 1975.
163p. (Das Wissenschaftliche Taschenbuch: Abt.
Geisteswissenschaft: 18).

*   ... (jnt. auth.) SEE also Buchloh, Paul Gerhard.

*   ... (jnt. ed.) SEE also Der Detektiverzählung auf
der Spur.

96. Becker, Lucille Frackman. Georges Simenon. Boston:
Twayne; 1977. 171p. (Twayne's world authors series; TWAS
456. France).

97. Becker, Stephen D. (1927-). Comic art in America; a
social history of the funnies, the political cartoons,
magazine humour, sporting cartoons, and animated cartoons.
N.Y.: Simon & Schuster; 1959. xi, 387p., illus.

98. Bedell, Jeanne F. Positive images of aging and active
retirement in detective fiction. - Reported as being in
progress in Popular Culture Association Newsletter and
Popular Culture Methods, vol.8:no.1 (March 1979) p.9.

99. Beekman, E. M. "Raymond Chandler and an American
genre." IN Massachusetts Review. v.14 (1973)
pp.149-173.

100. Behre, Frank (1896-). Get, come, and go; some aspects
of situational grammar: a study based on a corpus drawn
from Agatha Christie's writings. Stockholm: Almqvist &
Wiksell; 1973. 174p. (Acta Universitatis Gothoburgensis.
Gothenburg Studies in English 28).

101. ... Studies in Agatha Christie's writings; the
behaviour of "a good (great) deal, a lot, lots, much,
plenty, many, a good (great) many". Stockholm: Almqvist
and Wiksell; 1967. 203p. (Gothenburg Studies in English,
19).

*   Bell, Josephine. SEE Gilbert, M. F. Crime in good
company.

102. Bellak, Leopold. "Psychology of detective stories
and related problems." IN Psa. Review v.32 (1945).

103. Benét, Stephen Vincent. "Bigger and better murders."
IN Bookman [N.Y.] v.63 (May 1926) pp.291-296.

104. Benét, William Rose. "Here's to crime." IN
Saturday Review of Literature v.4 (18 February 1928)
pp.605-606.

105. Ben Guigui, Jacques. Israel Zangwill; penseur et
écrivain, 1864-1926. Toulouse: Impr. toulousaine R. Lion;
1975. 478p.

106. Bentley, Edmund Clerihew (1875-). "Introduction"
IN Bentley, Edmund Clerihew, (1875-). ed. The second
century of detective stories. London: Hutchinson; 1938.
761p.

107. ... Those days; [autobiography]. London: Constable;
1940. xv, 327p., illus.

108. Benton, Richard P. "The mystery of Marie Rogêt - a
defense." IN Studies in Short Fiction v.6:no.2 (Winter
1969) pp.144-151.

109. Bergier, Jacques. "Redécouverte du roman d'aventure
anglais." IN Le Planète (October-November 1961).

110. Bergler, Edmund. "Mystery fans and the problem of
potential murders." IN American Journal of
Orthopsychiatry v.15 (1945).

111. Bergonzi, Bernard. "The case of Mr. Fleming." IN
Twentieth Century v.163 (1958) pp.220-228.

112. Berkeley, Anthony. "Vorwort zu The second shot."
- orig. publ. 1930; repr. in German trans. IN Der
Detektiverzählung auf der Spur. (q.v.).

113. Berkowitz, L. (jnt. auth.). "The effects of film violence on inhibitions against subsequent aggression." By L. Berkowitz and E. Rawlings. IN Journal of Abnormal and Social Psychology v.66:no.5 (1963).

114. Bibliography of Dr. R. H. van Gulik (D.Litt.). [Boston: Boston University; 1968?] 82p.

  - compiled for the benefit of the Boston University Libraries - Mugar Memorial Library 'Robert van Gulik collection' Boston University.

115. Bien, Günter. "Abenteuer und verborgene Wahrheit; Gibt es den literarischen Detektivroman?" IN Vogt, Jochen (ed.) Der Kriminalroman. (q.v.) pp.457-472.

116. ... "Detektivroman im Unterricht." IN DU no.20 (1968) pp.98ff.

117. Bingham, John. "Vorwort zur deutschen Ausgabe von Murder Plan Six." - orig. publ. 1958; repr. IN Der Detektiverzählung auf der Spur.

118. Binyon, T. J. "A lasting influence?" IN Gross, M. (ed.). The world of Raymond Chandler. (q.v.) pp.171-183.

119. Bishop, John Peale. "Georges Simenon." IN New Republic v.104 (10 March 1941) pp.345-346.

120. Bittner, William Robert. Poe; a biography. Boston: Little, Brown; 1962. 306p. - U.K. ed.: London: Elek; 1963. xi, 306p.

*   Blair, Eric Arthur. SEE Orwell, George [pseud.].

121. Blair, Walter. "Dashiell Hammett; themes and techniques." IN Essays on American literature, in honor of Jay B. Hubbell. Ed. by Clarence Gohdes. Chapel Hill, N.C.: Duke University Press; 1967. viii, 350p. pp.295-306.

*   Blake, Nicholas [pseud.]. SEE Day Lewis, C.

*   Blakey, Dorothy. SEE London. Bibliographical Society.

122. Blanch, Robert J. "The background of Poe's 'Gold
Bug'." IN English Record [New York State English
Council] v.16:no.4 (April 1966) pp.44-48.

123-130. Bleiler, E.F. "Introduction" IN

123. Bramah, Ernest. Best Max Carrados detective stories.
N.Y.: Dover; 1972. x,245p. pp.v-vii.

124. Freeman, Richard Austin. The best Dr. Thorndyke
detective stories. N.Y.: Dover; 1973. xii,275p.
pp.v-ix.

125. Freeman, Richard Austin. The stoneware monkey & The
Penrose mystery; two Dr. Thorndyke novels. N.Y.: Dover;
1973. viii, 440p. pp.iii-viii.

126. Futrelle, Jacques. Best "Thinking Machine"
detective stories. N.Y.: Dover; 1973. xii, 241p.
pp.v-ix.

127. Gaboriau, Emile. Monsieur Lecoq. N.Y.: Dover; 1975.
xxviii, 278p., illus. pp.v-xxviii.

128. Three Victorian detective novels: 'The unknown
weapon' by Andrew Forrester; 'My Lady's money' by Wilkie
Collins; 'The Big Bow mystery' by Israel Zangwill. N.Y.:
Dover; 1978. xvi, 302p. pp.vii-xvi.

129. Vickers, Roy. The department of dead ends; 14
detective stories. N.Y.: Dover; 1978. x, 277p.
pp.iii-viii.

130. Wood, H. F. The passenger from Scotland Yard; a
Victorian detective novel. N.Y.: Dover; 1977. xvi, 295p.
pp.v-xii.

131. Bloch, E. "Philosophische Ansicht des Detektivromans."
IN Žmegač, V. (ed.) Der wohltemperierte Mord. (q.v.)

132. Block, Andrew (1892-). The English novel, 1740-1850;
a catalogue including prose romances, short stories, and
translations of foreign fiction. 2d ed., rev. London:
Dawsons; 1961. xv, 349p. - U.S. ed.: Dobbs Ferry, N.Y.:
Oceana Publn.; 1967. xv, 349p.

133. Bogan, Louise. "The time of the assassins." IN The Nation v.158 (22 April 1944, and, 27 May 1944) pp.475-6; 635.

134. Bogdanovich, Peter (1939-). The cinema of Alfred Hitchcock. N.Y.: Museum of Modern Art Film Library; 1963. 48p.

135. ... Fritz Lang in America. London: Studio Vista; 1967. 144p. (Movie paperbacks) - U.S. ed.: N.Y.: Praeger; 1969, 1976. 143p.

136. Boileau, Pierre (1906-). "Quelque chose de changé dans le roman policier." IN Lacassin, F. (jnt. ed.). Simenon. (q.v.) pp. 190-192.

137. ... (jnt. auth.) Le roman policier. By Boileau-Narcejac. Paris: Payot; 1964. 240p. (Petite bibliotheque Payot, 70. Ser. Science de l'homme) German ed.: Der Detektivroman. Neuwied a. Rh.: Luchterhand; 1967. 260 p.

138. ... Le roman policier. Paris: Presses universitaires de France; 1975. 127p. (Que sais-je?; 1623).

*   Boileau-Narcejac [pseud.]. SEE Boileau, Pierre (1906-) (jnt. auth.) Le roman policier. 1964.

139. Bond, Mary Wickham. How 007 got his name. London: Collins; 1966. 62p.

140. Bonaparte, Marie, Princess (1882-). Edgar Poe; étude psychanalytique. Paris: Denoël et Steele; 1933. 2 vols., illus. (Bibliotheque psychanalytique).

   German ed.: Edgar Poe; eine psychoanalytische studie. Vienna: Internationaler psychoanalytischer verlag; 1934. 3 vols., illus.

   U.K. (first English) ed.: The life and works of Edgar Allan Poe; a psycho-analytic interpretation. London: Imago Publ. House; 1949. xiv, 749p. - U.S. ed.: N.Y.: Humanities Press; 1971. xi, 749p.

141. ... "The murders in the Rue Morgue." IN The Psychoanalytic Quarterly v.4 (1935).

142. Borde, Raymond. (jnt. auth.) Panorama du film noir américain (1941-1953). By R. Borde and Étienne Chaumeton. Paris: Éditions de Minuit; 1955. x, 279p., illus.

  repr.: Paris: Éditions d'Aujourd'hui; 1975. x, 279p. (Les Introuvables).

143. Borges, Jorge Luis (1899-). "On Chesterton." IN Borges, Jorge Luis (1899-). Other inquisitions; 1937-1952. Austin, Texas: University of Texas Press; 1964. xviii, 205p. (Texas Pan-American series).

144. Borneman, Ernest. "'Black Mask'." IN Go [London] (February/March 1952).

145. Borowitz, Albert (1930-). Innocence and arsenic; studies in crime and literature. N.Y.: Harper & Row; 1977. xiv, 170p.

146. Borrello, Alfred. "Evelyn Waugh and Erle Stanley Gardner." IN Evelyn Waugh Newsletter v.4 (Winter 1970) pp.1-3.

147. Boston, R. E. "Mystery story." IN English Journal v.64 (January 1975) pp.83-84.

148. Boucher, Anthony [pseud.]. "critical discussion of locked room theory" IN Holmes, H. H. [pseud.] Nine times nine. N.Y.: Duell Sloan & Pearce; 1940. 296p. v. Chap.14.

  N.B.: Both "H. H. Holmes" and "Anthony Boucher" were pseudonyms of William Anthony Parker White (1911-1968).

149. ... Ellery Queen; a double profile. Boston: Little Brown; 1951. 12p.

150. ... "The ethics of the mystery novel." IN Tricolor [American ed. of 'La France Libre'] (October 1944)

  repr. IN Haycraft, H. (ed.) Art of the mystery story. (q.v.) pp.384-389.

151. ... "Introduction" IN Derleth, August. The reminiscences of Solar Pons. Sauk City, Wisc.: Mycroft & Moran; 1961. xii, 199p. pp.vii-xi.

152. ... "Introduction [on religious detectives]" IN
Chesterton, Gilbert Keith (1874-1936). Ten adventures of
Father Brown. N.Y.: Dell; 1961. (Chapel Books No. F133).

153. ... Multiplying villanies; selected mystery criticism,
1942-1968, by Anthony Boucher. Ed. by Robert E. Briney and
Francis M. Nevins. [n.pl.: n.publ.]; 1973. 136p. (A
Bouchercon book).

154. ... "Reply to N. Muhlen's 'Thinker and the tough guy';
Commonweal, 25 November 1949." (q.v.) IN Commonweal
v.51 (23 December 1949) p.315.

155. ... Reply with rejoinder to: John Paterson, 'A cosmic
view of the private eye'; Saturday Review of Literature, 22
August 1953. (q.v.) IN Saturday Review of Literature,
v.36. (31 October 1953) p.24.

156. ... (jnt. auth.). Sincerely, Tony/Faithfully,
Vincent; the correspondence of Anthony Boucher and Vincent
Starrett. Ed. by Robert W. Hahn. Chicago: Catullus Press;
1975. [4], 55p.

157. ... "Trojan horse opera." IN Haycraft, H. (ed.)
Art of the mystery story. (q.v.) pp.245-249.

158. Bourne, Michael. "An informal interview with Rex
Stout." IN Corsage. (q.v.) pp.103-152.

*   ... (ed.). SEE also Corsage.

159. Boverie, Dieudonné. "Georges Simenon, écrivain
liégeois." orig. publ. IN L'Essai (September 1962) - repr.
IN Lacassin, F. (jnt. ed.). Simenon (q.v.) pp.272-275.

160. Bowles, Paul Frederic (1911-). Without stopping; an
autobiography. N.Y.: Putnam's; 1972. 379p. - U.K. ed.:
London: Owen; 1972. 379p.

161. Boyd, Ann S. The devil with James Bond! Richmond,
Va.: John Knox Press; 1967. 123p. - U.K. ed.: London:
Collins; 1967. 126p. (Fontana Books).

162. Boyd, Ian. The novels of G. K. Chesterton; a study in art and propaganda. London: Paul Elek; 1975. xii, 241p. - U.S. ed.: N.Y.: Barnes and Noble; 1975. xii, 241p.

163. Boyd, Stuart. "Homicide in fiction." IN Macdonald, John Marshall (1920-). The murderer and his victim. Springfield, Ill.: Charles C. Thomas; 1961. xiv, 420p.

164. Boyle, Andrew. The riddle of Erskine Childers. London: Hutchinson; 1977. 351p., illus.

165. Boynton, Henry Walcott. "Adventure and riddles." IN Bookman [N.Y.] v.49 (May 1919) pp.321-327.

166. ... "In behalf of the puzzle novel." IN Bookman [N.Y.] v.58 (November 1923) pp.295-298.

167. Braddy, Haldeen (1908-). Glorious incense; the fulfillment of Edgar Allan Poe. Washington, D.C.: Scarecrow Press; 1953. 234p., illus. - U.K. ed.: London: Bailey & Swinfen; 1953. 263p. - 2d U.S. ed.: Port Washington, N.Y.: Kennikat Press; 1968. 234p.

168. Bragin, Charles. Bibliography of Dime novels, 1860-1928. Brooklyn, N.Y.: C. Bragin; 1938. 5p., 29 numb. ., illus.

   2d ed.: Dime novels; bibliography 1860-1928. Brooklyn, N.Y.: C. Bragin; 1938. 29p.

   rev. ed.: Dime novels, 1860-1964; bibliography. Brooklyn, N.Y.: C. Bragin; 1964. 20p., illus. (Dime Novel Club. No.63).

169. Braithwaite, W. S. "S. S. Van Dine - Willard Huntington Wright." IN Van Dine, S. S. [pseud.]. Philo Vance murder cases. N.Y.: Scribners; 1936. pp.29-45.

170. Brand, Mary Christina. "Inspector Cockrill." IN Penzler, O. M. The great detectives. (q.v.) pp.57-66.

171. ... "Miss Marple - a portrait." IN Agatha Christie. (q.v.) pp.193-204.

*   Brean, Herbert. SEE Mystery Writers of America.
Mystery writer's handbook. 1956.

172. Brecht, B. "Über die Popularität des Kriminalromans."
IN Žmegač, V. (ed.) Der wohltemperierte Mord. (q.v.).

173. Breen, Jon L. The girl in the pictorial wrapper; an
index to reviews of paperback original novels in the New
York Times' "Criminals at Large" column 1953-1970.
Dominguez Hills, Calif.: Library, California State College
- Dominguez Hills; [1970?, 1971?] 46

   rev. ed.: 1973. (Dominguez Hills Bibliographic series
   no.2).

174. Bremner, Marjorie. "Crime fiction for intellectuals."
IN 20th Century (September 1954) pp.246-252.

175. Briney, Robert E. "Death rays, demons, and worms
unknown to science; the fantastic element in mystery fiction."
IN The mystery story. (q.v.) pp.235-289.

176. ... "The literature of the subject; an annotated
bibliography." IN The mystery story. (q.v.) pp.365-390.

177. ... "Sax Rohmer; an informal survey." IN Xero
No. 10 (May 1963).

   rev. version IN The Rohmer Review No.1 (July 1968).

   re-rev. version IN Nevins, F. M. (comp.) The mystery
   writer's art. (q.v.) pp.42-78.

*   ... (jnt. ed.). SEE also Boucher, Anthony [pseud.].
Multiplying villainies.

*   Britto, José Gabriel de Lemos (1886-). SEE Lemos
Britto, José Gabriel de (1886-).

178. Broberg, Jan (1932-). "Lew Archer och hans värld."
IN Horisont [Stockholm] v.20:no.3 (1973) pp.57-60.

179.   ... (comp.).   Meningar om mord: 15 uppsatser om
deckare, deckarförfattare och deckarhjältar; En antologi.
Staffanstorp, Sweden: Cavefors/Solna, Sweden: Seelig; 1968.
136p., illus. (Kalejdoskop).

180.   ... Mord för ro skull; deckarens debut och dilemma.
Malmo, Sweden: Cavefors; 1964. 300p., illus.

181.   ... Mord i minne: 12 kapitel om deckare och
deckarförfattare. Goteborg: Zinderman/Solna: Seelig; 1976.
151p., illus.

182.   ... Mordisk familjebok. Göteborg [Uddevalla?]:
Zinderman/Solna, Sweden: Seelig; 1972. 261p., illus.

183.   ... "Reverens för Rinehart." IN Jury - tidskrift
för deckarvänner [Stockholm: Bromma] No.1 (1972)
pp.16-19.

*   ... (ed.).   SEE also Ord om mord.

184. Bronowski, Jacob (1908-). "Preface." IN Bronowski,
Jacob (1908-). The face of violence; an essay with a play.
London: Turnstile Press; 1954. 128p. - U.S. ed. - N.Y.:
G. Braziller; 1955. 128p.

185. Brookes, Joshua Alfred Rowland. Murder in fact and
fiction. London: Hurst & Blackett; [1925,1926] 284p.

186. Brophy, Brigid (1929-). "Detective fiction; a modern
myth of violence?" IN Hudson Review v. 18 (Spring 1965)
pp.11-30.

    repr. IN Brophy, Brigid (1929-). Don't never forget;
    collected views and reviews. N.Y.: Holt Rinehard Winston;
    [c1966] 1967. 319p. pp.121-142.

187. Brosnan, John. James Bond in the cinema. London:
Tantivy Press/South Brunswick, N.J.: A. S. Barnes; 1972.
176p., illus.

188. Brown, Ivor John Carnegie (1891-). Conan Doyle; a
biography of the creator of Sherlock Holmes. London:
Hamish Hamilton; 1972. 145p.

189. Browne, Nelson (1908-). Sheridan Le Fanu. London:
Arthur Barker; 1951. 135p. (English Novelist series) -
U.S. ed.: N.Y.: Roy Publishers; 1951. 135p.

*   Browne, Pat. SEE Landrum, Larry (et al.) Introduction.

*   Browne, Ray B. SEE Landrum, Larry (et al.)
Introduction.

190. Bruccoli, Matthew Joseph (1931-). "Afterword; Raymond
Chandler & Hollywood." IN Chandler, Raymond (1888-1959).
The Blue Dahlia; a screenplay. Carbondale, Ill.: Southern
Illinois University Press; 1976. xxi, 139p. pp.129-139.

191. ... (comp.) Kenneth Millar/Ross Macdonald; a
checklist. Intro. by Kenneth Millar. Detroit: Gale Research
Co.; 1971. xvii, 86 p., illus. (A Bruccoli-Clark book).

192. ... Raymond Chandler; a checklist. Kent, Ohio:
Kent State University Press; 1968. ix, 35p. (The Serif
series; bibliographies and checklists, no.2).

193. Bryce, Ivar. You only live once; memories of Ian
Fleming. London: Weidenfeld & Nicolson; 1975. 142p., illus.

194. Buchan, John (1875-1940). Memory hold-the-door.
London: Hodder & Stoughton; 1940. 327p. - Cdn. ed.:
Toronto: Musson; 1940. 327p., illus.

*   Buchan, Susan Grosvenor (1882-). SEE John Buchan;
by his wife and friends.

195. Buchloh, Paul Gerhard. (jnt. auth.). Der Detektivroman;
Studien zur Geschichte und Form der englischen und
amerikanischen Detektivliteratur. Mit Beiträgen von Antje
Wulff und Walter T. Rix. By P. G. Buchloh and Jens P. Becker.
Darmstadt: Wissenschaftliche Buchgesellschaft; 1973. vii,
199p.

*   ... (jnt. ed.) SEE also Der Detektiverzählung auf
der Spur.

196. Bullett, Gerald William (1894-1958). The innocence of
G. K. Chesterton. London: Cecil Palmer; 1923. viii, 233p.
- U.S. ed.: N.Y.: Holt; 1923. - repr. 1952.

197. Bullough, Vern L. "Deviant sex and the detective
story." IN Mystery and detection annual; 1973. (q.v.)
pp.326-330.

198. Bunnell, William Stanley. Wilkie Collins; 'The
Moonstone'. London: Brodie; 1961. 60p. (Notes on Chosen
English Texts).

199. Buono, Oreste Del. (jnt. auth.) Il caso Bond. By
O. Del Buono and Umberto Eco. Milan: Bompiani; 1965.

    U.K. (first English) ed.: London: Macdonald; 1966. 173p.

200. Burack, Abraham Saul (1908-). (ed.). Writing
detective and mystery fiction. Boston: Writer; 1945.
x, 237p. - rev. ed.: Boston: Writer; 1967. vii, 280p.
- Cdn. ed.: Toronto: Burns & MacEachern; 1967. vii, 280p.

*   ... (ed.). SEE also Writing suspense and mystery
fiction.

201. Buranelli, Vincent. Edgar Allan Poe. N.Y.: Twayne;
1961. 157p. (Twayne's United States Authors series no.4).

    also publ.: New Haven, Conn.: College & University
    Press; 1961.

*   Burger, Margaret A. (jnt. comp.). SEE Harmon, R. B.
(jnt. comp.).

202. Burton, Carl Taylor. The hero as detective ... Ph.D.
thesis, Columbia University, 1973. iii, 342ℓ.

203. Butler, William Vivian (1927-). The durable
desperadoes. London: Macmillan; 1973. 288p.

204. Buxbaum, Edith. "The role of detective stories in a
child analysis." IN The Psychoanalytic Quarterly v. 10
(1941).

205. Byrd, M. "Detective detected; from Sophocles to
Ross Macdonald." IN Yale Review v. 64 (Autumn 1974)
pp.72-83.

206.   Byrne, Evelyn B.   (jnt. comp.).   Attacks of taste.
Comp. and ed. by E. B. Byrne and Otto M. Penzler.   N.Y.:
Gotham Book Mart; 1971.   xii, 65p.

C

207. C., A. "Crime in current literature." IN Westminster Review [London] v.147 (April 1897) p.429.

 repr. in German trans. AS "Das Verbrechen in der Gegenwartsliteratur." IN Der Detektiverzählung auf der Spur. (q.v.).

208. Cabana, Roy. "Murder, mythology, and Mother Goose." IN Kaleidoscope v.2:no.3. pp.23-33.

209. Caillois, Roger (1913-). Le roman policier; ou, Comment l'intelligence se retire du monde pour se consacrer à ses jeux et comment la société introduit ses problèmes dans ceux-ci. Buenos Aires: Éditions des Lettres Françaises, SUR; 1941. 73p. (Half-title: Collection des amis des lettres françaises, no.1).

210. Cain, James Mallahan (1892-). "[Preface]" IN Cain, James Mallahan (1892-). Three of a kind. N.Y.: Alfred A. Knopf; 1943. xv, 327p.

211. ... "[Preface]" IN Cain, James Mallahan (1892-). Three of hearts. London: Robert Hale; 1949. 405p.

212. California. University. University at Los Angeles. Library. The boys in the Black mask; an exhibit in the UCLA Library, January 6-February 19, 1961. Los Angeles: UCLA; 1961. 12p.

 N.B.: attributed to Philip Durham by William F. Nolan (Nolan, W.F.: Dashiell Hammett (q.v.) p.175).

213. California. University. University at San Diego. University Extension. [The Mystery Library.] [La Jolla, Calif.: University of California, San Diego; 1976 [sic: 1977]] 4p.

214. Cambiaire, Célestin-Pierre (1880-). The influence of Edgar Allan Poe in France. N.Y.: G. E. Stechert; 1927. 332p. repr.: N.Y.: Haskell; 1970. 332p. - repr.: St. Clair Shores, Mich.: Scholarly Press; 1971. 332p.

*   Cameron, Elisabeth (jnt. auth.). SEE Cameron, Ian (jnt. auth.).

215. Cameron, Ian Alexander (1937-) (jnt. auth.). Broads. By I. and Elisabeth Cameron. London: Studio Vista; 1969. 144p., illus. (Movie paperbacks).

216. ... (jnt. auth.). The heavies. By I. and Elisabeth Cameron. London: Studio Vista; 1967. 144p., illus. (Movie paperbacks) - U.S. ed.: N.Y.: Praeger; 1969. 143p.

217. ... A pictorial history of crime films. London/N.Y.: Paul Hamlyn; 1975. 221p., illus.

218. Camp, Jocelyn. "John Buchan and Alfred Hitchcock." IN Literature/Film Quarterly vol.6:no.3 (Summer 1978) pp.230-240, illus.

219. Campbell, Frank D. (1915-). John D. MacDonald and the colorful world of Travis McGee. San Bernardino, Calif.: R. Reginald - The Borgo Press; 1977. 64p. (The Milford Series: Popular Writers of Today 5).

220. Campbell, Iain. Ian Fleming: a catalogue of a collection; a preliminary to a bibliography. Liverpool: Iain Campbell; 1978. viii, 71p.

221. Campbell, Killis (1872-1937). The mind of Poe; and other studies. Cambridge, Mass.: Harvard University Press; 1933. 237p. - repr.: N.Y.: Russell & Russell; 1962. 237p.

222. Campinchi, César. "Le crime et le mystère d'Edgar Poe à Geo. London." IN Les Annales Politiques et Littéraires [Paris] v.97 (15 July 1931). p.85.

*   Canby, Henry Seidel. SEE "Sherlock Holmes and after."

223. Carey, John. "Introduction" IN Hogg, James (1770-
1835). The private memoirs and confessions of a justified
sinner. Ed. by John Carey. London/N.Y.: Oxford University
Press; 1969. xxxiii, 262p. (Oxford English novels).

224. Carlisle, Charles R. "Strangers within, enemies
without; alienation in popular Mafia fiction." IN Dimensions
of detective fiction. (q.v.) pp.194-202.

225. Carlson, Eric W. (ed.). The recognition of Edgar Allan
Poe; selected criticism since 1829. Ann Arbor, Mich.:
University of Michigan Press; 1966. xv, 316p.

226. Carnillon, John. The androgynous orchid; or The
homophillic misogynist relationship in the Nero Wolfe tales
of Rex Stout. ... paper delivered at The Popular Culture
Association convention, 1973. Quoted in: Bourne, M. "An
informal interview with Rex Stout" (q.v.), p.134.

227. Carpenter, Richard C. "007 and the myth of the hero."
IN Journal of Popular Culture v.1:no.2 (1967). pp.79-89.

228. Carr, John Dickson. "The grandest game in the world."
IN Ellery Queen's Mystery Magazine (March 1963).

   repr. IN Nevins, F. M. (comp.). The mystery writer's
   art. (q.v.). pp.227-247.

229. ... The life of Sir Arthur Conan Doyle. London:
J. Murray; 1949. 361p. - U.S. ed.: N.Y.: Harper & Row;
1949. 304p.

230. ... "The locked room lecture." IN Carr, John Dickson.
The hollow man. London: Hamilton; 1935. v. Chap.17. -
U.S. ed. AS: The three coffins. N.Y.: Harper; 1935. -
various reprints under either title.

   repr. IN Haycraft, H. (ed.). The art of the mystery
   story. (q.v.). pp.273-286.

231. ... "The UNC detective collection." IN The Bookmark;
Friends of the UNCL [University of North Carolina]
(September 1968).

232. Carr, Nick. America's secret service ace. Oak Lawn,
Ill.: Robert Weinberg; 1974. 64p., illus. (Pulp classics, 7).

233. Carroll, Jon. "Ross Macdonald in raw California."
IN Esquire v.77 (June 1972). pp. 148-149ff.

234. Carter, John (1905-). "Detective fiction." IN
Carter, John (1905-). New paths in book collecting; essays
by various hands. London: Constable; 1934. v, 294p.
pp.33-63. - U.S. ed. - N.Y.: Scribners; 1934. v, 294p. -
repr. Freeport, N.Y.: Books for Libraries; 1967. v, 294p.
(Essay Index Reprint series).

   repr. AS Carter, John (1905-). Collecting detective
   fiction. London: Constable; 1938. 30p. [i.e. pp.33-63]
   (Aspects of book collecting) - Cdn. ed. - Toronto:
   Macmillan; 1938. 30p. - U.S. ed. - N.Y.: Scribner;
   1938. 30p.

   repr. AS "Collecting detective fiction." IN Haycraft, H.
   (ed.). The art of the mystery story. (q.v.) pp.453-475.

   repr. IN Carter, John (1905-). Books and book-collectors.
   Cleveland: World; 1957. 196p.

*   ... SEE also Scribner, firm, publishers, New York.

235. Carter, Steven R. "Ishmael Reed's neo-hoodoo detection."
IN Dimensions of detective fiction. (q.v.) pp.265-274.

236. ... "Ross Macdonald; the complexity of the modern
quest for justice." IN Mystery and Detection Annual; 1973.
(q.v.) pp. 59-82.

237. Cascudo, Luís da Câmara (1898-). Flor de romances
trágicos. Rio de Janeiro: Editôra do Autor; 1966. 185p.

238. Casey, Robert Joseph. "Oh, England! full of sin; as
discovered by a chronic reader of English detective and
mystery stories." IN Scribner's Magazine v.101 (April 1937).
pp.33-37.

   repr. IN Haycraft, H. (ed.). The art of the mystery
   story. (q.v.) pp.343-351.

239. Cashman, G. "Reply to: J. P. Sisk, 'Crime and criticism'
(Commonweal, 20 April 1956)." IN Commonweal v.64 (18 May
1956). p. 182.

240.   Caspary, Vera.   "Mark McPherson."   IN   Penzler, O. M.
The great detectives.   (q.v.)   pp.141-146.

241.   Cassill, R. V.   "'The killer inside me'; fear, purgation,
and the Sophoclean light."   IN   Madden, D. (ed.).   Tough guy
writers of the Thirties.   (q.v.)   pp.230-238.

242.   Catogan, Valère.   Le secret des rois de France, ou La
véritable identité d'Arsène Lupin.   Paris: Éditions de Minuit;
1955.   71p., illus.

243.   Cauliez, Armand Jean.   Le film criminel et le film
policier.   Paris: Éditions du Cerf; 1956.   121p., illus.
(Collection "7e art").

244.   Cawelti, John G.   Adventure, mystery and romance;
formula stories as art and popular culture.   Chicago:
University of Chicago Press; 1976.   335p.

245.   ...   (comp.).   Focus on 'Bonnie and Clyde'.   Englewood
Cliffs, N.J.: Prentice-Hall; 1973.   xi, 176p.   (Film focus).
(A Spectrum book).

*   Chacko, David (jnt. ed.).   SEE   Allen, R. S.   (jnt. ed.).

246.   Champigny, Robert (1922-).   What will have happened;
a philosophical and technical essay on mystery stories.
Bloomington, Ind.: Indiana University Press; 1977.   viii,
183p.

247.   Chandler, Frank Wadleigh (1873-1947).   The literature
of roguery.   Boston: Houghton Mifflin; 1907.   2 vols.
Vide Chap. 'The literature of crime detection'.

   repr.: N.Y.: B. Franklin; 1958.   2 vols. [i.e. viii, 584p.].
   (The Types of English literature).

248.   Chandler, Raymond (1888-1959).   "The detective story
as an art form."   IN   Crime Writer   (Spring 1959).

249.   ...   "Introduction".   IN   Chandler, Raymond (1888-1959).
The smell of fear.   London: Hamish Hamilton; 1965.   538p.

250. ... The notebooks of Raymond Chandler; and, English
summer, a gothic romance. Ed. by Frank MacShane. N.Y.:
Ecco Press; 1976. 113p., illus.

251. Chandler, Raymond. "Notes on the mystery." IN
Raymond Chandler speaking. (q.v.)

   repr. IN Chandler, Raymond. The notebooks of Raymond
   Chandler. (q.v.)

   repr. IN Antaeus; Popular Fiction Issue No.25/26
   (Spring/Summer 1977) pp.100-105.

   repr. IN Writing suspense and mystery fiction (1977)
   (q.v.) pp.297-305.

252. ... Raymond Chandler speaking. Ed. by Dorothy Gardner
and Kathrine Sorley Walker. Boston: Houghton Mifflin; 1962.
271p. - U.K. ed.: London: Hamish Hamilton; 1962. 271p. -
repr.: Freeport, N.Y.: Books for Libraries; 1971. 271p. -
repr.: Boston: Houghton Mifflin; 1977. 288p. (Houghton
Mifflin Paperbacks).

253. ... "The simple art of murder." IN Atlantic Monthly
v.174 (December 1944) pp.53-59.

   repr. IN The pocket Atlantic. Ed. by Edward Weeks.
   N.Y.: Pocket Books; 1946. 304p. pp.195-214.

   repr. IN Fiedler, Leslie Aaron (1917-) (ed.). The art
   of the essay. N.Y.: Thomas Y. Crowell; 1958. 640p.
   pp.453-465. - 2d ed. - N.Y.: Crowell; 1969. xii, 593p.

   repr. with revisions IN Haycraft, H. (ed.). The art of
   the mystery story. (q.v.) pp.222-237.

   repr. with further revisions IN Chandler, Raymond
   (1888-1959). The simple art of murder. Boston: Houghton
   Mifflin; 1950. xiv, 533p. - Cdn. ed. - Toronto: Thomas
   Allen; 1950. xiv, 533p. - U.K. ed. - London: Hamish
   Hamilton; 1950. xiv, 533p. - repr. - N.Y.: Pocket Books;
   1953. - repr. - N.Y.: Norton; 1968. (Seagull Library of
   mystery and suspense).

   repr. IN Allen, R. S. (jnt. ed.). Detective fiction.
   (q.v.) pp. 387-399.

254. ... "The simple art of murder." IN Saturday Review
of Literature v.33 (15 April 1950) pp.13-14.

   NOTE: This is a new and different essay from that in
   Atlantic Monthly (December 1944). (supra).

repr. AS "Introduction." IN Chandler, Raymond (1888-1959). The simple art of murder. (For publishing history of this title, see above.)

repr. IN Gilbert, M. F. (comp.). Crime in good company. (q.v.) pp. 85-104.

255. Chapman, John. "Introduction" IN Cartmell, Van H. (jnt. comp.). Famous plays of crime and detection; from 'Sherlock Holmes' to 'Angel Street'. Comp. by V. H. Cartmell and Bennett Cerf, with an intro. by John Chapman. Philadelphia: Blakiston; 1946. xv, 910p. pp.ix-xv. - repr.: Freeport, N.Y.: Books for Libraries; 1971. xv, 910p. (Play anthology reprint series).

256. Chassaing. De Zadig au Riffifi; ou, Du roman policier: discours. Audience solennelle du 16 septembre 1958, Cours d'appel de Montpellier. Montpellier: Impr. de la Charite; 1958. 23p.

257. Chastaing, M. "Le roman policier et vérité." IN Journal de Psychologie [Paris] (April-June 1938).

258. Charland, Maurice. "The private eye; from print to television." IN Journal of Popular Culture vol.12:no.2 (Fall 1979) pp.210-216.

259. Charney, Hanna. "Pourquoi le "nouveau roman" policier?" IN French Review v.46:no.1 (October 1972) pp.17-23.

*   Chaumeton, Etienne (jnt. auth.). SEE Borde, Raymond.

260. Chertok, Harvey (jnt. comp.). Quotations from Charlie Chan. Comp. and ed. by H. Chertok and Martha Torge. N.Y.: Golden Press; 1968. 51p., illus.

261. Chesler, Phyllis. "The amazon legacy; an interpretive [sic] essay." IN Wonder Woman. (q.v.) [unpag. (i.e. 16pp.)]

262. Chesterton, Cecil (1879-1918). "Art and the detective." IN Temple Bar [London] v.134 (10 October 1906) p.322ff.

repr. IN Living Age v.251 (24 November 1906) pp. 505-510.

263. Chesterton, Gilbert Keith (1874-1936). "About shockers." IN Chesterton, Gilbert Keith (1874-1936). As I was saying; a book of essays. London: Methuen; 1936. vi, 227p. pp.200-210. - U.S. ed. -- N.Y.: Dodd Mead; 1936. - repr. - Freeport, N.Y.: Books for Libraries; 1966. (Essay Index Reprint series) viii, 228p.

264. ... Autobiography. London: Hutchinson; 1936. 347p. - U.S. ed.: N.Y.: Sheed & Ward; 1936. vii, 360p. - repr.: London: Hutchinson; 1949, and, 1969.

265. ... "A defense of detective stories." IN Chesterton, Gilbert Keith (1874-1936). The defendant. London: R. Brimley Johnson & Ince; 1901. 131p. - also publ. - London: Dent; 1901. 172p. pp.155-162. - U.S. ed. - N.Y.: Dodd Mead; 1902. - repr. several times by both Dent and Dodd Mead.

repr. IN Pritchard, Francis Henry (1884-1942) (ed.). Essays of today; an anthology. London: G. Harrap; 1923. 258p. - U.S. ed. - Boston: Little Brown; 1924. x, 261p. - repr. several times by both Harrap and Little Brown.

repr. IN Jepson, Rowland Walter (188?-1954) (ed.). New and old essays, 1820-1935. London: Longmans; 1936. 256p. - U.S. ed. - N.Y.: Longmans; 1937.

repr. IN Haycraft, H. (ed.). The art of the mystery story. (q.v.) pp.3-6.

repr. IN Allen, R. S. (jnt. ed.). Detective fiction. (q.v.) pp.384-386.

repr. in German trans. AS "Verteidigung von Detektivgeschichten." IN Vogt, J. (comp.). Der Kriminalroman. (q.v.) pp.95-98.

repr. in German trans. AS "Verteidigung von Kriminalroman." IN Der Detektiverzählung auf der Spur. (q.v.)

266. ... "Detective stories. [preface]" IN Masterman, Walter Sidney (1876-). The wrong letter. With a preface by G. K. Chesterton. London: Methuen; 1926. ix, 186p. - U.S. ed. - N.Y.: Dutton; 1926. xi, 212p. - various reprints.

repr. IN Chesterton, Gilbert Keith (1874-1936). G.K.C. as M.C.; being a collection of thirty-seven introductions by G. K. Chesterton. Ed. by J. P. de Fonseka. London: Methuen; 1929. xxiv, 273p. pp.175-177. - repr. - Freeport, N.Y.: Books for Libraries; 1967. xxii, 273p. (Essay Index Reprint series).

267. ... "The divine detective." IN Chesterton, Gilbert
Keith (1874-1936). A miscellany of men. London: Methuen;
1912. viii, 267p. - U.S. ed.: N.Y.: Dodd Mead; 1912. xii,
314p. - repr. several times by Methuen.

268. ... "The domesticity of detectives." IN Chesterton,
Gilbert Keith (1874-1936). The uses of diversity; a book
of essays. London: Methuen; 1920. vi, 191p. - U.S. ed.:
N.Y.: Dodd Mead; 1921. 289p. - repr. several times by
Methuen.

269. ... "How to write a detective story." IN Chesterton,
Gilbert Keith (1874-1936). The spice of life and other essays.
Ed. by Dorothy Collins. Beaconsfield, Eng.: Darwin Finlayson;
1964. 175p. pp.15-21. - U.S. ed.: Philadelphia: Dufour;
1966. 175p.

270. ... "[Introduction]" IN Capes, Bernard Edward
Joseph (?-1918). The skeleton key. London: Collins; 1917.
- U.S. ed.: N.Y.: Doran; 1918. - repr. several times by
both Collins and Doran.

271. ... "[Introduction]" IN A century of detective
stories. With an intro. by G. K. Chesterton. London:
Hutchinson; 1935. 1019p.

272. ... "On detective novels." IN Chesterton, Gilbert
Keith (1874-1936). Generally speaking; a book of essays.
London: Methuen; 1928. v, 249p. - U.S. ed.: N.Y.: Dodd
Mead; 1929. 291p. - also publ.: Leipzig: B. Tauchnitz;
1929. 271p.

    repr. IN Noyes, Edward Simpson ed. Readings in the
    modern essay. Boston: Houghton Mifflin; 1933. viii, 561p.

    repr. IN Chesterton, Gilbert Keith (1874-1936). The man
    who was Chesterton; the best essays, stories, poems, and
    other writings of G. K. Chesterton. Comp. and ed. by
    R. T. Bond. N.Y.: Dodd Mead; 1937. xi, 801p. - repr.:
    Freeport, N.Y.: Books for Libraries Press; 1970. xi, 801p.
    (Essay Index Reprint series).

    repr. AS "A propos du roman policier." IN Cellules
    Grises No.4 (October 1955).

273. ... "On detective story writers." IN Chesterton,
Gilbert Keith (1874-1936). Come to think of it ... a book
of essays. Selected and arranged by J. P. de Fonseca. London:
Methuen; 1930. xiii, 243p. - U.S. ed.: N.Y.: Dodd Mead;
1931. xiv, 272p.

274. Chianese, Robert L. "James Hogg's 'Confessions of a
justified sinner'; an anatomy of terror." IN Mystery and
Detection Annual; 1973. (q.v.) pp.97-112.

275. Chimera; a special issue on detective fiction. (Ed. by
Barbara Howes) [New York] v.5:no.4 (Summer 1947). 80p.

276. "The Chinese apathy toward crime detection." IN
Literary Digest v.116 (23 September 1933). pp.14ff.

277. Christensen, Peter. "William Hope Hodgson; 'Carnacki
the ghost-finder'." IN Armchair Detective vol.12:no.2
(Spring 1979) pp.122-124.

278. Christie, Dame Agatha Mary Clarissa Miller (1890-1976).
An autobiography. London: Collins; 1977. 542p., illus. -
repr.: London: Fontana; 1978.

279. Christopher, Joseph R. "The mystery of social reaction;
two novels by Ellery Queen." IN The Armchair Detective
v.6:no.1 (October 1972). pp.28-32.

280. ... "Poe and the detective story." IN The Armchair
Detective v.2:no.1 (October 1968). pp.49-51.

     rev. and repr. AS 'Poe and the tradition of the detective
     story' IN Nevins, F. M. (comp.). The mystery writer's
     art. (q.v.) pp.19-36.

281. Ciǵánek, Jan. Umění detektivky; o smyslu a povaze
detektivky. Prague: Státní nakl. detské knihy; 1962. 410p.
(Knižnice teorie detské literatury, 13).

282. City of San Francisco Magazine. vol.9:No.17
(4 November 1975) - "Souvenir edition" devoted to
Dashiell Hammett; ed. by Warren Hinckle.

283. Clarens, Carlos. "Hooverville West; the Hollywood
G-Man, 1934-1945." IN Film Comment vol.13:no.3 (May-June
1977) pp.10-16.

284. Clipper, Lawrence J. G. K. Chesterton. N.Y.: Twayne;
1974. 190p. (Twayne's English Authors series no.166).

285. Clurman, Robert. "Introduction" IN Dey, Frederick
Marmaduke Van Rensselaer. Nick Carter, detective; the
adventures of fiction's most celebrated detective. N.Y.:
Dell; 1963. pp.7-14.

286. Cockburn, Claud. "'The riddle of the sands', Erskine
Childers." IN Cockburn, Claud. Bestseller; the books that
everyone read 1900-1939. London: Sidgwick & Jackson; 1972.
[viii], 182p. pp.75-82.

287. Cohen, Ralph. "Private eyes and public critics."
IN Partisan Review v.24 (Spring 1957) pp.235-243.

288. Colbron, Grace Isabel. "Detective story in Germany
and Scandinavia." IN Bookman [N.Y.] v.30 (December 1909)
pp.407-412.

289. Cole, Margaret I. "Senility of detective novels?"
IN Spectator No.5,355 (14 February 1931) pp.230-231.

290. Collins, Carvel. "Simenon" IN Paris Review.
Writers at work; the 'Paris Review' interviews. Ed. by
Malcolm Cowley. First Series. N.Y.: Viking; 1958. 390p.,
illus. - U.K. ed. - London: Secker & Warburg; 1958. 276p.

291. Collins, Philip Arthur William. Dickens and crime.
London: Macmillan; 1962. xiii, 371p. (Cambridge Studies
in Criminology, vol.17) - U.S. ed.: N.Y.: St. Martin's
Press; 1962. xiii, 371p. - 2d ed.: London: Macmillan/N.Y.:
St. Martin's Press; 1964. xiv, 371p. - repr.: 1965, and,
1966. - repr. pbk.: Bloomington, Ind.: Indiana University
Press; 1968. ix, 371p. (A Midland book, MB119).

292. Colum, Pádraic. "Introduction" IN Poe, Edgar Allan
(1809-1849). Tales of mystery and imagination. London:
Dent; 1966. xv, 527p. (Everyman's Library) - U.S. ed.:
N.Y.: E. P. Dutton.

293. Comber, Leon. "An introduction to the world of
Magistrate Pao." IN Comber, Leon. (trans. and ed.).
The strange cases of Magistrate Pao; Chinese tales of crime
and detection. Rutland, Vt.: Charles E. Tuttle; 1964. 137p.
pp.9-31.

294. Conan Doyle, Adrian M. The true Conan Doyle. London:
John Murray; 1945. 24p., illus.

295. Conan Doyle, Sir Arthur (1859-1930). Memories and adventures. London: Hodder & Stoughton; 1924. 408p. - U.S. ed.: Boston: Little Brown; 1924. ix, 410p. - 2d ed.: London: John Murray; 1930. 460p.

296. Conlon, D. J. G. K. Chesterton; the critical judgments. Antwerp: Antwerp Studies in English Literature; 1977 - 2 vols.

    Pt.1: 1900-1937. 1977. 555p.

297. Connor, Edward. "The four Ellery Queens." IN Films in Review v.11:no.6 (June-July 1960) pp. 338-342.

    rev. and repr. IN The Queen Canon Bibliophile (April 1971).

298. ... "The mystery film." IN Films in Review v.5:no.3 (March 1954) pp.120-123.

299. ... "The nine Philo Vances." IN Films in Review v.9:no.3 (March 1958) pp.133-137, 154.

300. ... "Sherlock Holmes on the screen has never been exactly the man Conan Doyle's readers imagined." IN Films in Review v.12:no.7 (August-September 1961) pp.409-418.

301. ... "The 6 Charlie Chans." IN Films in Review v.6 (January 1955) pp.23-27.

302. ... "The twelve Bulldog Drummonds." IN Films in Review v.7:no.8 (October 1956) pp.394-397.

303. Conrad, Horst (1943-). Die literarische Angst; das Schreckliche in Schauerromantik und Detektivgeschichte. Düsseldorf: Bertelsmann-Universitäts-verlag; 1974. 230p. (Literatur in der Gesellschaft, 21).

304. Cook, Bruce. "Ross Macdonald; the prince in the poorhouse." IN Catholic World vol.214 (October 1971) pp.27-30.

305. Cook, Michael L. Murder by mail; inside the mystery book clubs - with complete checklist. Evansville, Ind.: Cook Publications; 1979. 109p.

306.   Cooke, Alistair.   "Epitaph for a tough guy; Humphrey
Bogart."   IN   Atlantic Monthly   v.199   (May 1957)   pp.31-35.

   rev. and repr.   IN   Cooke, Alistair.   Six men.   N.Y.:
   Knopf; 1956.   -   repr. - N.Y.: Berkley; 1978.   237p.,
   illus.   pp.205-233.

307.   Cookridge, E. H.   "The train in fiction and on the
screen."   IN   Cookridge, E. H.   Orient Express; the life and
times of the world's most famous train.   N.Y.: Random House;
1978.   288p., illus.   Chap.XII: pp.228-246.

308.   Corbett, James Edward.   "Art of writing thrillers."
IN   Contemporary Review   v.182   (October 1952)   pp.240-243.

309.   Cordell, Richard.   Somerset Maugham; a biographical and
critical study.   Bloomington, Ind.: Indiana University Press;
1961.   xii, 250p.   -   U.K. ed.: London: Heinemann; 1961.
xii, 250p.

310.   Cornell Woolrich; a catalogue of first and variant
editions of his work.   Pocono Pines, Pa.: Gravesend Books;
1975.   [n.pag.].

*   Corrigan, Beatrice (ed.).   SEE   Cortona Codex.

311.   Corsage; a bouquet of Rex Stout and Nero Wolfe.   Ed. by
Michael Bourne.   Bloomington, Ind.: James A. Rock; 1977.
xiv, 163p., illus.

312.   Cortona Codex.   Curious annals; new documents relating
to Browning's Roman murder story.   Trans., ed., and with an
intro. by Beatrice Corrigan.   Toronto: University of Toronto
Press; 1956.   142p., illus.

*   Couperie, Pierre.   SEE   Musée des Arts Decoratifs,
Paris.

313.   Courtine, Robert-Jullien.   Le cahier de recettes de
Madame Maigret.   Paris: Robert Laffont; 1974.   269p., illus.

314.   ...   "Simenon ou l'appétit de Maigret."   IN   Lacassin,
F. (jnt. ed.).   Simenon.   (q.v.)   pp.204-219.

315. Cowley, Malcolm. "Sex murder incorporated." IN
New Republic v.126 (1952) pp.17-18.

316. Cox, J. Randolph. "John Buchan; a philosophy of high
adventure." IN Armchair Detective (July 1969).

    repr. IN Buchan, John. The thirty-nine steps. San Diego:
    University Extension, University of California-San Diego/Del
    Mar, Calif.: Publisher's Inc.,; 1978. xvi, 207p., illus.
    pp.170-184.

317. Cox, Reginald. "The Sexton Blake file; characteristics,
methods & manners of a great British detective." IN The
Saturday Book:6. London: Hutchinson; 1946. 288p., illus.
pp. 161-176.

318. Coxe, George Harmon. "Flash Casey." IN Penzler, O. M.
The great detectives. (q.v.) pp.37-46.

*   Craigie, Dorothy. SEE Glover, Dorothy.

319. Creasey, John. "John Creasey - fact or fiction."
IN Armchair Detective v.2:no.1 (October 1968) pp.1-5.

320. Crider, Allen Billy. The private eye hero; a study of
the novels of Dashiell Hammett, Raymond Chandler and Ross
Macdonald ... Ph.D. dissertation, University of Texas at
Austin, 1972. 176p.

321. ... "Race Williams - private investigator." IN
Dimensions of detective fiction. (q.v.) pp.110-113.

322. "Crime; 'Little Caesar' starts a crime wave." IN
The Hamlyn history of the movies. Comp. by Mary Davies
et al. London: Hamlyn; 1975. 224p. pp.98-113.

323. "Crime in fiction." IN Blackwood's Edinburgh
Magazine. v.148:898 (August 1890) pp.172-189.

324. "Crime should be credible." IN Saturday Review
[London] v.154:no.4015 (8 October 1932) p.365.

325. Crime writers; reflections on crime fiction. Ed. by
H. R. F. Keating and Michael Pavett. London: British
Broadcasting Corporation; 1978. 160p., illus.

326. Crispin, Edmund. "Introduction" IN Crispin, Edmund (ed.). Best detective stories. Ed. with an intro. by Edmund Crispin. London: Faber; 1959. 287p. - repr.: London: Faber; 1961.

repr. in German trans. AS Vorwort zu Best Detective Stories IN Der Detektiverzählung auf der Spur. (q.v.).

327. ... "The mistress of simplicity; a conversation with H. R. F. Keating." IN Agatha Christie. (q.v.) pp.39-48.

328. Cristea, Valeriu. "Voluptatea teroarei." IN Interpretări critice [Bucharest, Cartea romănească] (1970) pp.304-305.

329. Cromie, Robert. "Dr. Conan Doyle's place in modern literature." IN The Twentieth Century London v.2:no.5 (May 1901) pp.187-205.

* Cross Country. SEE "A poetic investigation of detectives, mystery and murder".

330. Crossen, Ken. "There's murder in the air." IN Haycraft, H. (ed.). The art of the mystery story. (q.v.) pp.304-307.

331. Crouse, Russel (1893-). "The murder of Mary Cecilia Rogers." IN Crouse, Russel (1893-). Murder won't out. Garden City, N.Y.: Doubleday Doran; 1932. xx, 261p.

332. Crowther, Bosley. "film history of 'The Thin Man'" IN Crowther, Bosley. The lion's share; the story of an entertainment empire. N.Y.: Duton; 1957. 320p.

333. ... "'The Maltese Falcon'." IN Crowther, Bosley. The great films; fifty golden years of motion pictures. N.Y.: G. P. Putnam's Sons; 1967. 258p.

334. Cruse, Amy (1870-). "Crime fiction." IN Cruse, Amy (1870-). After the Victorians. London: Allen & Unwin; 1938. 264p. - repr.: St. Clair Shores, Mich.: Scholarly Press; 1971. 264p.

335. Cruttwell, Patrick. "On 'Caleb Williams'." IN Hudson Review v.9 (Spring 1958) pp.87-95.

336. Cullaz, Maurice. "Chester Himes, interview." IN
Jazz-Hot No.285 (July-August 1972).

337. Cummings, J. C. "Detective stories." IN Bookman
[N.Y.] v.30 (January 1910) pp.499-500.

338. Cuppy, Will. "How to read a whodunit." IN Mystery
Book Magazine (January 1946).

  repr. IN Haycraft, H. (ed.). The art of the mystery
  story. (q.v.) pp.373-376.

339. Curry, Nancy Ellen Loudenslager. The life and works
of Emile Gaboriau ... Ph.D. thesis, University of Kentucky,
1970. 273p. - repr. - N.Y.: Graland; 1978. 273p.

340. Cushing, Charles Phelps. "Who writes these mystery
yarns?" IN Independent v.118 (9 April 1927) pp.382-388.

D

341. Dahl, Willy. Blå briller og løsskjegg i Kristiania. Oslo: Gyldendal; 1975. 116p., illus. (En Fakkel-bok: 327).

342. Dahncke, Walter. Kriminalroman und Wirklichkeit; ein versuch, dem verehrlichen publiko beides zu demonstrieren. Hamburg: Verlag Kriminalistik; 1958. 260p., illus.

343. Daiber, Hans. "Nachahmung der Vorsehung." IN Vogt, J. (comp.) Der Kriminalroman. (q.v.).

344. Dale, Alzina Stone. Maker and craftsman; the story of Dorothy L. Sayers. Grand Rapids, Mich.: William B. Eerdmans; 1978. 158p., illus.

345. Daley, Robert. "Police report on the TV cop shows". IN The New York Times (19 November and 24 December 1972).

  repr. IN Allen, R. S. (jnt. ed.). Detective fiction. (q.v.) pp.430-445.

* Dalliba, William Swift. (jnt. ed.). SEE Ruber, Peter A.

346. Dalziel, Margaret. Popular fiction 100 years ago; an unexplored tract of literary history. London: Cohen & West; 1957. vii, 188p., illus.

347. Dameron, J. Lasley. Edgar Allan Poe; a bibliography of criticism, 1827-1967. Charlottesville, Va.: pub. for

Bibliographical Society [of the] University of Virginia by
University Press of Virginia; 1974. xvi, 386p.

348. Dane, Clemence [pseud.]. "Best detective story in the
world." IN Bookman [N.Y.] v.75 (October 1972) pp.539-541.

349. Daniel, Peter. Bleak House (Charles Dickens). Oxford:
Blackwell; 1968. 85p. (Notes on English Literature 34).

350. Daniel-Rops. "Les romans policiers de M. Georges
Simenon." orig. publ. IN La Nouvelle Revue des Jeunes
(15 July 1932) - repr. IN Lacassin, F. (jnt. ed.).
Simenon. (q.v.) pp.223-226.

351. Daniell, David. The interpreter's house; a critical
assessment of John Buchan. London: Thomas Nelson; 1975.
xxi, 226p.

352. Daniels, Les. Comix; a history of comic books in
America. N.Y.: Bonanza; c1971. 198p., illus.

353. Dannay, Frederic (1905-). The golden summer. By
Daniel Nathan [pseud.]. Boston: Little Brown; 1953. 215p.

*   ... SEE also Queen, Ellery [pseud.].

354. Dansk og udenlandsk kriminallitteratur. Ed. by Tage
la Cour, Harald Mogensen, [and] Else Larsen. Copenhagn:
Politiken; 1975. 350., illus. (Politikens literaturhåndbøger).

355. Davenport, Basil. "The devil is not dead." IN
Saturday Review of Literature v.13 (15 February 1936)
pp.3-4ff.

356. Davidson, Edward Hutchins. Poe; a critical study.
Cambridge, Mass.: Harvard University Press; 1957. xiii,
296p. - U.K. ed.: London: Oxford University Press; 1957.
xiii, 296p.

357. Davies, Russell. "Omnes me impune lacessunt." IN
Gross, M. (ed.). The world of Raymond Chandler. (q.v.)
pp.32-42.

358. Davis, Brian. The thriller; the suspense film from
1946. London: Studio Vista; 1973. 159p., illus. (Studio
Vista/Dutton pictureback).

359. Davis, David Brion. Homicide in American fiction,
1798-1860; a study in social values. Ithaca, N.Y.: Cornell
University Press; 1957. xviii, 346p. - U.K. ed.: London:
Oxford University Press; 1957. xviii, 346p.

360. Davis, Nuel Pharr (1915-). The life of Wilkie Collins.
Urbana, Ill.: University of Illinois Press; 1956. 360p.

361. Davis, Paxton. "The world we live in; the novels of
Eric Ambler." IN The Hollins Critic [Hollins College]
(February 1971).

362. Day Lewis, Cecil (1904-1972). The buried day;
[autobiography]. London: Chatto & Windus; 1960. 244p.
- U.S. ed.: N.Y.: Harper; 1960. 243p.

363. ... "Introduction" IN Haycraft, Howard (1905-).
Murder for pleasure; the life and times of the detective
story. Intro. by Nicholas Blake [pseud.]. London: Peter
Davies; 1942. 376p.

   N.B.: This introduction was written specially for and
   only appeared in the U.K. edition.

   - a selection from this introduction was excerpted and
   reprinted AS "The detective story - why?" IN Haycraft,
   H. (ed.). The art of the mystery story. (q.v.) pp.398-405.

   repr. in German trans. AS "Wozu Detektivgeschichten?" IN
   Der Detektiverzählung auf der Spur. (q.v.).

364. Dear, A. "Intellectuals and 007; high comedy and total
stimulation." IN Dissent [Melbourne]. v.23 (Winter 1966).

365. Debray-Ritzen, Pierre. "Mon maître Simenon." IN
Lacassin, F. (jnt. ed.). Simenon. (q.v.) pp.59-68.

366. Degn, Peer. Blodige fotspor; litt om eldre utenlandsk
kriminallitteratur. Oslo: [n.publ.]; 1943. 19p.

   Not verified. Cited in: la Cour, T. 'The murder book'.
   (q.v.) p.176.

*   Del Buono, Oreste. SEE Buono, Oreste Del.

367. Del Monte, Alberto. Breve storia del romanzo poliziesco.
Bari: G. Laterza e F.; 1962. 285p. (Biblioteca di cultura
moderna. 568).

368. Denbie, R. "Reply to: Waite, J. B. 'If judges wrote
detective stories'; Scribner's Magazine, April 1934." (q.v.)
IN Scribner's Magazine v.95 (April 1934) Supp. p.22.

369. Denby, D. "Stolen privacy; Coppola's 'The
conversation'." IN Sight and Sound v.43:no.3 (Summer
1974) pp.131-133.

370. Deniker, Professeur. "Georges Simenon, clinicien de
l'âme." IN Lacassin, F. (jnt. ed.). Simenon. (q.v.)
pp.69-70.

371. Depken, Friedrich. Sherlock Holmes, Raffles, und Ihre
Vorbilder; Ein Beitrag zur Entwicklungsgeschichte und Technik
der Kriminalerzahlung. Heidelberg: Carl Winter; 1914. xi,
105p. (Anglistische forschungen ... hft 41) - repr. -
N.Y.: Garland; 1978.

     abr. vers. repr. AS "Sherlock Holmes, Raffles und
     Ihre Vorbilder (Auszuge)." IN Der Detektiverzählung
     auf der Spur. (q.v.).

     U.S. (first English lang.) ed. - Sherlock Holmes, Raffles,
     and their prototypes. Trans. by Jay Finley Christ.
     Chicago: Fanlight House; 1949. xii, 89p.

372. Derleth, August William (1909-1971). A Praed Street
dossier. Sauk City, Wisc.: Mycroft & Moran; 1968. 108p.,
illus.

373. Desilets, Michael. "Raymond Chandler and Hollywood."
IN Filmograph (April 1972) n.v.

374. Detectionary; a biographical dictionary of the leading
characters in detective and mystery fiction. Comp. by Chris
Steinbrunner et al. Lock Haven, Pa.: Published privately by
Hammerhill Paper Co., Lock Haven Division: 1971 [1972]. xiv,
590p., illus.

     repr. Detectionary; a biographical dictionary of leading
     characters in detective and mystery fiction, including

famous and little-known sleuths, their helpers, rogues
both heroic and sinister, and some of the most memorable
adventures, as recounted in novels, short stories, and
films. Ed. by Otto Penzler et al. Woodstock, N.Y.:
Overlook Press; 1977. xii, 299p.

375. Detective fiction: a century of crime; first and early
editions. Hastings, Eng.: R. A. Brimmell; [1966?]. 45p.,
illus.

376. Detective fiction; [catalogue]. Buntingford, [Herts,
Eng.?]: Charles Rare Books; 1955. 25p.

377. Detective fiction; mysteries and crime, first editions.
Chicago: J. & S. Graphics; 1972. 340p. (J & S Catalogue 15).

378. "Detective stories." IN Atlantic Monthly v.81
(April 1898). pp.573-574.

379. "Detectives [in fiction; a study in literary fashions]."
IN The Times Literary Supplement No.1,280 (12 August 1926).
pp.529-530.

    repr. IN Living Age v.330 (18 September 1926).
    pp.638-643.

380. Der Detektiverzählung auf der Spur. Essays zur Form
und Wertung der englischen Detektivliteratur. Hrsg. von
Paul G. Buchloh und Jens Peter Becker. Darmstadt:
Wissenschaftliche Buchgesellschaft; 1977. vii, 395p.
(Wege der Forschung, Vol.387).

381. de Traz, Georges Albert Edouard (1881-). Histoire et
technique du roman-policier. By François Fosca [pseud.].
Paris: Éditions de la Nouvelle Revue Critique; 1937. 228p.

382. De Voto, Bernard. "Alias Nero Wolfe." IN Harper's
Magazine v.209 (whole no.1,250) (July 1954) pp.8-9, 12-15.
("Easy Chair" column).

383. ... "Reply to Edmund Wilson on detective stories."
IN Harper's Magazine v.190 (whole no.1,135) (December 1944)
pp.36-37. ("Easy Chair" column).

384. De Waal, Ronald Burt. "Solar Pons and Dr. Parker; a
bibliography, 1929-1969." IN American Book Collector v.20
(May 1970) pp.19-26.

385. ... The world bibliography of Sherlock Holmes and
Dr. Watson; a classified and annotated list of materials
relating to their lives and adventures. Boston: New York
Graphic Society; 1974. xiv, 526p., illus.

*   Dexter, Walter (1877-). (ed.). SEE Dickens, Charles.

386. Díaz, César E. La novela policíaca; síntesis histórica
a través de sus autores, sus personajes y sus obras.
Barcelona: Ediciones Acervo; 1973. 202p.

387. Dickens, Charles (1812-1870). Some rogues and vagabonds
of Dickens. Selections from Dickens, with explanatory comment
by Walter Dexter. London: C. Palmer; 1927. 284p. - U.S.
ed.: Philadelphia: Lippincott; 1927.

388. Dickinson, Peter. "Superintendent Pibble." IN
Penzler, O.M. The great detectives. (q.v.) pp.175-182.

389. Dikty, Alan S. The American boys' book series
bibliography 1895-1935. Naperville, Ill.: BBC Publications;
[1977]. 170p., illus.

390. Dimensions of detective fiction. Ed. by Larry N.
Landrum et al. Bowling Green, Ohio: Bowling Green University
Popular Press; 1976. 290p.

391. Disher, Maurice Willson (1893-). Blood and thunder;
mid-Victorian melodrama and its origins. London: Muller;
1949. 280p. - U.S. ed.; N.Y.: Haskell House Pub.; 1974.
280p.

392. ... Melodrama; plots that thrilled; illustrated from
the Raymond Mander and Joe Mitchenson Theatre Collection.
London: Rockliff; 1954. xiv, 210p., illus. - U.S. ed.:
N.Y.: Macmillan; 1954. 210p.

393. Diskin, Patrick. "Poe, LeFanu, and the sealed room
mystery." IN Notes and Queries. o.s.vol.211/n.s.vol.13:no.9
(September 1966) pp.337-339.

394. Dolmetsch, Carl. "The writer in America; the strange
case of S. S. Van Dine." IN Literatur und Sprache der
Vereinigten Staaten. Heidelberg: Winter-Universitäts-verlag;
1969. 247p.

395. Donaldson, Norman. *In search of Dr. Thorndyke; the story of R. Austin Freeman's great scientific investigator and his creator*. Bowling Green, Ohio; Bowling Green University Popular Press; 1971. xii, 288p.

- a portion of Chap.VI, 'Thorndyke moves ahead',
(pp.98-105) was reprinted with slight revision AS
R. Austin Freeman; the inventor of inversion.   IN
Nevins, F. M. (comp.) *The mystery writer's art*.
(q.v.) pp.79-87.

396. ... "Introduction" IN Braddon, Mary Elizabeth
(1837-1915). *Lady Audley's secret*. N.Y.: Dover; 1974.
xvi, 286p. pp.v-xiv.

397. ... "Introduction." IN Childers, Erskine. *The riddle of the sands; a record of secret service*. N.Y.:
Dover; 1976. 284p. pp.1-11.

398. ... "R. Austin Freeman." IN *Armchair detective*
v.1:no.2 (January 1968) pp.32-37.

*   Donovan, Dick. SEE Preston-Muddock, Joyce Emmerson
(1843-1934).

399. Dorset, Gerald. *An aristocrat of intellect*. London:
G. Dorset; 1959. 51p.

400. Doulis, Thomas. "John D. MacDonald; the liabilities
of professionalism." IN *Journal of Popular Culture* v.10:no.1
(Summer 1976) pp.38-53.

401. *The Dover Detective Library*. N.Y.: Dover Publications;
1976. 1⅛. [i.e. 2p.].

402. Downer, Alan S. "The monitor image." IN *Man and the movies*. Ed. by William Ronald Robinson with assistance from
George Garrett. Baton Rouge, La.: Louisiana State University
Press; 1967. 371p.

*   Dresser, Davis. SEE Halliday, Brett [pseud.].

403. Drew, Bernard. "The land of the Midnight Pulps; Who
knows what evil lurks in the hearts of Canadians? The Shadow
knows ..." IN *The Canadian* (27 August 1977) pp.10-12.

404. Droom en onthulling, lezingen gehouden voor het
Criminologisch Instituut. By E. C. M. Frijling-Schreuder
et al. Utrecht: Dekker & Van de Vegt; 1948. 94p.
(Criminalologische studiën, deel 8).

405. Druxman, Michael B. (1941-). Basil Rathbone; his life
and his films. South Brunswick, N.J.: A. S. Barnes; 1975.
359p. - U.K. ed.: London: Tantivy Press; 1975. 359p.

406. Dubourg, Maurice. "Géographie de Simenon." IN
Lacassin, F. (jnt. ed.). Simenon. (q.v.) pp.139-156.

407. ... "Maigret and Co.; the detectives of the Simenon
agency."

   orig. publ. IN Mystère-Magazine No.203 (December 1964).

   repr. in Engl. IN Armchair Detective v.4:no.2 (January
   1971) pp.79-86.

408. Du Maurier, Daphne. Growing pains; the shaping of a
writer. London: Gollancz; 1977. 172p.

409. Duperray, Jean. "Au nom du Père." IN Lacassin, F.
(jnt. ed.). Simenon. (q.v.) pp.99-129.

410. Dupuy, Josée. Le roman policier. Paris: Larousse;
1974. 192p. (Textes pour aujourd'hui).

411. Durgnat, Raymond. "Spies and ideologies." IN Cinema
No.2 (March 1969) pp.5-13.

412. ... "The strange case of Alfred Hitchcock." IN
Films and Filming v.16:no.5 (February 1970) through
v.17:no.2 (November 1970) 10 pts.

   repr.: The strange case of Alfred Hitchcock; or, The
   plain man's Hitchcock. London: Faber & Faber; 1974.
   3, 419p. - U.S. ed.: Cambridge, Mass.: MIT Press;
   1974. 419p.

413. Durham, Philip C. "The 'Black Mask' school." IN
Madden, D. (ed.) Tough guy writers of the Thirties. (q.v.)
pp.51-79.

   repr. IN Nevins, F. M. (comp.) The mystery writer's art.
   (q.v.) pp.197-226.

414. ... <u>Down these mean streets a man must go; Raymond</u>
<u>Chandler's knight</u>. Chapel Hill, N.C.: University of North
Carolina Press; 1963. 173.

415. ... "Introduction" IN Chandler, Raymond (1888-1959).
<u>Killer in the rain</u>. With an intro. by Philip Durham. Boston:
Houghton Mifflin; 1964. xii, 394p. - U.K. ed.: London:
Hamish Hamilton; 1964. xii, 394p.

416. ... <u>The objective treatment of the hard-boiled hero</u>
<u>in American fiction; a study of the frontier background of</u>
<u>modern American literature</u> ... Ph.D. dissertation,
Northwestern University, 1949. n.p.

*   ... SEE also California. University. University
at Los Angeles. Library.

*   ... (jnt. comp.) SEE also Hagemann, E. R.

417. Dworak, Anselm. <u>Der Kriminalroman der D.D.R.</u>
Marburg/Lahn: IM SELBSTVERLAG des Herausgehers Hans-Friedrich
Foltin; 1974. viii, 549p. (Aussagenanalysen: 1).

418. Dyer, Peter John. "The murderers among us." IN
<u>Films and Filming</u> v.5:no.3 (December 1958) pp.13-15,
32-33.

419. ... "Some silent sinners." IN <u>Films and Filming</u>
v.4:no.6 (March 1958) pp.13-15, 34.

420. ... "Young and innocent." IN <u>Sight and Sound</u>
v.30:no.2 (Spring 1961) pp.80-83.

421. Dyson, Anthony Edward. <u>Dickens 'Bleak House'; a</u>
<u>casebook</u>. London: Macmillan; 1969. 284p. (Casebook ser.)

E

422. Eames, Hugh. Sleuths, Inc.; studies of problem solvers: Doyle, Simenon, Hammett, Ambler, Chandler. Philadelphia: J. B. Lippincott; 1978. 228p.

423. Earley, Steven C. An introduction to American movies. N.Y.: New American Library; 1978. xii, 337p., illus. (A Mentor Book 451-ME1638) vide Chapter 11: "The gangster film", pp.127-137; Chapter 12: "Film noir, or black cinema", pp.138-145.

424. East, Andy R. Agatha Christie quizbook. N.Y.: Drake; 1975. 169p. - repr.: N.Y.: Pocket Books; 1976.

425. Eckley, Wilton. T. S. Stribling. Boston: Twayne; 1975. 127p. (Twayne's United States Authors ser. no.255).

426. Eco, Umberto. "James Bond; une combinatoire narrative." IN Communications [Paris] No. 8 (1966).

*   Eco, Umberto (jnt. auth.) SEE also Buono, Oreste Del.

427. Edenbaum, Robert I. "The poetics of the private eye; the novels of Dashiell Hammett." IN Madden, D. (ed.). Tough guy writers of the Thirties. (q.v.) pp.80-103.

  repr. IN Nevins, F. M. (comp.) The mystery writer's art. (q.v.) pp.98-121.

428. Edgar, George (1877-). "The unromantic detective."
IN Outlook [London] (3 December 1910).

    repr. IN Living Age v.267 (24 December 1910) pp.825-827.

429. Edmiston, S. "Nine most devilish murders." IN
Esquire v.84 (August 1975) pp.66-67ff.

430. Edwards, Peter David. Some mid-Victorian thrillers;
the sensational novel, its friends and its foes. St. Lucia,
Queensland: University of Queensland Press; 1971. 34p.
(University of Queensland inaugural lectures).

431. Egloff, Gerd (1939-). Detektivroman und englisches
Bürgertum; Konstruktions schema und Gesellschaftsbild bei
Agatha Christie. Düsseldorf: Bertelsmann Universitätsverlag;
1974. 137p. (Literatur in der Gesellschaft, 33).

432. Eisinger, Erica M. "Crime and detection in the novels
of Marguerite Duras." IN Contemporary Literature v.15
(Autumn 1974) pp.503-520.

433. ... "Maigret and women; 'la maman' and 'la putain'."
IN Journal of Popular Culture vol.12:no.1 (Summer 1978)
pp.52-60.

434. Eisner, Lotte. Fritz Lang. Oxford University Press;
1977.

435. Elgström, Jörgen (jnt. auth.). Mord i biblioteket;
detektivromanens märkvärdiga historia. By J. Elgström,
Tage la Cour, and Åke Runniquist. Stockholm: Bonnier; 1961.
222p., illus.

    A Danish ed. - Copenhagen: [n.publ.]; 1965 - is cited in:
    la Cour, T. 'The murder book' (q.v.), p.176; but has not
    proved possible to verify.

436. ... (jnt. auth.). Svensk mordbok; den svenska
detektivromanens historia, 1900-1950. By J. Elgström and
Åke Runniquist. Stockholm: Sällskapet Bokvännerna; 1957.
160p., illus. (Bokvännens bibliotek, nr.36).

437. Eliot, Thomas Stearns. "Dickens and Collins." IN
Eliot, Thomas Stearns. Selected essays, 1917-1932. London:
Faber & Faber; 1932. 454p. pp.373-382. - U.S. ed.: N.Y.:
Harcourt Brace; 1932.

438. ... "Introduction." IN Collins, Wilkie. The
moonstone. With an intro. by T. S. Eliot. London: Oxford
University Press; 1928. xx, 522p. (World's Classics CCXVI)
- repr. many times by OUP.

  repr. in German trans. AS "Einleitung zu Wilkie Collins'
  'The Moonstone'." IN Der Detektiverzählung auf der Spur.
  (q.v.).

439. Ellin, Stanley. "The crime short story; an American
view." IN Gilbert, M. (ed.). Crime in good company.
(q.v.) pp.163-177.

440. Elliott, George Paul. "A country full of blondes."
IN Nation v.190 (23 April 1960) pp.354-356, 358-360.

441. Ellis, Stewart Marsh. Wilkie Collins, Le Fanu, and
others. London: Constable; 1931. 343p. - repr. 1951
(Constable Lives).

442. ... William Harrison Ainsworth and his friends.
London: John Lane; 1911. 2 vols., illus. - repr. -
N.Y.: Garland; 1978. 2 vols.

443. Elsen, Claude. "Faulkner et le roman noire." IN
Réforme (16 February 1952).

444. Encyclopedia of comic book heroes. N.Y.: Macmillan;
1976 - 8 vols.

  Vol.1: Batman. By Michael L. Fleisher. 1976. 387p.,
  illus.

  Vol.2: Wonder Woman. By Michael L. Fleisher and Janet
  E. Lincoln. 1976. 253p., illus.

445. Encyclopedia of mystery and detection. Ed. by Chris
Steinbrunner and Otto M. Penzler. N.Y.: McGraw-Hill; 1976.
436p., illus. - U.K. ed.: London: Routledge & Kegan Paul;
1976.

446. Ennok, E. "'Myshelovka'." IN Sovetskaya Estoniya
[Tallin] (12 October 1973).

447. Epstein, Hans (1905-). Der Detektivroman der
Unterschicht. Frankfurt-am-Main: Neuer Frankfurter Verlag;
1930. 68p.

448. Ercoli, Emma. "Agatha Christie." IN Nuova Antologia
v.109 (1974) pp.245-248.

449. Erisman, Fred. "'Where we plan to go'; the Southwest
in Utopian fiction." IN Southwestern American Literature
(April 1971).

450. Evans, Verda. "The mystery as mind-stretcher." IN
English Journal vol.61:no.4 (April 1972) pp.495-503.

451. Everson, William K. The bad guys; a pictorial history
of the movie villain. Secaucus, N.J.: Citadel Press; 1964,
1974. xiv, 241p., illus.

452. ... The detective in film. Secaucus, N.J.: Citadel
Press; 1972. viii, 247p., illus. - repr. pap.: 1974. -
Cdn. ed.: Toronto: George J. McLeod; 1972.

453. ... "'The Kennel Murder Case'" from "Six mystery
movies and their makers." (q.v.) pp.190-192 - repr.
and expanded IN Everson, William K. The detective in film.
(q.v.) pp.38ff.

454. ... Six mystery movies and their makers. IN Nevins,
F. M. (comp.) The mystery writer's art. (q.v.) pp.180-195.

455. Eyles, Allen. "Great films of the century: 'The Maltese
Falcon'." IN Films and Filming v.11:no.2 London (November
1964) pp.45-50.

F

456. Fairlie, Gerard. With prejudice; almost an autobiography. London: Hodder & Stoughton; 1952. 255p.

457. Falk, Doris V. "Poe and the power of animal magnetism."
IN PMLA v.82:no.3 (May 1969) pp.536-546.

458. Fallois, Bernard de. Simenon. Paris: Gallimard; 1961.
305p. (La Bibliothèque idéale) - rev. ed.: - Paris:
Éditions Rencontre; 1971.

459. The fantastic pulps. Ed. by Peter Haining. London:
Gollancz; 1975. 419p., illus. - U.S. ed. - N.Y.:
St. Martin's Press; 1976. 419p.

460. Farber, Stephen. "The bloody movies; why film violence
sells." IN New York vol.9:no.48 (29 November 1976)
pp.39-45.

461. Farrar, John Chipman. "Have you a detective in your
home?; today's craze for a crime in fiction and its causes."
IN Century v.118 (May 1929) pp.84-89.

462. Farrell, James Thomas (1904-). "Cain's movietone
realism." IN Farrell, James Thomas (1904-). Literature
and morality. N.Y.: Vanguard; 1947. xv, 304p. pp.79-89.

*   Farris, Miriam (jnt. auth.) SEE Allott, Kenneth

463. Feiffer, Jules (ed.). The great comic book heroes.
N.Y.: Dial Press; 1965. 189p., illus.

464. Feinman, Jeffrey. The mysterious world of Agatha
Christie. N.Y.: Award Books; 1975. 190p., illus. (An
Award biography).

465. Ferguson, Otis C. "Cops and robbers." IN New Republic
vol.83 (15 May 1935) pp.19-20.

466. Ferkiss, Victor. "Cops, robbers, and citizens." IN
Commonweal v.62 (1955) pp.251-253.

467. Ferri, Enrico (1856-1929). I delinquenti nell'arte.
Commento et note di Bruno Cassinelli. Milan: Dall'Oglio;
1954. 315p., illus.

468. Fiedler, Leslie Aaron. Love and death in the American
novel. N.Y.: Criterion; 1960 [i.e. 1961]. xxxiv, 603p. -
U.K. ed.: London: Secker & Warburg; 1961. xxxiv, 603p. -
rev. ed.: N.Y.: Stein and Day; 1966. 512p. - U.K. ed.:
London: Cape; 1967. 512p. - 2d (U.K.) ed., repr.: London:
Paladin; 1970. 474p. - rev., with new data; pbk. ed.:
N.Y.: Delta; 1966.

469. Field, Louise Maunsell. "Philo Vance & Co., benefactors."
IN North American Review v.235 (March 1933) pp.254-260.

470. Finch, George. Raymond Chandler. Boston: Twayne;
197? . (Twayne's United States Authors series).

   Announced as forthcoming in publisher's Spring 1974
   catalogue but not verified to date.

471. Fischer, P. "Neue Häuser in der Rue Morgue."
Quellennachweis. IN Žmegač, V. (ed.) Der wohltemperierte
Mord. (q.v.).

472. ... "Neue Häuser in der Rue Morgue; Entwicklungslinien
des modernen Kriminalromans." IN Vogt, J. (comp.)
Der Kriminalroman. (q.v.) pp.185-200.

473. Fish, Robert L. "Captain José Da Silva." IN Penzler,
O. M. The great detectives. (q.v.) pp.67-77.

474. Fisher, Benjamin Franklin. "Poe in the seventies;
the poet among the critics." IN Mystery and detection
annual; 1973. (q.v.) pp.129-141.

475. Fishman, Katherine Davis. "Professionals in crime."
IN New York Times Book Review (26 April 1970) p.2.

476. Fitt, Mary. "Crime on the radio; basic demands."
IN Gilbert, M. (ed.). Crime in good company. (q.v.)
pp.210-231.

*   Fleisher, Michael L. SEE The Encyclopedia of comic
book heroes.

477. Fleishman, Avron. "The symbolic world of 'The secret
agent'." IN English Literary History v.32 (1965)
pp.205-211.

   repr. IN Watt, I. (ed.). Conrad; 'The secret agent'.
   (q.v.) pp.170-178.

478. Fleming, Ian (1908-1964). "Raymond Chandler." IN
London Magazine v.6 (December 1959) pp.43-54.

479. Flint, R. W. "A Cato to the cruelties." IN Partisan
Review v.14 (May-June 1947) pp.328-330.

*   Fosca, François [pseud.]. SEE de Traz, G.

480. Fouyé, Yves. Guy de Maupassant et les criminels,
discours de rentrée prononcé. par M. le Conseiller à la
cour Fouyé, Cour d'appel de Rouen, audience solennelle de
rentrée du 2 octobre 1951. Rouen: Impr. commerciale; 1952.
36p.

481. Frank, Nino. "Hypothèse à propos de Maigret." IN
Lacassin, F. (jnt. ed.). Simenon. (q.v.) pp.193-196.

482. Franklin, Howard Bruce. The victim as criminal and
artist; literature from the American prison. N.Y.: Oxford
University Press; 1978. xxiv, 337p.

483. Frayling, Christopher. "Sax Rohmer and the devil
doctor." IN London Magazine v.13:no.2 (1973) pp.65-80.

484. Freeling, Nicolas. "Inspector Van der Valk." IN
Penzler, O. M. The great detectives. (q.v.) pp.247-257.

485. Freeman, Richard Austin (1862-1943). "The art of the
detective story." IN 19th Century and After [London]
v.95 (May 1924) pp.713-721.

   repr. IN Rhode, J. [pseud.] (ed.) Detection medley.
   (q.v.).

   repr. IN Haycraft, H. (ed.) The art of the mystery
   story. (q.v.) pp.7-17.

   repr. IN Freeman, Richard Austin (1862-1943).
   Dr. Thorndyke's crime file; a selection of his most
   celebrated cases, containing, also, hitherto unpublished
   material about the famous detective and his methods.
   Ed. by P. M. Stone. N.Y.: Dodd Mead; 1941. xv, 838p.

   repr. in Swedish trans. IN Broberg, J. (comp.)
   Meningar om mord. (q.v.)

   repr. in German trans. AS "Die Kunst der Detektivgeschichte" IN Der Detektiverzählung auf der Spur.
   (q.v.)

486. ... (jnt. auth.) "Thorndykiana." By R. A. Freeman
and P. M. Stone. IN Freeman, R. A. Dr. Thorndyke's crime
file. (for descriptive entry for this title, see above).

487. Fremlin, Celia. "The Christie everybody knew." IN
Agatha Christie. (q.v.) pp.111-120.

488. French, Philip. "Cops." IN Sight and Sound v.43:no.2
(Spring 1974) pp.113-115.

   cf. Sparne, K. "Reply to..."

489. ... "Incitement against violence." IN Sight and
Sound v.37 (Winter 1967-1968) pp.2-8.

490. ... "Media Marlowes" IN Gross, M. (ed.). The world
of Raymond Chandler. (q.v.) pp.67-79.

491. French, Warren. "William Faulkner and the art of the
detective story." IN French, Warren, (ed.). The Thirties;
fiction, poetry, drama. Deland, Fla.: Everett Edwards; 1967.
pp.55-62.

492. Frenzel, Elisabeth. "Kriminalgeschichte." IN
RL. 2.Aufl. Bd.I pp.895-899.

493. Freund, Winfried (1938-). Die deutsche Kriminalnovelle
von Schiller bis Hauptmann; Einzelanalysen unter sozial-
geschichtlichen und didaktischen Aspekten. Paderborn:
Schöningh; 1975. 115p. (Wort, Werk, Gestalt).

494. ... "Der Mörder des Juden Aaron. Zur Problematik von
Annette von Droste-Hülshoffs Erzählung "Die Judenbuche"."
IN WW v.19 (1969) pp.244-253.

495. Freustié, Jean. "Une petite tente au milieu du jardin."
IN Lacassin, F. (jnt. ed.) Simenon. pp.52-58.

496. Friedland, Susan. South African detective stories in
English and Afrikaans from 1951-1971; a bibliography.
Johannesburg: University of Witwatersrand, Dept. of
Bibliography, Librarianship and Typography, 1973. ii, 46p.

*   Frijling-Schreuder, E. C. M. SEE Droom en onthulling.

497. Frohock, Wilbur Merrill. The novel of violence in
America; 1920-1950. Dallas, Texas: Southern Methodist
University Press; 1950. 216p. - 2d ed.: Dallas, Texas:
Southern Methodist University Press; 1957. 238p. - 2d ed.:
(U.K.), rev.: London: Barker; 1959. xi, 238p. - 2d ed.
rev. repr.: Boston: Beacon Press; 1964. 238p. (Beacon
paperbacks no.BP176).

G

498. Gabree, John. Gangsters; from 'Little Caesar' to
'The Godfather'. N.Y.: Pyramid Books; 1973. 160p., illus.
(Pyramid illustrated history of the movies) - repr.:
N.Y.: Galahad Books; [1975?, c1973] 160p., illus. (The
Pictorial treasury of film stars).

499. Gallagher, T. "Night moves." IN Sight and Sound
v.44:no.2 (Spring 1975) pp.86-89.

500. Galligan, Edward L. "Simenon's mosaic of small novels."
IN South Atlantic Quarterly v.66 (Autumn 1967) pp.534-543.

501. Galtier-Boissiere, Jean. "Origines du roman policier."
IN Gaboriau, Émile. Petit vieux des Batignolles; un chapitre
des Memoirs d'un agent de la sûrete. Paris: Grund; 1946.
109p.

502. "Gang films." IN Commonweal vol.14 (10 June 1931)
pp.143-144.

503. Gant, Richard. Ian Fleming; the man with the golden pen.
London: Mayflower Books; 1966. 172p. (Mayflower-Dell
paperback) - U.S. ed. AS Ian Flaming; the fantastic
007 man. N.Y.: Lancer; 1966. 174p.

504. Garden, Y. B. [pseud.?]. "Impressionistic biography."
IN Van Dine, S. S. Philo Vance murder cases. N.Y.:
Scribners; 1936. pp.46-73.

505. Gardiner, Harold Charles (1904-). "The barbarians
are within the gates." IN Gardiner, Harold Charles (1904-).
In all conscience; reflections on books and culture. Garden
City, N.Y.: Doubleday; 1959. 288p.   - repr.: Freeport, N.Y.:
Books for Libraries Press; 1972. (Essay Index reprint series).

*   Gardner, Dorothy. (jnt. ed.). SEE Chandler, Raymond.
Raymond Chandler speaking.

506. Gardner, Erle Stanley. "The case of the early
beginning." IN Haycraft, H. (ed.) The art of the mystery
story. (q.v.) pp.203-207.

507. ... "Getting away with murder." IN The Atlantic
v.215 (January 1965) pp.72-75.

   repr.: Ellery Queen's Mystery Magazine (November 1965).

508. Gardner, Frank Matthias (comp.) Sequels. 6th ed.
[Harrogate]: Association of Assistant Librarians; 1974 -
2 vols.

   Vol.1: Adult books. 1974. 288p.
   Vol.2: Children's Books.

   - useful for title listings of crime-detective-mystery
   novels in series in which the same character appears.

509. Garland Publishing, Inc., publishers, New York. Fifty
classics of crime fiction 1900-1950. N.Y.: Garland Publ.;
1975. 15p.

510. Gass, Sherlock Bronson (1878-). "Desipere in loco."
IN Gass, Sherlock Bronson (1878-). The criers of the shops.
Boston: Marshall Jones; 1925. 364p.

*   Gerahty, Digby George. SEE Standish, Robert [pseud.].

511. Gerber, Richard. "Namen als Symbol; Über Sherlock
Holmes und das Wesen des Kriminalromans." IN Neue Rundschau
v.83 (1972). pp.504-509.

512. Gerhardt, Mia I. "Homicide West - some observations on
the Nero Wolfe stories of Rex Stout." IN English Studies;
a journal of English letters and philogy. v.49:no.2
(April 1968) pp.107-127.

513. Gerould, Katharine Fullerton. "Men, women, and
thrillers." IN Yale Review NS.v.19 (June 1930)
pp.689-701.

514. ... "Murder for pastime." IN Saturday Review of
Literature v.12 (3 August 1935) pp.3-4ff.

515. Gerteis, Walter (1906-). Detektive, Ihre Geschichte
im Leben und in der Literatur. Munich: Heimeran; 1953. 187p.

516. Gibson, Walter B. "My years with The Shadow." IN
Grant, Maxwell [pseud.]. The Crime Oracle and The Teeth
of the Dragon; two adventures of The Shadow. N.Y.: Dover;
1975. xxvi, 163p. pp.vii-xix.

517. Gide, André. "Afterword". IN Hogg, James (1770-1835).
The private memoirs and confessions of a justified sinner.
N.Y.: W. W. Norton; 1970. xiv, 242p. (The Norton Library
N515).

518. Gidley, Mick. "Elements of the detective story in
William Faulkner's fiction." IN Journal of Popular Culture
v.7:no.1 (Summer 1973) pp.97-123.

     repr. IN Dimensions of detective fiction. (q.v.)
     pp.228-246.

519. Gilbert, Elliot G. "The detective as metaphor in the
nineteenth century." IN The Journal of Popular Culture
v.1:no.3 (Winter 1967) pp.256-262.

     repr. IN Nevins, F. M. (comp.) The mystery writer's
     art. (q.v.) pp.285-294.

     N.B.: An expansion of this into a full-length study is
     announced as being in preparation in Nevins (op. cit.)
     p.294; unverified to date.

520. ... "'McWatters' Law'; the best kept secret of the
Secret Service." IN Dimensions of detective fiction. (q.v.)
pp.22-36.

521. Gilbert, Michael Francis (1912-). "Autumn in London."
IN Gross, M. (ed.). The world of Raymond Chandler. (q.v.)
pp.103-114.

522. ... (comp.). Crime in good company; essays on criminals and crime-writing. By Josephine Bell and others. Collected by Michael Gilbert on behalf of the Crime Writers' Association. London: Constable; 1959. x, 242p. - U.S. ed.: Boston: Writer; 1960. x, 242p.

523. ... "Introduction." IN Buchan, John. The thirty-nine steps. San Diego: University Extension, University of California-San Diego/Del Mar, Calif.: Publisher's Inc.; 1978. xvi, 207p., illus. pp.vii-xiv.

524. ... "Introduction" IN Hare, Cyril [pseud.]. Best detective stories of Cyril Hare. Chosen, with an intro. by Michael Gilbert. London: Faber; 1959. 272p.

525. ... "The moment of violence." IN Gilbert, M. (ed.). Crime in good company. (q.v.) pp.105-125.

526. ... "Paţrick Petrella." IN Penzler, O. M. The great detectives. (q.v.) pp.165-174.

527. ... "The spy in fact and fiction." IN The mystery story. (q.v.) pp.205-221.

528. ... "A very English lady." IN Agatha Christie. (q.v.) pp.49-78.

529. Gill, Richard (1922-). Happy rural seat; the English country house and the literary imagination. New Haven, Conn.: Yale University Press; 1972. xix, 305p.

530. Girvan, Waveney (ed.). Eden Phillpotts; an assessment and a tribute. London: H. Hutchinson; 1953. 159p., illus.

531. Glass, Robert. "The gunnery of James Bond." IN Snakes Alive; the journal of the Belfast Medical School. (1963).

532. Glover, Dorothy (jnt. auth.). Victorian detective fiction; a catalogue of the collection made by Dorothy Glover and Graham Greene bibliographically arranged by Eric Osborne and introduced by John Carter, with a preface by Graham Greene. London: Bodley Head; 1966. 151p. Ltd. ed. 500 copies.

533. Godfry, Lionel. "Martinis without olives." IN
Films and Filming v.14:no.7 (April 1968) pp.10-14.

534. Godshalk, William. "a critical biography of Hammett"
Twayne Press. - mentioned as being in progress in Gores, J.
'Hammett' (q.v.) pp.247-248; unverified to date.

535. Goldin, Hyman E. A dictionary of American underworld
lingo. N.Y.: Twayne; 1950. 327p.

  Of peripheral interest.

536. Goll, August (1866-1936). Criminal types in Shakespeare.
N.Y.: Haskell House; 1966. 271p.

537. Goncourt, Edmond Louis Antoine de (jnt. auth.).
Pages from the Goncourt journal. Ed. by Robert Baldick.
London: Oxford University Press; 1962. xxii, 434p., illus.

*   Goncourt, Jules Alfred de (jnt. auth.). SEE Goncourt,
E. L. A. de.

538. Gonda, Manji (1936-). Shukumei no bigaku. Tokyo:
Daisan Bunmeisha; 1973. 300p.

539. Goodstone, Tony (comp.). The pulps; fifty years of
American pop culture. N.Y.: Bonanza; 1971. xvi, 239p.,
illus. - repr.: N.Y.: Chelsea House; 1976. xvi, 239p.,
illus.

*   Goodwin, Archie [pseud.]. SEE Stout, Rex.

540. Gores, Joseph N. Hammett; a novel. By Joe Gores.
N.Y.: G. P. Putnam's Sons; [c1975]. 251p. vide "Author's
note" pp.243-251. - Simult. publ. (Cdn. ed.): Toronto:
Longmans Canada; 1975. - U.K. ed.: London: Macdonald/Raven
Books; 1975.

541. ... Hammett the writer. - speech delivered at Hammett
Conference sponsored by the University of California as a
U.C. Extension Program, San Francisco, July 1976. - repr.
Xenophile (q.v.) No.38 (March-April 1978) pp.5-10.

542. Gose, Elliott B. ""Cruel devourer of the world's
light"; 'The secret agent'." IN Nineteenth-Century Fiction
v.15:no.1 (June 1960) pp.39-51.

543. Gossett, Louise Young. "The climate of violence; Wolfe,
Caldwell, Faulkner." IN Gossett, Louise Young. Violence in
recent Southern fiction. Durham, N.C.; Duke University Press;
1965. xi, 207p. pp.3-52.

544. Goulart, Ron (1933-). Cheap thrills; an informal
history of the pulp magazines. New Rochelle, N.Y.: Arlington
House; 1972. 192p., illus. - repr. AS An informal history
of the pulp magazines. N.Y.: Ace; 1973.

545. ... (ed.). The hardboiled dicks; an anthology and
study of pulp detective fiction. Los Angeles: Sherbourne
Press; 1965. xviii, 296p. - repr.: N.Y.: Pocket Books;
1967. xviii, 268p. - U.K. ed.: London: Boardman; 1967.
xv, 296p.

546. Gould, Chester. "Dick Tracy." IN Penzler, O. M.
The great detectives. (q.v.) pp.235-245.

547. Gould, James A. (1922-). (jnt. auth.). Violence
in modern literature. By J. A. Gould and John J. Iorio.
San Francisco: Boyd & Fraser; 1972. 203p.

548. Gow, Gordon. "Success ... without the excess." IN
Films and Filming v.4:no.11 (August 1958) pp.7, 33.

549. ... Suspense in the cinema. London: Zwemmer; 1968.
167p. (International film guide series) - U.S. ed.: N.Y.:
Barnes; 1968. 167p. (International film guide series). -
repr.: N.Y.: Paperback Library; 1971. 222p., illus.
(International film guide series #8).

550. Grace, Harry. "A taxonomy of American crime film
themes." IN Journal of Social Psychology v.42 (August
1955) pp.129-136.

551. Grant, Maxwell [pseud.]. "The Shadow." IN Penzler,
O. M. The great detectives. (q.v.) pp.205-216.

552. Graphic violence on the screen. Ed. by Thomas R. Atkins.
N.Y.: Monarch Press; 1976. viii, 96p., illus. (Monarch film
studies).

553. Graves, Robert (1895-). "After a century, will anyone care whodunit?" IN New York Times Book Review (25 August 1957) p.5.

554. ... (jnt. auth.). The long weekend; a social history of Great Britain (1918-1939). By R. Graves and Alan Hodge. London: Faber and Faber; 1940. - repr.: Harmondsworth: Penguin; 1971. - U.S. ed.: N.Y.: The Macmillan Co.; 1941. - repr.: N.Y.: Norton; 1963.

555. Great Britain. British Council. British crime fiction. By the British Council and the National Book League. London: British Council/National Book League; 1974. 51p.

556. Grebstein, Sheldon N. "The tough Hemingway and his hard-boiled children." IN Madden, D. (ed.) Tough guy writers of the Thirties. (q.v.)

557. Green, Roger Lancelyn. A. E. W. Mason. London: Max Parrish; 1952. 272p.

558. Greene, Graham (1904-). The last Buchan. IN Greene, Graham (1904-). Collected essays. London: Bodley Head; 1969. - repr.: Harmondsworth, Eng.: Penguin; 1970. 345p.

559. ... (jnt. ed.). The spy's bedside book; an anthology. Ed. by G. and Hugh Greene. London: Rupert Hart-Davis; 1968. 256p., illus.

*   ... (jnt. auth.). SEE also Glover, Dorothy.

560. Greene, Sir Hugh (ed.). The rivals of Sherlock Holmes. London: Bodley Head; 1970-1976. 4 vols. - repr.: Harmondsworth: Penguin.

Vol.1: The rivals of Sherlock Holmes; early detective stories. 1970. 352p. vide 'Introduction' pp.7-20.

Vol.2: More rivals of Sherlock Holmes; cosmopolitan crimes. 1971. 348p. vide 'Introduction' pp.9-18 - U.S. title: Cosmopolitan crimes.

Vol.3: The crooked counties; further rivals of Sherlock Holmes. 1973. 318p. vide 'Introduction' pp.11-20.

Vol.4: The American rivals of Sherlock Holmes. 1976. 349p. vide 'Introduction' pp.7-14. - U.S. ed.: N.Y.: Pantheon; 1976. 349p.

*   ... (jnt. ed.). SEE also Greene, G. The spy's
bedside book.

561. Gregory, E. R. "Wilkie Collins and Dorothy L. Sayers."
IN As her whimsey took her. (q.v.) pp.51-64.

562. Greiner-Mai, Herbert (jnt. ed.). Die deutsche
Kriminalerzählung von Schiller bis zur Gegenwart. Hrsg. von
H. Greiner-Mai und Hans-Joachim Kruse, mit einer Einleitung
von Hans-Joachim Kruse. Berlin: Das Neue Berlin; 1967.
1 vol.

563. Grella, George. "Evil plots." IN New Republic v.173
(26 July 1975) pp.24-26.

564. ... "The gangster novel; the urban pastoral." IN
Madden, D. (ed.) Tough guy writers of the Thirties. (q.v.)
pp.186-198.

565. ... "Murder and manners; the formal detective novel."
IN Novel v.4:no.1 (Fall 1970) pp.30-48.

   repr. IN Dimensions of detective fiction. (q.v.)
   pp.37-57.

566. ... "Murder and the mean streets; the hard-boiled
detective novel." IN Contempora v.1:no.1 (March 1970)
pp.6-15.

   repr. IN Allen, R. S. (jnt. ed.). Detective fiction.
   (q.v.) pp.411-429.

567. ... "Simenon and Maigret." IN Adam International
Review [University of Rochester, N.Y.] v.34:no.328-330 (1969).

568. Gribbin, Lenore S. Who's whodunit; a list of 3218
detective story writers and their 1100 pseudonyms. Chapel
Hill, N.C.: University of North Carolina Student Stores;
[1968, c1969]. 174p. (University of North Carolina Library
Studies Number 5).

569. Grogg, Samuel L. Gangster and crime movies. Boston:
G. K. Hall; [1977].

   - announced as forthcoming in publisher's 1976-1977
   catalogue; unverified to date.

570.   ...   "Ross Macdonald; at the edge. [interview]"   IN
Journal of Popular Culture   v.7:no.1   (Summer 1973)   pp.211-222.

repr.   IN   Dimensions of detective fiction.   (q.v.)
pp.182-192.

571.   Gross, Miriam (ed.).   The world of Raymond Chandler.
London: Weidenfeld and Nicolson; 1977.   [x], 190p., illus.
- U.S. ed. - N.Y.: A & W; 1978.   190p.

572.   Grotjahn, Martin.   "Sex and the mystery story."   IN
Human sexuality   v.6:no.3   (March 1972)   pp.126-137.

573.   Gruber, Frank (1904-1969).   The pulp jungle.   Los
Angeles: Sherbourne Press; 1967.   189p.

574.   Gubern, Román (comp.).   La novela criminal.   By
R. Gubern et al.   Barcelona: Tusquets Editor; 1970.   80p.
(Cuadernos infimos, 10).

575.   Guérard, Albert Joseph (1914-).   "Aversion of anarchy."
IN   Guérard, Albert Joseph (1914-).   Conrad the novelist.
Harvard UP; 1958.   xiv, 322p.   pp.218-231.

repr.   IN   Watt, I. (ed.).   Conrad; 'The secret agent'.
(q.v.)   pp.150-165.

*   Gulik, Robert Hans van (1910-1968).   SEE   van Gulik,
R. H.

576.   Gurko, Leo.   "'The secret agent'; Conrad's vision of
Megalopolis."   IN   Modern Fiction Studies   v.4:no.1   (Winter
1958-1959)   pp.307-318.

repr.   IN   Gurko, Leo.   Joseph Conrad; giant in exile.
N.Y.: Collier-Macmillan; 1962.   Chap.10.

577.   Guymon, E. T.   "Why do we read this stuff?"   IN
The mystery story.   (q.v.)   pp.361-363.

H

578. Hagan, John. "The design of Conrad's 'The secret agent'." IN English Literary History v.22 (June 1955) pp.148-164.

579. Hagemann, E. R. "Focus on 'You play the black and the red comes up'; no bet." IN Madden, D. (ed.). Tough guy writers of the Thirties. (q.v.) pp.163-170.

580. Hagemann, E. R. (jnt. comp.). "James M. Cain, 1922-1958; a selected checklist." Comp. by E. R. Hagemann and Philip C. Durham. IN Bulletin of Bibliography v.23 (September-December 1960) pp.57-61.

581. Hagen, Ordean A. Who done it?; a guide to detective, mystery, and suspense fiction. N.Y.: Bowker; 1969. xx, 834p.

   Additions, corrections, and alterations, have been
   appearing in 'The Armchair Detective' beginning with
   the October 1969 issue.

*   Hahn, Robert W. (ed.). SEE Boucher, Anthony [pseud.] Sincerely, Tony/Faithfully, Vincent.

582. Haining, Peter. Mystery!; an illustrated history of crime and detective fiction. London: Souvenir Press; 1977. 176p., illus.

*   Haining, Peter (ed.). SEE The fantastic pulps [and] The penny dreadfuls.

583. Hall, Adam [pseud.]. "Quiller." IN Penzler, O. M.
The great detectives. (q.v.) pp.183-192.

584. Hall, Stuart (jnt. auth.). "The avenging angels."
By S. Hall and Paddy Whanel. IN Hall, Stuart (jnt. auth.).
The popular arts. By S. Hall and Paddy Whanel. 480.,
illus. pp.142-163.

585. Halliday, Brett [pseud.]. "Michael Shayne." IN
Penzler, O. M. The great detectives. (q.v.) pp.217-225.

586. Halliwell, Leslie. The filmgoer's companion. London:
MacGibbon & Kee; 1965. 468p. - U.S. ed.: N.Y.: Hill & Wang;
1965. 468p.

    2d ed.: 1967; 3d ed.: 1970; 4th ed.: 1976 - available
    in both hardbound and paperback.

587. Hamblen, Abigail Ann. "The inheritance of the meek;
two novels by Agatha Christie and Henry James." IN Discourse
v.12 (1969) pp.409-413.

588. Hamilton, Donald. "Matt Helm." IN Penzler, O. M.
The great detectives. (q.v.) pp.119-126.

589. Hamilton, Kenneth Morrison. "Murder and morality; an
interpretation of detective fiction." IN Dalhousie Review
v.33 (Summer 1953) pp.102-108.

590. Hammett, [Samuel] Dashiell (1894-1961). "Introduction"
IN Hammett, [Samuel] Dashiell (1894-1961). The Maltese
falcon. N.Y.: Random House; 1934. ix, 267p. (Modern
Library).

591. ... "Poor Scotland Yard" [Review of 'The Benson Murder
Case' among others] IN Saturday Review of Literature [N.Y.]
v.3:no.25 (15 January 1927) p.510.

    - section of review article pertaining to 'The Benson
    Murder Case' repr. IN Haycraft, H. (ed.). The art of
    the mystery story. (q.v.) pp.382-383.

592. Hammond, Lawrence. Thriller movies; classic films of
suspense and mystery. London: Octopus Books; 1974. 160p.,
illus. (The Movie treasury). - U.S. ed. - N.Y.:
Derbibooks; 1975. 160p., illus.

593. Handlin, Oscar. "Reader's choice." IN Atlantic
Monthly v.218 (July 1966) pp.136-138.

594. Hankiss, Jean. "Littérature 'populaire' et roman-
policier." IN Revue de Littérature Comparée [Paris] v.8
(July 1928) pp.556-563.

595. Hanna, Archibald. John Buchan, 1875-1940; a bibliography. Hamden, Conn. Shoe String Press; 1953. xi, 135p.

596. Hannay, Margaret P. "Harriet's influence on the
characterization of Lord Peter Wimsey." IN As her whimsey
took her. (q.v.) pp.36-50.

*   Hannay, Margaret P. (ed.). SEE As her whimsey took her.

597. Hansen, Robert. Kriminal romaner. Med en bibliografi.
By Jens Anker [pseud.] Copenhagn: Forum; 1948. 127p.

598. Hardacre, Kenneth. Rudyard Kipling; 'Kim'. London:
Brodie; 1956. 80p. (Notes on Chosen English Texts series).

599. Hardwick, John Michael Drinkrow (jnt. auth.). The man
who was Sherlock Holmes. By Michael and Mollie Hardwick.
London: Murray; 1964. 92p., illus.

*   Hardwick, Michael. SEE Hardwick, J. M. D.

*   Hardwick, Mollie (jnt. auth.). SEE Hardwick, J. M. D.

600. Hardy, A. E. Gathorne. "Novels of Émile Gaboriau."
IN National Review [London] v.3 (July 1884) p.591.

601. Hardy, Thomas John (1868-). "The romance of crime."
IN Hardy, Thomas John (1868-). Books on the shelf. London:
Philip Allan; 1934. 253p. - repr.: Freeport, N.Y.: Books
for Libraries Press; 1970. 253p. (Essay Index reprint
series).

602. Hare, C. "The classic form." IN Gilbert, M. (ed.).
Crime in good company. (q.v.) pp.55-84.

603. Harmon, Jim. The great radio heroes. N.Y.: Doubleday;
1967. 263p. - repr.: N.Y.: Ace; [n.d.]. 253p.

604. Harmon, Robert Bartlett (1932-) (jnt. comp.).
An annotated guide to the works of Dorothy L. Sayers.
Comp. by R. B. Harmon and Margaret A. Burger. N.Y.: Garland;
1977. 286p.

605. Harper, Ralph (1915-). The world of the thriller.
Cleveland, Ohio: The Press of Case Western Reserve University;
1969. xii, 139p. - repr.: Cleveland, Ohio: The Press of
Case Western Reserve University; 1974. - repr., pap.:
Baltimore, Md.: Johns Hopkins Press; 1975.

606. Harris, James B. "Translator's preface." IN Rampo,
Edogawa [pseud.]. Japanese tales of mystery & imagination.
Trans. by James B. Harris. Tokyo: Charles E. Tuttle; 1956,
1970. xii, 222p. pp.vii-xii.

607. Harrison, Barbara Grizulti. "Dorothy L. Sayers and
the tidy art of detective fiction." IN Ms. Magazine
v.3:no.5 (November 1974) pp.66-69, 84-89.

608. Harrison, Michael. "Dupin; the reality behind the
fictions." IN Harrison, Michael. The exploits of the
Chevalier Dupin. Sauk City, Wisc.: Mycroft and Moran; 1968.
xi, 138p. pp.3-14.

609. ... Peter Cheyney; prince of hokum. London: Neville
Spearman; 1954. viii, 303p., illus.

610. Harrison, Richard (1901-). "The detective in fact
and fiction." IN Harrison, Richard (1901-). Whitehall
1212; the story of the police of London. London: Jarrolds;
1948. 240p., illus. pp.219-230 (Chap.21). - U.S. ed. AS
Scotland Yard. Chicago: Ziff-Davis; 1949. xi, 269p., illus.

611. Hart, Harold. "Accident, suicide, or murder?; a
question of stereochemistry." IN Journal of Chemical
Education v.52 (July 1975) pp.444.

612. Hart, James David (1911-). The popular book; a history
of America's literary taste. N.Y.: Oxford University Press;
1950. 351p. - repr. - Berkeley, Calif.: California
University Press/London: Cambridge University Press; 1961,
1963. - repr. - Westport, Conn.: Greenwood Press; 1976.

613. Hartman, Geoffrey H. "Literature high and low; the
case of the mystery story." IN Hartman, Geoffrey H.
The fate of reading and other essays. Chicago: University
of Chicago Press; 1975. xvi, 352p. pp.203-222.

614. ... "The mystery of mysteries." IN New York Review
of Books (18 May 1972) pp.31-34.

615. Harwood, H. C. "The detective story." IN Outlook
[London] (1 January 1927).

616. ... "Holiday homicide." IN Saturday Review [London]
v.148 (whole no. 3,851) (17 August 1929) pp.181-182.

617. Haslinger, A. "Friedrich Schiller und die
Kriminalliteratur." IN Sprachkunst v.2 (1971)
pp.173-187.

618. Hasubek, Peter (1937-). Die Detektivgeschichte für
junge Leser. Bad Heilbrunn/Obb.: J. Klinkhardt; 1974. 143p.
(Schriften des Arbeitskreises für Jugendliteratur).

619. Hawke, Jessica. Follow my dust!; a biography of Arthur
Upfield; with an intro. by Detective Inspector Napoleon
Bonaparte. London: Heinemann; 1957. xii, 238p., illus.

620. Hawkins, John. "Poe's 'The murders in the Rue Morgue'."
IN Explicator v.23:no.6 (February 1965) Item 49.

621. Haworth, Peter. "Introduction." IN Haworth, Peter
(ed.). Before Scotland Yard; classic tales of roguery and
detection. Oxford: Basil Blackwell; 1927. xx, 303p.
pp.vii-xix. - U.S. ed. AS: Classic crimes in history
and fiction. N.Y.: D. Appleton; 1927. xviii, 286p.

622. Haycraft, Howard (1905-). (ed.). The art of the
mystery story; a collection of critical essays; with a
commentary. N.Y.: Simon & Schuster; 1946. ix, 545p. -
Cdn. ed.: Toronto: Musson; 1946. ix, 545p. - repr.:
N.Y.: Grosset & Dunlap; 1961. ix, 565p. (Universal
Library UL91).

623. ... "Dictators, democrats, and detectives." IN
Saturday Review of Literature [New York] v.20 (7 October
1939) p.8ff.

  repr. IN Spectator [London] (17 November 1939).

  repr. IN Kort en Goed [Johannesburg] (April 1940).

  repr. in part IN Haycraft, H. (ed.). Murder for pleasure.
  (q.v.) pp.312-318 (Chap.15).

624. ... "From Poe to Hammett; a foundation list of detective
fiction." IN Wilson Bulletin for Librarians v.12 (February
1938) pp.371-377.

  repr. AS "A readers' list of detective story 'cornerstones'" IN Haycraft, H. (ed.) Murder for pleasure.
  (q.v.) pp.302-306 (Chap.14: 'A detective story bookshelf;
  pp.298-311).

  rev. and repr. AS "Notes on additions to a cornerstone
  library" IN Ellery Queen's Mystery Magazine (October
  1951).

  repr. AS "A decennial detective digest" IN Wilson
  Library Bulletin (November 1951) pp.242-246.

  repr. AS "Notes on additions to a cornerstone library"
  IN Haycraft, H. (ed.) Murder for pleasure. (enlg. ed.,
  1968) (q.v.) pp.xxi-xxxiv.

  N.B.: This last incorporates "The Haycraft-Queen definitive
  library of detective-crime-mystery fiction; two centuries
  of cornerstones, 1748-1948".

625. ... "Introduction" IN Fourteen great detective
stories. Ed. by Howard Haycraft. rev. ed. N.Y.: Random
House; 1949. xiv, 464p. (The Modern Library) pp.vii-xiv.

626. ... "Murder for pleasure." IN Haycraft, H. (ed.)
The art of the mystery story. (q.v.) pp.158-177.

  Condensation of his chapter on Poe from: Haycraft, H.
  'Murder for pleasure'. (q.v.)

627. ... Murder for pleasure; the life and times of the
detective story. N.Y.: Appleton-Century; 1941. xviii, 409p.
- Cdn. ed.: Toronto: Ryerson Press; 1941. xviii, 409p.

  U.K. ed.: Intro. by Nicholas Blake [pseud.] (q.v.) London:
  Peter Davies; 1942. 376p.

repr.: Newly enlarged edition with Notes on Additions
to a Cornerstone Library and The Haycraft-Queen Definitive
Library of Detective-Crime-Mystery Fiction. N.Y.: Biblo
and Tannen; 1968. xviii, [1r], 409p., illus.

N.B.: repr. of 1941 ed. (Appleton-Century) with two
articles from 'Ellery Queen's Mystery Magazine', 1951,
unpaged at front. (SEE Item 499).

628. ... "The rules of the game." FROM (his) Murder for
pleasure.

   repr. IN Writing suspense and mystery fiction (1977).
   (q.v.) pp.273-296.

629. ... "The whodunit in World War II and after."   IN
New York Times Book Review (12 August 1945) p.7.

   repr. IN Haycraft, H. (ed.).   The art of the mystery
   story. (q.v.) pp.536-542.

630. Hayden, George Allen.   "Courtroom plays of the Yüan
and early Ming periods." IN Harvard Journal of Asiatic
Studies v.34 (1974) pp.192-220.

631. ... The Judge Pao plays of the Yüan Dynasty ... Ph.D.
dissertation, Stanford University, 1972. viii, 453ℓ

632. Hazard, Johnnine. "Ph.D. dissertation on Ross
Macdonald, University of Chicago, 1974".

   Not verified. Cited in: Cawelti, J. G.   'Adventure,
   mystery, and romance' (q.v.), p.327.

633. Heald, Tim. John Steed; an authorized biography.
Toronto: McGraw-Hill Ryerson; 1978 - vols.

   Vol.1: Jealous in honour. 1978. 197p.

634. Hecht, Ben. "Whistling corpse." IN Ellery Queen's
Mystery Magazine (September 1945).

   repr. IN Haycraft, H. (ed.). The art of the mystery story.
   (q.v.) pp.339-342.

*   Hecke, B. C. Van. (jnt. auth.). SEE Lee, Raymond.

635. Hedman, Iwan (1931-). (jnt. auth.). Fyra decennier
med Dennis Wheatley; en biografi och bibliografi. By I. Hedman
and Jan Alexandersson. Strängnäs, Sweden: Dast forlag; 1973.
191p., illus. (Dast dossier nr.1).

636. ... Svensk deckare- & thrillerbibliografi. Strängnäs:
författaren (Flodinsv. 5); 1972. 7, 524p., illus.

2d ed.: Deckare och thrillers på svenska 1864-1973; i orig.
och övers., med titel- och pseudonym-register samt
förteckning över utgivna antologier i genern med
innehållsforteckning. 2d rev. ed. Strängnäs, Sweden:
Dast; 1974. 377p., illus. (Dast dossier nr.3).

*   ... (jnt. auth.). SEE Alexandersson, J. (jnt. auth.).
Leslie Charteris och Helgonet.

637. Heilbrun, Carolyn G. "Sayers, Lord Peter, and God."
IN American Scholar v.37:no.2 (Spring 1968) pp.324-334.

repr. IN Sayers, Dorothy Leigh (1893-1957). Lord Peter;
a collection of all the Lord Peter Wimsey stories. Comp.
and with an intro. by James Sandoe. Coda by Carolyn
Heilbrun. Codetta by E. C. Bentley. N.Y.: Harper and
Row; 1971, [c1972]. xiv, 487p. pp.454-469. - repr. -
N.Y.: Avon; 1972.

638._ Heissenbüttel, H. "Spielregein des Kriminalromans."
IN Zmegač, V. (ed.). Der wohltemperierte Mord. (q.v.)

639. Hellman, Lillian (1905-). [autobiography] Boston:
Little, Brown/London: Macmillan; 1969-1976. 3 vols.

vol.1: An unfinished woman; a memoir. 1969. 280p.
vol.2: Pentimento. 1973, U.K. 1974. 297p.
vol.3: Scoundrel time. 1976. iv, 155p., illus.

640. ... "Dashiell Hammett; a memoir." IN New York Review
of Books (25 November 1965).

repr. AS "Introduction." IN Hammett, Dashiell (1894-
1961). The big knockover; selected stories and short
novels. Ed. and with an intro. by Lillian Hellman.
N.Y.: Random House; 1966. xxi, 355p. pp.vii-xxi. -
U.K. ed. AS The Dashiell Hammett story omnibus. London:
Cassell; 1966. xxi, 355p. - repr. - Penguin.

641. Helman, Alicja. Filmy kryminalne. Warsaw: Wydawnictwa
Artystyczne i Filmowe; 1972. 233p., illus. (Mały leksykon
filmowy, 1).

*   Hennisart, Martha.   SEE   Lathen, Emma [pseud.].

642. Henry, Clayton. "Crime films and social criticism."
IN Films in Review v.2:no.5 (May 1951) pp.31-34.

643. Henry, Gilles. Commissaire Maigret, qui êtes-vous?
Paris: Plon; 1977. 285p., illus., maps.

644. Heppenstall, Rayner (1911-). French crime in the
Romantic age. London: Hamilton; 1970. xiii, 306p.

645. ... Reflections on the Newgate calendar. London:
W. H. Allen; 1975. xiii, 226p., illus.

646. Herman, Linda. (jnt. auth.). Corpus delicti of mystery
of mystery fiction; a guide to the body of the case. By
L. Herman and Beth Stiel. Metuchen, N.J.: Scarecrow Press;
1974. viii, 180p.

647. Herzel, Roger. "John Dickson Carr." IN Minor American
novelists. Ed. by Charles Alva Hoyt. With a preface by
Harry T. Moore. Carbondale, Ill.: Southern Illinois University
Press; 1970. xx, 140p. (Crosscurrents/Modern Critiques)
pp.67-80.

648. Higgins, George V. "The private eye as illegal hero."
IN Esquire v.68:no.6 (December 1972) pp.348-351.

649. Higham, Charles (1931-). The adventures of Conan
Doyle; the life of the creator of Sherlock Holmes. N.Y.:
W. W. Norton; 1976. 368p., illus. - U.K. ed.: London:
Hamish Hamilton; 1976. 384p., illus.

650. Highsmith, Patricia (1921-). "Introduction". IN
Gross, M. (ed.). The world of Raymond Chandler. (q.v.)
pp.1-6.

651. ... Plotting and writing suspense fiction. Boston:
The Writer; 1966. 149p. - 2d ed.: Boston: The Writer;
1972. viii, 149p.

652. Hill, Lew. "The Hero in criminal literature." IN
Pacific Quarterly [Hamilton, New Zealand] v.3:no.1
(January 1978) pp.33-41.

653. Hill, Reginald. "Holmes; the Hamlet of crime fiction."
IN Crime writers (q.v.) pp.20-41.

654. Hill, Wycliffe Aber (1883-). Index book for use with
the plot genie: Supplementary formula no.3; detective-mystery.
Los Angeles: Ernest E. Gagmon; 1933. 160p.

655. Hills, L. Rust. "Awesome beige typewriter; calling on
John D. MacDonald." IN Esquire v.84 (August 1975)
pp.68ff.

656. Himes, Chester B. (1909-). The autobiography of
Chester Himes. Garden City, N.Y.: Doubleday; 1972-1976.
2vols.

  Vol.1: The quality of hurt. 1972. 351p.

  Vol.2: My life of absurdity. 1976. 398p., illus.

  U.K. ed.: London: Michael Joseph; 1973-

657. Himmelfarb, Gertrude. "John Buchan; an untimely
appreciation." IN Encounter (September 1960) pp.46-53.

  repr. with small changes AS "John Buchan; the last
  Victorian." IN Himmelfarb, Gertrude. Victorian minds.
  N.Y.: Knopf; 1968. xiii, 392, vp. - repr. - N.Y.:
  Harper & Row; 1970. xiii, 397p. (Harper Torchbooks
  TB 1536) - U.K. ed. - London: Weidenfeld and Nicolson;
  1968. xiii, 397p.

*   Hinckle, Warren. (ed.). SEE City of San Francisco
Magazine.

658. Hirsh, Michael. (jnt. auth.). The great Canadian comic
books. By M. Hirsh and Patrick Loubert. Toronto: Peter
Martin Associates; 1971. 264p., illus.

*   A history of the comic strip. By Pierre Couperie,
Maurice C. Horn, et al. SEE Musée des Arts Decoratifs,
Paris.

659. Hitchman, Janet (1916-). Such a strange lady; an
introduction to Dorothy L. Sayers (1893-1957). London:
New English Library; 1975. 203p. - repr., pbk.: London:
New English Library; 1976. - U.S. ed.: N.Y.: Harper & Row;
1975.

660. Hodder Williams, J. E. "Sir Arthur Conan Doyle."
IN The Bookman [London] v.22:no.127 (April 1902)
pp.6-13, illus.

  repr. IN The Bookman [New York] v.17 (August 1903)
  pp.647-651.

*   Hodge, Alan. (jnt. auth.). SEE Graves, Robert. (jnt.
auth.). The long weekend.

661. Hoffman, Daniel (1923-). Poe Poe Poe Poe Poe Poe Poe.
Garden City, N.Y.: Doubleday; 1972. xvi, 339p. - repr.,
pbk.: N.Y.: Doubleday; 1973. (Anchor Books).

662. Hoffman, Nancy Y. "Mistresses of malfeasance." IN
Dimensions of detective fiction. (q.v.) pp.97-101.

663. Hofsess, John. "Death Valley, U.S.A." IN Take One
v.1:no.11 (May-June 1968) pp.6-9.

664. Hogarth, Basil (1908-). Writing thrillers for profit;
a practical guide. London: A. & C. Black; 1936. xii,
13-158p. (The writers' and artists' library v.6).

665. Hollingsworth, Keith. The Newgate novel, 1830-1847;
Bulwer, Ainsworth, Dickens and Thackeray. Detroit: Wayne
State University Press; 1963. 279p., illus.

666. Hollis, Christopher (1902-). G. K. Chesterton.
London: pub. for the British Council and The National Book
League by Longmans Green; 1964. 32p. (Writers and Their
Work ser. no.3).

667. ... The mind of Chesterton. London: Hollis & Carter;
1970. 303p. - U.S. ed.: Coral Gables, Fla.: University
of Miami Press; 1970. 303p.

668. Hollyer, Cameron. "Arthur Conan Doyle; a case of
identity." IN Pacific Quarterly v.3:no.1 (January 1978)
pp.50-61.

669.   ...   The body in the library; an inquest into the
materials available for the study of detective fiction.
Compiled by Cameron Hollyer, Literature Section, Metropolitan
Toronto Central Library, for the Workshop on the Other
Literatures, November 9, 1974, sponsored by the University
of Toronto School of Continuing Studies.   Toronto: Metropolitan
Toronto Central Library; 1974.   15p.

*   Holmes, H. H. [pseud.].   SEE   Boucher, Anthony [pseud.].

670.   Holquist, Michael.   "Murder she says."   IN   New Republic
v.173   (26 July 1975)   pp.26-28.

671.   ...   "Whodunit and other questions; metaphysical
detective stories in post-war fiction."   IN   New Literary
History   v.3:no.1   (Autumn 1971)   pp.135-156.

672.   Holtan, Judith (jnt. auth.).   "The time-space dimension
in the Lew Archer detective novels."   By J. Holtan and
I. Orley.   IN   North Dakota Quarterly   (Autumn 1972)
pp.30-41.

673.   Holton, Leonard [pseud.].   "Father Bredder."   IN
Penzler, O. M.   The great detectives.   (q.v.)   pp.23-35.

674.   Homberger, Eric.   "The man of letters (1908-12)"
IN   Gross, M. (ed.).   The world of Raymond Chandler.
(q.v.)   pp.7-18.

675.   Honce, Charles Ellsworth (1895-).   "Detective stories
as literature."

  Not verified.   Cited in: Queen, E.   'The detective short
  story'   (q.v.), p.iv.

676.   Hone, Ralph E.   Dorothy L. Sayers; a literary biography.
Kent, Ohio: Kent State University Press; 1979.   xviii,
217p., illus.

677.   Hopkins, Joel.   "An interview with Eric Ambler."
IN   Journal of Popular Culture   v.9:no.2   (Fall 1975)
pp.285-293.

678.   Horn, Maurice C.   Women in the comics.   N.Y.: Chelsea
House; 1978.

*   ... (jnt. comp.). SEE Musée des Arts Decoratifs, Paris.

679. Hossent, Harry. Gangster movies; gangsters, hoodlums, and tough guys of the screen. London: Octopus Books; 1974. 160 p., illus. (The Movie treasury).

*   Hotchin, F. E. (jnt. auth.). SEE Allinson, A. A.

680. Hottinger, M. "Vorwort zu Mord, Angelsächsische Kriminalgeschichten." - orig. publ. 1959; repr. IN Der Detektiverzählung auf der Spur. (q.v.)

681. Household, Geoffrey. "Introduction." IN Childers, Erskine. The riddle of the sands; a record of the Secret Service. Harmondsworth, Eng.: Penguin; 1978. 328p., maps. pp.7-15.

682. Houseman, John. "Lost fortnight: a memoir; 'The Blue Dahlia' and how it grew out of Raymond Chandler's alcoholic dash for a deadline." IN Harper's Magazine v.231 (August 1965) pp.55-66.

  repr. IN Chandler, Raymond (1888-1959). The Blue Dahlia; a screenplay. With a memoir by John Houseman. Ed., with an Afterword by Matthew J. Bruccoli. Carbondale, Ill.: Southern Illinois University Press; 1976. xxiii, 139p. pp.ix-xxi.

  repr. IN Gross, M. (ed.). The world of Raymond Chandler. (q.v.) pp.53-66.

683. ... "Today's here; a review." IN Hollywood Quarterly v.2:no.2 (January 1947) pp.161-163.

684. Houston, Penelope. "The figure in the carpet." IN Sight and Sound v.32:no.4 (Autumn 1963) pp.158-164.

685. ... "007." IN Sight and Sound v.34:no.1 (Winter 1964-1965) pp.14-16.

686. ... "The private eye." IN Sight and Sound v.26:no.1 (Summer 1956) pp.22-23, 55.

687. Hoveyda, Fereydoun. Petite histoire du roman policier. Paris: Éditions du Pavillon; 1956. 94p.

688. ... Histoire du roman policier. Paris: Les Éditions du Pavillon; 1965. 264p.

*   Howard, Herbert Edmund. SEE Philmore, R. [pseud.].

689. Howarth, Patrick. Play up and play the game; the heroes of popular fiction. London: Eyre Methuen; 1973. 178p.

690. Howe, Irving. "Joseph Conrad; order and anarchy: the political novels." IN Kenyon Review v.15:no.4 and v.16:no.1 (1953 and 1954) pp.505-521 and pp.1-19.

   repr. IN Howe, Irving. Politics and the novel. N.Y.: Horizon Press; 1957. 251p. pp.93-100. - repr. - N.Y.: Meridian Books. (No. M46) - U.K. ed. - London: Stevens; 1961. 251p. (New Left books).

   repr. IN Watt, I. (ed.). Conrad; 'The secret agent'. (q.v.) pp.140-149.

*   Howes, Barbara. (ed.). SEE Chimera.

691. Hoyt, Charles Alva. "'The damned'; good intentions: the tough guy as hero and villain." IN Madden, D. (ed.). Tough guy writers of the Thirties. (q.v.) pp.224-230.

692. Hubin, Allen J. The bibliography of crime fiction 1749-1975; listing all mystery, detective, suspense, police, and gothic fiction in book form published in the English language. Del Mar, Calif.: Publisher's Inc.; 1979. xvi, 697p.

693. ... "Patterns in mystery fiction; the durable series character." IN The mystery story (q.v.) pp.291-318.

694. Hughes, Dorothy Belle Flanagan. "The Christie nobody knew." IN Agatha Christie. (q.v.) pp.121-130.

695. ... Erle Stanley Gardner; the case of the real Perry Mason. N.Y.: Morrow; 1978. 350p., illus.

696. Hughes, Rupert (1872-1956). "The detective in fact and fiction." IN Hughes, Rupert (1872-1956). The complete detective; being the life and strange and exciting cases of Raymond Schindler, master detective. N.Y.: Sheridan House; 1950. 319p.

*   Hulsewe, A. F. P.   SEE   Necrology of R. H. van Gulik.

*   Hunter, Evan.   SEE   McBain, Ed [pseud.].

697. Hutchinson, Horatio Gordon.   "Detective fiction."
IN Quarterly Review [London]   v.253   (July 1929)
pp.148-160.

698. Hutter, Albert D. (jnt. auth.).   ""Who can be trusted?";
'The Detective', an early journal of detection."   By A. D.
Hutter and Mary W. Miller.   IN Mystery and Detection Annual;
1973. (q.v.) pp.167-192.

699. Hyder, Clyde Kenneth (1902-).   "Wilkie Collins and
'The woman in white'."   IN P.M.L.A.   v.54   (March 1939)
pp.297-303.

700. Hyneman, Esther F.   Edgar Allan Poe; an annotated
bibliography of books and articles in English, 1827-1973.
Boston: G. K. Hall; 1974.   xvi, 335p.   (Literature series)
(Research bibliographies in American literature, no.2).

I

701. Ikushima, Jirō. Hangyaku no kokoro o torimodose.
Tokyo: Futaba Sha; 1974. 293p.

702. Ilyina, N. (jnt. auth.). "Detective novels; a game
and life." By N. Ilyina and A. Adamov. IN Soviet Literature
No.3 (1975) pp.142-150.

703. Indiana. University. Lilly Library. The first hundred
years of detective fiction, 1841-1941; by one hundred authors
on the hundred thirtieth anniversary of the first publication
in book form of Edgar Allan Poe's 'The murders in the Rue
Morgue', Philadelphia, 1843. Comp. by David A. Randall.
Bloomington, Ind.: The Lilly Library, Indiana University;
1973. 64p., illus. (Lilly Library publication no.18).
"An exhibition held at the Lilly Library, Indiana University,
Bloomington, July-September, 1973."

704. Indianapolis, Ind. Public Library. Some less known
detective stories. [Indianapolis, Ind.: Indianapolis Public
Library; n.d., i.e. ca.1915] 21ℓ.

705. Innes, Michael [pseud.]. "Death as a game." IN
Esquire v.63 (January 1965) pp.55-56.

706. ... "John Appleby." IN Penzler, O. M. The great
detectives. (q.v.) pp.9-15.

*   Iorio, John J. (jnt. auth.). SEE Gould, J. A.

J

*   J. & S. Graphics. SEE <u>Detective fiction; mysteries and crime</u>.

707. Jacobs, Jack. "William Powell". IN <u>Films in Review</u> v.9:no.9 (November 1958) pp.497-509.

708. Jacobs, Jay. "Simenon's mosaic." IN <u>The Reporter</u> (14 January 1965) pp.38-40.

709. James, Clive. "The country behind the hill." IN Gross, M. (ed.). <u>The world of Raymond Chandler</u>. (q.v.) pp.115-126.

710. ... "Eric Ambler." IN <u>New Review</u> London v.1:no.6 (September 1974) pp.63-69. ("Prisoners of clarity" column, no.2).

711. James, P. D. "Dorothy L. Sayers; from puzzle to novel." IN <u>Crime writers</u>. (q.v.) pp.64-75.

712. Jameson, Fredric. "On Raymond Chandler." IN <u>Southern Review</u> v.6 (1970) pp.624-650.

713. Janeczko, Paul. <u>It's elementary; great detectives greatest cases</u>. N.Y.: Bantam; 1977.

714. Janvier, Ludovic. <u>Une parole exigeante; le nouveau roman</u>. Paris: Éditions de Minuit; 1964. 188p.

715.   Jarrett, C.   "Jane Austen and detective stories."
IN Saturday Review of Literature   v.13   (7 December 1935)
p.15.

716.   Jenkinson, Philip.   "The Agatha Christie films."   IN
Agatha Christie.   (q.v.)   pp.155-182.

717.   Jensen, P.   "Film noir: the writer; Raymond Chandler -
the world you live in."   IN Film Comment   v.10   (November
1974)   pp.18-22ff.

718.   Jensen, Vagn.   Stene for brød; de kulørte hefters
problem.   Copenhagn: G. E. C. Gad; 1961.   126p., illus.

719.   Jesse, Fryniwyd Marsh Tennyson (1889-1958).
"Introduction."   IN Jesse, Fryniwyd Marsh Tennyson (1889-
1958).   The Solange stories.   London: Wm. Heinemann; 1931.
xxii, 285p.   pp.ix-xxi.   -   U.S. ed.: N.Y.: Macmillan; 1931.
xvi, 182p.

720.   Jinka, Katsuo.   "Mystery stories in Japan."   IN
Armchair Detective   v.9:no.2   (February 1976)   pp.112-113.

721.   John Buchan; by his wife and friends.   Ed. by Susan
Grosvenor Buchan.   London: Hodder & Stoughton; 1947.   304p.

  A supplement, complementary to: Buchan, J.   'Memory
  hold-the-door'.   (q.v.)

722.   Johannsen, Albert (1871-1962).   The House of Beadle
and Adams; and its dime and nickle novels: the story of a
vanished literature.   Norman, Okla.: University of Oklahoma
Press; 1950-1962.   3 vols.

723.   Johnson, Ian.   "007 + 4."   IN   Films and Filming
v.12:no.1   (October 1965)   pp.5-11.

724.   Johnston, Alva.   "The case of Erle Stanley Gardner."
IN Saturday Evening Post   vol.219   (5, 12, 19 October 1946)
pp.9-11ff; 26-27ff; 24ff.

  - repr. abrgd.   IN Readers Digest   vol.50 (January 1947)
  pp.11-15.

  - repr.   The case of Erle Stanley Gardner.   N.Y.: Wm. Morrow;
  1947.   87p., illus.

725. Johnston, Charles (1867-). "The detective story's origin." IN Harper's Magazine v.54 (12 February 1910) pp.16-17.

726. Jones, Archie H. "Cops, robbers, heroes and anti-heroes; the American need to create." IN Journal of Popular Culture v.1:no.2 (Fall 1967) pp.114-127.

727. Jones, James P. "Nancy Drew, WASP Super Girl of the 1930's." IN Journal of Popular Culture v.6:no.4 (Spring 1973) pp.707-717.

728. Jones, James P. "Negro stereotypes in children's literature; the case of Nancy Drew." IN The Journal of Negro Education v.40:no.2 (Spring 1971) pp.121-125.

729. Jones, Robert Kenneth (1926-). The shudder pulps; a history of the weird menace magazines of the 1930's. West Linn, Or.: FAX Collector's Editions; 1975. xv, 238p., illus.

730. Juin, Hubert. "Un roman ininterrompu." IN Lacassin, F. (jnt. ed.). Simenon. (q.v.) pp.77-88.

731. Just, Klaus Günther. "Edgar Allan Poe und die Folgen." IN Vogt, J. (comp.) Der Kriminalroman. (q.v.) pp.9-32.

K

732. Kabatchnik, Amnon. "Retrospective review." IN
The Armchair Detective (February 1974) pp.131-132.

733. Kaemmel, E. "Literatur unterm Tisch." IN Žmegač, V.
(ed.). Der wohltemperierte Mord.

734. Kaminsky, Stuart M. American film genres; approaches
to a critical theory of popular film. N.Y.: Dell; 1974,
1977. 288p., illus. (Laurel Editions).

   - v. Chap.2: "The individual film; 'Little Caesar' and
   the gangster film.", pp.23-48; Chap.4: "Literary adaptation
   and change; 'The killers' - Hemingway, Film Noir, and the
   Terror of Daylight.", pp.62-84; Chap.5: "Contemporary
   problems; the white hot violence of the 1970's", pp.85-99;
   Chap.6: "Variations on a major genre; the Big Caper film.",
   pp.100-129.

735. ... "Chicago letter." IN Take One v.1:no.3-7
(September-October 1971) pp.42-45.

736. ... "'Little Caesar' and its role in the gangster film
genre." IN Journal of Popular Film v.1:no.3 (Summer 1972)
pp.209-227.

737. Kane, Patricia. "Perry Mason; modern culture hero."
IN Browne, Ray Broadus (jnt. comp.). Heroes of popular
culture. Ed. by R. B. Browne, Marshall Fishwick, and Michael
T. Marsden. Bowling Green, Ohio: Bowling Green University
Popular Press; 1972. 190p. (Probings in popular culture)
pp.125-133.

738. Kanfer, Stefan. "The spy who came in for the gold;
meet John le Carré, alias David Cornwell." IN Time; the
weekly newsmagazine. v.110:no.14 (3 October 1977) pp.50-55.

739. Kanin, Garson. Remembering Mr. Maugham. With a
foreword by Noel Coward. London: Hamish Hamilton; 1966.
[iv], 240p.

740. Kanters, Robert. "Sur la vieillesse et sur la mort."
IN Lacassin, F. (jnt. ed.). Simenon. (q.v.) pp.71-76.

741. Kanzog, K. "E. T. A. Hoffmanns Erzählung "Das Fraulein
von Scuderi" als Kriminalgeschichte." IN Mitteleilangen der
E. T. A. Hoffman - Gesellschaft. v.11 (1964) pp.1-11.

742. Karimi, Amir Massoud. Toward a definition of the
American 'film noir' (1941-1949) ... Ph.D. dissertation,
University of Southern California, 1970. - N.Y.: Arno
Press; 1976. 255p. (Dissertations on Film series).

743. Karpf, Stephen Louis. The gangster film; emergence,
variation and decay of a genre, 1939-1940 ... Ph.D.
dissertation, Northwestern University, 1970. iv, 300p.

   - publ. - N.Y.: Arno Press; 1973. viii, 299p. (The
   Arno Press cinema program. Dissertations on film series).

744. Katholische Akademie Stuttgart-Hohenheim. Für und
wider den Krimi. Stuttgart-Hohenheim: Akadaemie der Diozese
Rottenburg; 1965. 79p. (Beitrage zur Begegnung von Kirche
und Welt, Nr.77).

745. Keating, Henry Reymond Fitzwalter (1926-). "Hercule
Poirot - a companion portrait." IN Agatha Christie. (q.v.)
pp.205-216.

746. ... "Inspector Ghote." IN Penzler, O. M. The great
detectives. (q.v.) pp.109-117.

747. ... Murder must appetize. London: Lemon Tree Press;
1975. 64p., illus. (Time Remembered).

748. ... "New patents pending." IN Crime writers. (q.v.)
pp.138-155.

*   ...   (ed.).   SEE   Also   <u>Agatha Christie</u>.

*   ...   (jnt. ed.).   SEE   also   <u>Crime writers</u>.

749.   Keddie, James.   "Freeman Wills Crofts."   IN   <u>Armchair</u>
<u>Detective</u>   v.2:no.3   (April 1969)   pp.137-142.

750.   Keene, Carolyn [pseud.].   "Nancy Drew."   IN   Penzler,
O. M.   <u>The great detectives</u>.   (q.v.)   pp.79-86.

751.   ...   <u>The Nancy Drew cookbook; clues to good cooking</u>.
N.Y.: Grosset & Dunlap; c1973, 1977.   159p.

752.   Kelly, R. Gordon.   "The precarious world of John D.
MacDonald."   IN   <u>Dimensions of detective fiction</u>.   (q.v.)
pp.149-161.

753.   Kemelman, H.   "Vorwort zur deutschen Ausgabe von <u>The</u>
<u>nine mile walk</u>."   -   orig. publ. 1969; repr. in German trans.
IN   <u>Der Detektiverzählung auf der Spur</u>.   (q.v.)

754.   Kendrick, Baynard H.   "Duncan Maclain."   IN   Penzler,
O. M.   <u>The great detectives</u>.   (q.v.)   pp.127-140.

755.   Kennedy, J. G.   "Limits of reason; Poe's deluded
detectives."   IN   <u>American Literature</u>   v.47   (May 1975)
pp.184-196.

756.   Kenney, William Patrick.   <u>The Dashiell Hammett tradition</u>
<u>and the modern detective novel</u>   ...   Ph.D. dissertation,
University of Michigan, 1964.   171p.

757.   Kermode, J. F.   "Novel and narrative."   IN   Halperin,
John (1941-).   (ed.).   <u>The theory of the novel; new essays</u>.
N.Y.: Oxford University Press; 1974.   xi, 396p.   pp.155-174.

758.   Kinder, M.   "Return of the outlaw couple."   IN   <u>Film</u>
<u>Quarterly</u>   v.27:no.4   (Summer 1974)   pp.2-10.

759. Kittle, Charles Frederick. "Arthur Conan Doyle; doctor
and writer (1859-1930)." IN Journal of the Kansas Medical
Society v.61:no.1 (January 1960) pp.13-18.

  rev., enlg., and repr. AS "Arthur Conan Doyle;
  detective-doctor." IN University of Minnesota Medical
  Bulletin v.36:no. 8 (April 1965) pp.278-292.

  orig. vers. repr. with slight changes AS "The case
  of the versatile A. Conan Doyle." IN The University
  of Chicago Magazine v.42:no.2-3 (September-December
  1969) pp.8-14.

760. Kittredge, William (jnt. auth.). "Introduction."
By W. Kittredge and Steven M. Krauzer. IN The great American
detective. Ed. and with an intro. by William Kittredge and
Steven M. Krauzer. N.Y.: New American Library; 1978.
xxxiv, 414p. (A Mentor Book) pp.x-xxxiv.

  repr. AS "The evolution of the great American detective;
  the reader as detective hero." IN Armchair Detective
  vol.11:no.4 (October 1978) pp.319-330.

761. Knight, Damon Francis (1922-). ["... A careful analysis
of Curme Gray's 'Murder in Millennium VI ..."] IN Knight,
Damon Francis (1922-). In search of wonder; essays on modern
science fiction. 2d (rev.) ed. Chicago: Advent Publishers;
1967. xi, 306p., illus. pp.181-187.

762. Knobel, Bruno. Krimifibel. Solothurn, Germany:
Schweizer Jugend-Verlag; 1968. 80p., illus. - also
publ.: Stuttgart: Eulen-Verlag; 1968. 80p., illus.

763. Knoepflmacher, U. S. "The counterworld of Victorian
fiction and 'The woman in white'." IN The worlds of
Victorian fiction. Ed. by Jerome H. Buckley. Cambridge,
Mass./London: Harvard University Press; 1975. x, 416p.
(Harvard English Studies, 6) pp.351-369.

764. Knopf, Jan. Friedrich Dürrenmatt. Munich: Verlag
C. H. Beck; 1976. 173p. (Autorenbücher; 3).

765. Knox, Ronald A. "Introduction." IN Best detective
stories; first series. Ed. by Ronald A. Knox and Henry
Harrington, with an intro. by R. A. Knox. London: Faber &
Faber; 1929. 480p. pp.9-25. - U.S. ed.: N.Y.: Liveright;
1929. - repr. often by Faber. - also repr.: Paulton,
Eng.: Purnell and Sons; 1948.

Section containing 'A detective story decalogue. repr.
IN Haycraft, H. (ed.). The art of the mystery story.
(q.v.) pp.194-196.

repr. in German trans. AS "Zehn Regeln für einenguten
Detektivroman." IN Der Detektiverzählung auf der Spur.
(q.v.)

766. ... "Introduction." IN Chesterton, Gilbert Keith
(1874-1936). Father Brown; selected stories. With an
intro. by Ronald Knox. London: Oxford University Press;
1955. xvii, 411p. (World's Classics No.547) - repr.:
OUP; 1966.

767. Kolker, R. P. "Night to day." IN Sight and Sound
v.43:no.4 (Autumn 1974) pp.236-239.

768. Korg, Jacob. (ed.). Twentieth century interpretations
of 'Bleak House'; a collection of critical essays. Englewood
Cliffs, N.J.: Prentice-Hall; 1968. ix, 114p. (Spectrum
Books).

769. Kosakai, Fuboku (1890-1929). Kindai hanzai kenkyū.
Tokyo: Shunyodo; 1925. 364p.

770. Kracauer, Siegfried. Schriften. Frankfurt/Main:
Suhrkamp Verlag; 1971-

    Bd.1: Soziologie als Wissenschaft. Der Detektivroman.
    Die Angestellten. 1971. 308p.

*   Krauzer, Steven M. (jnt. auth.). SEE Kittredge, W.
(jnt. auth.).

771. Krkošková, Mária. (comp.). Magazín Labyrintu. Zost.
a zred. Mária Krkošková ... Illustr. [za fot. spoluprace
J. V. Frica] a graf. upr. Sláva Jílek. Bratislava: Smena,
t. Nitrianske tlač., Nitra; 1970. 111p., illus. (Labyrint).

*   Kruse, Hans-Joachim. (jnt. ed.). SEE Greiner-Mai, H.

772. Krutch, Joseph Wood (1893-1970). "Only a detective
story." IN Nation v.159 (25 November 1944) pp.647-648ff.

    repr. IN Haycraft, H. (ed.). The art of the mystery
    story. (q.v.) pp.178-185.

repr. in German trans. AS "Nur ein Detektivroman"
IN Der Detektiverzahlung auf der Spur. (q.v.)

773. Kuki, Shirō (1910-). Tantei shōsetsu hyakka. Tokyo:
Kanazono-sha; 1975. 12, 516p., illus. Cover title: The
detective story and all that.

774. Kusumoto, Kenkichi (1922-). Ninkyō eiga no sekai.
Tokyo: Arachisha; 1969. 237p.

775. Kvam, Lorentz Normann (1891-). Om norsk kriminallitteratur. Oslo: Damm; 1942. 20p.

L

776. Lacassin, Francis. "Alan Resnais; the quest for Harry Dickson." IN Sight and Sound v.42:no.4 (Autumn 1973) pp.212-217.

777. ... Mythologie du roman policier. Paris: Union générale d'éditions; 1974. 2 vols. (10/18: Inédit; 867).

   Vol.1: 320p.

   Vol.2: 317p.

778. ... (jnt. comp.). Simenon. Ed. by F. Lacassin and Gilbert Sigaux. Paris, Plon; 1973. 481p.

779. ... "Simenon et la fugue initiatique." IN Lacassin, F. (jnt. ed.). Simenon. (q.v.) pp.157-183.

780. Lach, Donald F. "Introduction." IN Van Gulik, Robert H. The Chinese Bell murders. Chicago: University of Chicago Press; [c1958], 1977. xi, 288p. pp.1-13.

   also contained IN Van Gulik, Robert H. The Chinese nail murders. Chicago: University of Chicago Press; [c1961, 1977]. xi, 209p. pp.1-13.

781. Lacombe, Alain. Le roman noir américain. Paris: Union générale d'éditions; [c1975]. 188p. (Inédit 10/18; 918).

782. la Cour, Tage. "Damer på den litteraere forbryderbane." IN la Cour, T. 'Kaleidoskop'. (q.v.)

783. ... "Dr. Jekyll og Mr. Brodie." IN la Cour, T.
'Kaleidoskop'. (q.v.)

784. ... Den grønne ø i fantasiens hav og andre egne i
den lettere bogverden. Copenhagn: Selskabet bogvennerne;
1973. 124p., illus.

785. ... "Jules Maigret's privatliv." IN la Cour, T.
'Kaleidoskop'. (q.v.)

786. ... Kaleidoskop; causerier, noveller, parodier og
rimerier fra den lettere bogverden. Copenhagn: Bogvennerne -
Carit Andersen; 1975. 176p.

787. ... "Monsieur Hercule Poirot." IN la Cour, T.
'Kaleidoskop'. (q.v.)

788. ... Mord i Biblioteket. Stockholm: Sällskapet
Bokvännerna; 1953. 83p., illus. (Bokvännens småskrifter,
nr.9).

   repr. in Danish under same title IN la Cour, T.
   'Studier i rødt'. (q.v.) pp.7-96.

789. ... Mord mem moral - og uden. Copenhagn: [n.publ.];
1963. 51p.

   Not verified. Cited in: la Cour, T. 'The murder book'
   (q.v.), p.176.

790. ... (jnt. auth.). Mordbogen; Kriminal - og
detektivhistorien i billeder og tekst. By T. la Cour and
Harald Mogensen. Copenhagn: Lademann; 1969. 192p., illus.

   U.K. (first English) ed. AS The murder book; an
   illustrated history of the detective story. London:
   Allen & Unwin; 1971. 192p., illus. - U.S. ed.: N.Y.:
   McGraw-Hill; 1971. 191p.

*   ... (jnt. auth.). The murder book. SEE la Cour, T.
(jnt. auth.). Mordbogen.

791. ... "Mysteriet om en Hansom Cab." IN la Cour, T.
'Studier i rødt'. (q.v.) pp.123-135.

792. ... The Scandinavian crime-detection story. Chicago:
Arthur Lovell; n.d.

  Not verified. Cited in: la Cour, T. 'Studier i rødt'.
  (q.v.), p.5.

  repr. in Danish AS "Skandinaviske Kriminalfortaellinger."
  IN la Cour, T. 'Studier i rødt'. (q.v.) pp.97-122.

793. ... Studier i rødt; causerier om kriminalliteratur.
Copenhagn: Carit Andersens Forlaf; 1956. 135, [9]p.

  Cover sub-title has "essays on kriminallitteratur".

  Contents: Mord i Biblioteket; Skandinaviske Kriminalfortaellinger; Mysteriet om en Hansom Cab.

*   ... (jnt. ed.). SEE also Dansk og udenlandsk
kriminallitteratur.

*   ... (jnt. auth.). SEE also Elgström, J. Mord i
biblioteket.

794. La Farge, Christopher. "Mickey Spillane and his bloody
Hammer." IN Saturday Review (6 November 1954) pp.11-12,
54-59.

  repr. IN Rosenberg, Bernard (1923-). (jnt. comp.).
  Mass culture; the popular arts in America. Ed. by
  B. Rosenberg and David Manning-White. Glencoe, Ill.:
  Free Press/N.Y.: Macmillan; 1957. 561p. pp.176-185.

795. Lahue, Kalton C. Bound and gagged; the story of the
silent serials. South Brunswick, N.J.: Barnes & Noble; 1968.
352p., illus. - repr. - N.Y.: Castle Books; [1968]. 352p.,
illus.

796. Lambert, Gavin. The dangerous edge. London: Barrie &
Jenkins; 1975. xv, 271p. - U.S. ed.: N.Y.: Grossman; 1976.
xiii, 271p.

797. Lamond, John. Arthur Conan Doyle; a memoir. London:
John Murray; 1931. xiv, 310p. - repr.: Port Washington,
N.Y.: Kennikat Press; 1972. xiv, 310p. (No.1588).

798. Landrum, Larry N. "Detective and mystery novels." IN
Inge, M. Thomas (ed.). Handbook of American popular culture.
Westport, Ct.: Greenwood Press; 1978. x, 404p. (Vol.I)
pp.103-120.

799. ... (et al.). "Introduction." By L. N. Landrum,
Pat Browne, and Ray Broadus Browne. IN Dimensions of
detective fiction. (q.v.) pp.1-10.

*   ... (jnt. ed.). SEE also Dimensions of detective
fiction.

800. Lane, Margaret (1907-). Edgar Wallace; the biography
of a phenomenon. London: Wm. Heinemann; 1938. viii, 423p. -
var. reprints.

    rev. ed.: Intro. by Graham Greene. London: H. Hamilton;
    1964. xiv, 338p., illus.

801. Lane, Sheldon (comp.). For Bond lovers only. London:
Panther; 1965. 175p. - U.S. ed.: N.Y.: Dell; 1965. 156p.,
illus.

802. Langbaum, Robert. "Crime in modern literature." IN
American Scholar v.26 (Summer 1957) pp.360ff.

803. Langenbrucher, E. (et al.). "Geistes' Blitze aus
Kriminal-Romanen." IN Die Buchbesprechung [Leipzig]
Jahrg.3 (1939).

804. Larka, Robert. Television's private eye; an examination
of twenty years programming of a particular genre, 1949 to
1969 ... Ph.D. dissertation, Ohio University, 1973.

805. Larkin, Mark. "The philosophy of crime." IN
Photoplay (April 1929) pp.71, 135-137.

806. Larmoth, Jeanine. Murder on the menu; [food and drink
in the English mystery novel]. Recipes by Charlotte Turgeon.
N.Y.: Charles Scribner's; 1972. xv, 268p.

807. Larsen, A. P. (1871-). Sagen mod praesten i Vejlby,
og de sager der fulgte; fremstillet efter akterne. Copenhagn:
Gyldendal; 1951. 111p., illus.

*   Larsen, Else. (jnt. ed.). SEE Dansk og udenlandsk
kriminallitteratur.

808. Lasić, Stanko (1927-). Poetika kriminalističkog
romana; Pokušaj strukturalne analize. Zagreb: "Liber",
"Mladost"; 1973. 176p.

809. Lathen, Emma [pseud.]. "Cornwallis's revenge."
IN Agatha Christie. (q.v.) pp.79-94.

*   Latis, Mary J. SEE Lathen, Emma [pseud.].

810. Lauritzen, Henry. Mesterdetektiver under Lup.
Copenhagn: (L. C. Lauritzens Boghandel), (D.B.K.); 1970.
67 p., illus.

811. Leah, Gordon N. "Dürrenmatt's detective stories."
IN Modern Languages v.48 (1967) pp.65-69.

812. Leavis, Frank Raymond (1895-). "['The secret agent']".
IN Leavis, Frank Raymond (1895-). The great tradition;
George Eliot, Henry James, Joseph Conrad. London: Chatto &
Windus; 1948. 266p. pp.209-221. - repr. - 1950. -
U.S. ed. - N.Y.: G. W. Stewart; [1948?]. - repr. - Garden
City, N.Y.: Doubleday; 1954. 319p. (Anchor books A40).

    repr. IN Watt, I. (ed.). Conrad; 'The secret agent'.
    (q.v.) pp.118-132.

813. Leavis, Q. D. "The case of Miss Dorothy Sayers."
IN Scrutiny vol.6 (1937) pp.334-340.

*   Lee, Manfred Bennington. SEE Queen, Ellery [pseud.].

814. Lee Raymond (jnt. auth.). Gangsters and hoodlums; the
underworld in the cinema. By R. Lee and B. C. Van Hecke.
South Brunswick, N.J.: A. S. Barnes; 1971. 264p., illus.

815. Lee, Robert A. Alistair MacLean; the key is fear.
San Bernardino, Calif.: R. Reginald, The Borgo Press; 1976.
60p. (The Milford Series: Popular Writers of Today vol.2).

816. Lee, Stan. The superhero women. N.Y.: Simon and
Schuster; 1977. 255p., illus.

817. Leftwich, Joseph (1892-). Israel Zangwill. London:
J. Clark; 1957. 306p., illus. - U.S. ed.: N.Y.: T. Yoseloff;
1957. 306p.

818. Legman, Gershon (1917-). Love and death; a study in censorship. N.Y.: Breaking Point; 1949. 95p. (Direction 8) - repr.: N.Y.: Hackert Art Books; 1963. 95p.

*   Leites, Nathan. (jnt. auth.). SEE Wolfenstein, M.

819. Leithead, J. Edward. "The great detective team: Old and Young King Brady." IN American Book Collector v.20:no.3 (November-December 1969) pp.25-31.

820. Lejeune, A. "Age of the great detective." IN The Times Literary Supplement. Crime, detection and society. (q.v.)

821. Lemonnier, Léon. Edgar Poe et les conteurs français. Paris: Éditions Montaigne; 1947. 168p. (Coll. L'Histoire littéraire 13).

822. Lemos Britto, José Gabriel de (1886-). O crime e os criminosos na literatura brasileira. Rio de Janeiro: J. Olympio; 1946. 336p.

823. Lennig, Walter. Edgar Allan Poe in Selbstzeugnissen und Bilddokumenten. Hamburg: Rowohlt; 1959. 177p.

824. Leonard, John. "I care who killed Roger Ackroyd." IN Esquire v.84 (August 1975) pp.60-61.

825. ... "Ross Macdonald, his Lew Archer, and other secret selves." IN The New York Times Book Review (1 July 1969) p.19.

826. Le Queux, William (1864-1927). Things I know; about kings, celebrities, and crooks: [autobiography]. London: E. Nash & Grayson; 1923. 320p., illus.

827. Lerner, Max (1902-). "Cain in the movies." IN Lerner, Max (1902-). Public journal; marginal notes on wartime America. N.Y.: Viking Press; 1945. xii, 414p.

*   Lewis, C. Day. SEE Day Lewis, C.

*   Lewis, Gogo (jnt. comp.). SEE Manley, Seon.

828. Lewis, Sinclair. "Foreword". IN Long, Gabrielle
Margaret Vere Campbell. The golden violet; the story of
a lady novelist. By Joseph Shearing [pseud.]. N.Y.: Smith &
Durrell; 1941. 321p. - Orig. publ.: London: Heinemann;
1936. 348p.

829. Lichtenstein, Alfred. Der Kriminalroman; Eine
Literarische und forensisch-medizinische Studie, mit Anhang:
Sherlock Holmes zum Fall Hau. Munich: Ernst Reinhardt; 1908.
61p. (Grenzfragen der Literatur und Medizin in
Einzeldarstellungen von Dr. S. Rahmer. Heft 7).

830. Lid, R. W. "Philip Marlowe speaking." IN Kenyon
Review v.31;No.2 (1969) pp.153-178.

831. Liebman, Arthur (1926-). (comp.). Thirteen classic
detective stories; a critical history of detective fiction.
N.Y.: Richards Rosen Press; 1974. xii, 237p. (Masterworks
of Mystery series).

*   ... (ed.). SEE also Ms. mysteries.

*   Lincoln, Janet E. SEE The encyclopedia of comic
book heroes.

832. Lind, Sidney E. "Poe and mesmerism." IN Publications
of the Modern Languages Association v.62:no.4 (December 1947)
pp.1077-1094.

833. Lindsay, Philip (1906-). The haunted man; a portrait
of Edgar Allan Poe. London: Hutchinson; 1953. 256p. -
U.S. ed.: N.Y.: Philosophical Library; 1954.

834. Lingeman, R. R. "How to tell Sam Spade from Philip
Marlowe from Lew Archer." IN Esquire v.84 (August 1975)
pp.62-65.

*   Linington, Elizabeth. SEE Shannon, Dell [pseud.].

835. Lins, Alvaro. No mundo do romance policial. Rio de
Janeiro: Ministério da Educação e Saúde, Serviço de
Documentaçoa; 1953. 26p. (Õs Cadernos de cultura).

836. Locard, Edmond (1877-1966). La criminalistique, à
l'usage des gens du monde et des auteurs de roman policiers.
Lyon: J. Desvigne; 1937. 156p.

837. ... Edgar A. Poe as a detective ... [N.Y.: 1941?] -
typescript in a loose-leaf binder; 25ℓ.

- Translation by John Hugh Hulla of an excerpt from:
La Revue hebdomadaire no. 31, (30 July 1921). Held
New York Public Library.

838. ... Policiers de roman et policiers de laboratoire.
Paris: Payot; 1924. 277p.

839. Locke, Harold. A bibliographical catalogue of the
writings of Sir Arthur Conan Doyle, M.D., LL.D., 1879-1928.
Tunbridge Wells: D. Webster; 1928. 84p.

840. Lockridge, Richard. "Mr. and Mrs. North." IN
Penzler, O.M. The great detectives. (q.v.) pp.155-163.

841. Lodge, David (1935-). Graham Greene. N.Y.: Columbia
University Press; 1966. 48p. (Columbia essays on modern
writers no. 17).

   rev. vers. IN Six contemporary British novelists.
   Ed. by George Stade. N.Y.: Columbia University Press;
   1976. x, 357p.

842. Lofts, William Oliver Guillemont (jnt. auth.). The
British bibliography of Edgar Wallace. Comp. by W. O. G.
Lofts and Derek J. Adley. London: H. Baker; 1969. xiv,
246p.

843. ... (jnt. auth.). The men behind boys' fiction.
By W. O. G. Lofts and Derek J. Adley. London: Howard Baker;
1970. [5], 361p.

844. ... (jnt. auth.). The Saint and Leslie Charteris;
[a biography: the full life-story, plus a complete
bibliography of his work]. London: Howard Baker; 1970.
134p. - repr.: London: Hutchinson; 1971. - U.S. ed.:
Bowling Green, Ohio: Bowling Green University Popular
Press; 1972. 134p.

845. London. Bibliographical Society. The Minerva Press,
1790-1820. By Dorothy Blakey. London: Bibliographical
Society; [1935], 1939. 339p., illus.

846. "Looking backward; detective stories." IN Literary
Review v.4 (24 November 1923) p.283.

*   Loubert, Patrick (jnt. auth.). SEE Hirsh, Michael.

*   Loucks, James F. (jnt. auth.). SEE Altick, R. D.
(jnt. auth.). Browning's Roman murder story.

847. Lowndes, Mrs. Belloc. "Murder in fiction." IN
Saturday Review of Literature v.3:no.25 (15 January 1927)
pp.509-510.

848. Lowndes, Robert A. W. "The contributions of Edgar
Allan Poe." IN Startling Mystery Stories (Spring 1969
and Summer 1969) 2 pts.

    rev. vers. IN Nevins, F. M. (comp.) The mystery
    writer's art. (q.v.) pp.1-18.

849. Lucas, Alec. Studies in the Newgate novel of early
Victorian England, 1830-1845 ... Ph.D. thesis, Harvard
University, 1952. n.pag.

850. Lucas, Edward Verrall (1868-1938). "The search."
IN Outlook [London] (22 September 1906).

    repr. IN Living Age v.251 (8 December 1906) pp.632-634.

851. ... "Murder and motives." IN Lucas, Edward Verrall
(1868-1938). A fronded isle; and other essays. London:
Methuen; 1927. vi, 216p. - U.S. ed.: N.Y.: Doubleday
Doran; 1938. vi, 216p. - repr.: Freeport, N.Y.: Books
for Libraries; [n.d.].

    repr. IN Haycraft, H. (ed.). The art of the mystery
    story. (q.v.) pp.352-354.

852. ... "My murder story." IN Lucas, Edward Verrall
(1868-1938). Only the other day; a volume of essays.
London: Methuen; 1936. vi, 211p. - U.S. ed.: Philadelphia:
Lippincott; 1937. 211p.

853. Ludwig, Hans-Werner. "Der Ich-Erzähler im englisch-
amerikanischen Detektiv- und Kriminalroman." IN Deutsche
Vierteljahresschrift v.45 (1971) pp.438-441.

*   Ludwig, Myles Eric (jnt. auth.). SEE Smyth, Frank.
The detectives.

854. Lundin, Bo (1941-). "Den gamle mästaren." IN
Jury-tidskrift för deckarvänner [Stockholm: Bromma]
No.3-4 (1972) pp.16-18.

855. ... Mordets enkla konst; stencil för tvåbetygsseminarium.
Lund, Sweden: [n.publ.]; 1965. 21p.

  Not verified. Cited in: la Cour, T. The murder book.
  (q.v.), p.177.

856. ... "Poeten och deckaren." IN Jury-tidskrift för
deckarvänner [Stockholm: Bromma] No. 1 (1972). pp.21-23.

857. ... "Den skarpsinnige snobben." IN Jury-tidskrift
för deckarvänner [Stockholm: Bromma] No.2 (1972) pp.5-7.

858. ... Spårhundarna; Berömda detektiver i närbild.
Stockholm: Rabén & Sjögren; 1973. 251p., illus.

859. Lundquist, James. Chester Himes. N.Y.: Ungar; 1976.
ix, 166p. (Modern literature monographs).

*   Lupoff, Dick (jnt. ed.). SEE Thompson, Don. The
comic-book book.

860. Lynch, Judge [pseud.]. "Battle of the sexes; the judge
and his wife look at mysteries." IN Haycraft, H. (ed.).
The art of the mystery story. (q.v.) pp.367-372.

M

861. McAleer, John. _Rex Stout; a biography_. Boston: Little Brown; 1977. xvi, 621p., illus.

862. McArthur, Colin. _Underworld U.S.A._ N.Y.: Viking Press; 1972. 176p., illus. (Cinema one, 20) - U.K. ed.: London: Secker & Warburg; 1972. 176p., illus. (Cinema One series).

863. McBain, Ed [pseud.]. "The 87th Precinct." IN Penzler, O. M. _The great detectives_. (q.v.) pp.87-97.

864. McCann, J. "Graham Greene; the ambiguity of death." IN _Christian Century_ v.92 (30 April 1975) pp.432-435.

865. McCarthy, Mary. "Murder and Karl Marx; class-conscious detective stories." IN _Nation_ v.142 (25 March 1936) pp.381-383.

cf. Seagle, W. "Murder, Marx, and McCarthy".

866. McCleary, George Frederick (1867-). _On detective fiction and other things_. London: Hollis & Carter; 1960. 161p. - repr.: Norwood, Penn.: Norwood Editions; 1974. 161p. - repr.: Folcroft, Pa.: Folcroft Library Editions; [1976?].

Contains, among other essays: The popularity of detective fiction (pp.11-18); A Victorian masterpiece - 'The Moonstone' (pp.19-25); The apotheosis of Sherlock Holmes (pp.26-33); The original of Sherlock Holmes (pp.34-51); Three examination papers - Pickwick, Sherlock Holmes, Jane Austen (pp.52-65); Stevenson's early writings (pp.116-122).

867. McCloy, Stephen A. Rock my socks off, baby - shoes
ain't news; gunsels, yeggs, natural language and you; a
chronological bibliography of critical treatment of Dashiell
Hammett and Raymond Chandler, 1929-1974, selected, annotated
and indexed, with additional prefatory, introductory and
explanatory material. Wellington, N.Z.: Library School,
National Library of New Zealand; 1975. 52p.

868. McCormick, Donald (1911-). Who's who in spy fiction.
London: Hamish Hamilton; 1977. 215p. (Elm Tree Books)   -
U.S. ed.: N.Y.: Taplinger; 1977.   - repr. pbk. London:
Sphere; 1979. 254p.

869. McCracken, David. "Introduction." IN Godwin, William
(1756-1836). Caleb Williams. Ed. by David McCracken.
London: Oxford University Press; 1970. xxx, 351p. (Oxford
English Novels series) pp.vii-xxvi.

870. McDade, Thomas M. "Gallows literature of the streets."
IN The New Colophon [New York] v.3 (1950) pp.120-127.

871. Macdonald, Ross [pseud.] (1915-). "Cain X 3." IN
New York Times Book Review (2 March 1969) p.1.

872. ... "Down these streets a mean man must go." IN
Antaeus; Popular Fiction Issue No.25/26 (Spring/Summer 1977)
pp.211-216.

873. ... "Homage to Dashiell Hammett." IN Mystery Writers'
Annual; 1964. pp.8, 24.

874. ... "Introduction." IN Bruccoli, M. J. (comp.)
Kenneth Millar/Ross Macdonald. (q.v.) pp.xi-xvii.

875. ... "Introduction." IN Macdonald, Ross [pseud.]
(1915-). Archer in Hollywood; 3 exciting novels: The moving
target, The way some people die, and The barbarous coast.
N.Y.: Knopf; 1967. xi, 528p.

876. ... "Lew Archer." IN Penzler, O. M. The great
detectives. (q.v.) pp.17-24.

   repr. AS "Introduction." IN Macdonald, Ross [pseud.]
   (1915-). Lew Archer, private investigator. Yonkers, N.Y.:
   Mysterious Press; 1977. 272p.

877. ... On crime writing. Santa Barbara, Calif.: Capra
Press; 1973. viii, 9-45p. (Yes! Capra chapbook series;
no.11).

   Contents: The writer as detective hero; Writing 'The
   Galton case'.

878. ... "A preface to 'The Galton case'." IN McCormack,
Thomas (comp.). Afterwords; novelists on their novels.
N.Y.: Harper & Row; 1969. 231p.

   repr. AS "Writing 'The Galton case'." IN Macdonald, R.
   [pseud.]. On crime writing. (q.v.) pp.25-45.

879. ... "The writer as detective hero." IN Show v.1
(January 1965) pp.34-36ff.

   repr. IN Lid, Richard Wald (1928-). (comp.).
   Essays; classics and contemporary. Philadelphia:
   J. B. Lippincott; 1967. ix, 398p. (Lippincott College
   English series).

   repr. IN Macdonald, R. [pseud.]. On crime writing.
   (q.v.) pp.9-24.

   repr. IN Nevins, F. M. (comp.). The mystery writer's
   art. (q.v.) pp.295-305.

880. MacDonell, A. G. "The present conventions of the
mystery story." IN London Mercury v.23 (December 1930)
pp.158-165.

   cf. Sayers, D. L. "The present status of the mystery
   story."

881. McElroy, C. F. "The cliché of the mystery writers;
it doesn't make sense." IN Saturday Review of Literature
v.21 (13 January 1940) p.9.

882. McFarlane, Leslie (1902-). Ghost of the Hardy Boys;
[an autobiography]. Toronto: Methuen; 1976. 208p. -
U.S. ed.: N.Y.: Two Continents; 1976. 211p.

883. McGill, Vivian Jerauld. "Henry James, master detective."
IN Bookman [N.Y.2 v.72 (November 1930) pp.251-256.

884. MacGowan, Kenneth (1888-). (ed.). Sleuths; twenty-
three great detectives of fiction and their best stories.
N.Y.: Harcourt Brace; 1931. xix, 595p.

   "This ... is a collection of fictional detectives,
   not of detective stories. It aims to present the best
   twenty-three detectives in English and American fiction,
   not the best twenty-three detective stories." - Introd.

885. McHaney, Thomas L. William Faulkner; a reference guide.
Boston: G. K. Hall; 1976. xx, 568p. (Reference guides in
literature, no. 7).

886. McInnes, Graham. "Elementary, my dear Watson." IN
University of Toronto Quarterly v.16:no.4 (July 1947)
pp.411-419.

887. Mackenzie, Compton (1883-1972). "The man behind
Sherlock Holmes." IN Mackenzie, Compton (1883-1972).
On moral courage. London: Collins; 1962. 255p. -
U.S. ed. AS Certain aspects of moral courage. Garden
City, N.Y.: Doubleday & Co.; 1962. pp.164-186 (Chap.10).

888. McLaren, J. Ross. "Chandler and Hammett." IN
The London Magazine n.s.v.3:no.12 (March 1964) pp.70-79.

889. McLuhan, Herbert Marshall. "Footprints in the sands
of crime." IN Sewanee Review v.54 (October 1946)
pp.617-634.

890. MacShane, Frank. The life of Raymond Chandler.
N.Y.: Dutton; 1976. xii, 306p., illus. - U.K. ed.:
London: Cape; 1976. xii, 306p., illus.

*   ... (ed.). SEE also Chandler, Raymond. The notebooks.

891. McSherry, Frank D. "A new category of the mystery
story." IN The Armchair Detective v.2:no.1 (October 1968)
pp.23-24.

   rev. vers. AS "The Janus resolution." IN Nevins,
   F. M. (comp.). The mystery writer's art. (q.v.)
   pp.263-271.

892. ... "The shape of crimes to come." IN Nevins, F. M.
(comp.). The mystery writer's art. (q.v.) pp.326-338.

893.   ...   "Under two flags; the detective story in science fiction."   IN   The Armchair Detective   v.2:no.3   (April 1969)   pp.171-173.

894.   ...   "Who-really-dun-it?; two sub-branches of the detective story."   IN   The Armchair Detective   v.2:no.2   (January 1969)   pp.88-93.

*   Madden, Cecil.   SEE   Meet the detective.

895.   Madden, David T.   (1933-).   "Cain's 'The postman always rings twice' and Camus' 'L'Etranger'."   IN   Papers on Language and Literature   v.6:no.4   (Fall 1970)   pp.407-419.

896.   ...   James M. Cain.   N.Y.: Twayne; 1970.   200p.   (Twayne's United States Authors Series no.171).

897.   ...   "James M. Cain and the movies of the thirties and forties."   IN   Film Heritage   v.2   (Summer 1967)   pp.9-25.

898.   ...   "James M. Cain and the pure novel."   IN   The University Review - Kansas City   v.30   (December 1963 and March 1964)   2 pts.   [Dec. 1963: pp.143-148; Mar. 1964: pp.235-239].

899.   ...   "James M. Cain and the tough guy novelists of the 30's."   IN   French, Warren (ed.).   The thirties; fiction, poetry, drama.   Deland, Fla.: Everett Edwards; 1967.   ix, 253p.   -   2d ed.: Deland, Fla.: Everett Edwards; 1976.   ix, 259p.

900.   ...   "James M. Cain; twenty-minute egg of the hard-boiled school."   IN   Journal of Popular Culture   v.1:no.3   (Winter 1967)   pp.178-192.

901.   ...   (ed.).   Tough guy writers of the Thirties.   Carbondale, Ill.: Southern Illinois University Press/London: Feffer & Simons; 1968.   xxxix, 247p.   (Crosscurrents: modern critiques).

902.   Mager, Hasso.   Krimi und crimen; Zur Moral der Unmoral.   Halle (Saale): Mitteldeutscher Verlag; 1969.   142p.

903. Maggs Brothers, London, booksellers. A gallery of
rogues: outlaws of society in fact and fiction; highwaymen,
murderers, pirates, plotters, robbers, smugglers, witches, etc.
London: Maggs Bros.; 1936. 85, 5p., illus. (Maggs catalogue
630).

904. Magny, Claude-Edmonde. L'âge du roman américain; roman
et cinéma: Dos Passos, Hemingway, Faulkner, Steinbeck. Paris:
Éditions du Seuil; 1948. 256p. (Coll. Pierres vives) –
U.S. (first English) ed. AS The age of the American novel;
the film aesthetic of fiction between the two wars. N.Y.:
Ungar; 1972. 239p.

905. Malin, Irving. "Focus on 'The Maltese Falcon'; the
metaphysical falcon." IN Madden, D. T. (ed.). Tough-guy
writers of the thirties. (q.v.) pp.102-109.

906. Maloney, Martin. "A grammar of assassination." IN
ETC.; a review of general semantics. The use and misuse of
language; selections from 'Etc.; a review of general semantics'.
Ed. by Samuel Ichiye Hayakawa. N.Y.: Harper & Row; 1962.
x, 240p., illus. – also publ.: Greenwich, Conn.: Fawcett;
1962. x, 240p., illus. (A Premier book) (Premier behavioral
sciences) (Premier book M441) – repr.: same publ.; 1964.
(A Premier book: t166) – repr.: same publ.; 1966.

907. Malraux, André. "Preface to William Faulkner's
'Sanctuary'." IN Southern Review v.10 (October 1974)
pp.889-891.

908. Maltin, Leonard. "Philo Vance at the movies." IN
Tuska, J. (et al.). Philo Vance. (q.v.) pp.35-47.

909. Mambrino, Jean. "Le mot du coffre." IN Lacassin, F.
(jnt. ed.). Simenon. (q.v.) pp.23-51.

910. Manchel, Frank. Gangsters on the screen. N.Y.:
Franklin Watts; 1978. viii, 120p.

911. Manley, Seon (jnt. comp.). Grande dames of detection;
two centuries of sleuthing stories by the gentle sex.
Selected by S. Manley & Gogo Lewis. N.Y.: Lothrop Lee &
Shepard Co.; 1973. 224p.

912. ... Mistresses of mystery; two centuries of suspense
stories by the gentle sex. Selected and with introductions
by S. Manley and Gogo Lewis. N.Y.: Lothrop Lee & Shepard;
1973. 220p. - large print ed.: Boston: G. K. Hall; 1973.
x, 367p.

913. Mann, Thomas. "Joseph Conrad's 'The secret agent'.
IN Conrad, Joseph. Der Geheimagent. Berlin: S. Fischer;
1926, repr. 1938. 382p. pp.5-13.

   repr. IN Mann, Thomas. Past masters; and other papers.
   London: M. Secker; 1933. 275p. pp.231-247. - U.S. ed.
   - N.Y.: Knopf; 1933. 275p.

   repr. IN Watt, I. (ed.). Conrad; 'The secret agent'.
   (q.v.) pp.99-112.

914. Marcel, G. "Roman policiers." IN L'Europe Nouvelle
[Paris] (1 October 1932).

915. Marcus, Steven. "Dashiell Hammett and the Continental
Op." IN Partisan Review v.41;No.3 (1974) pp.362-377.

   repr. AS "Introduction." IN Hammett, Dashiell
   (1894-1961). The Continental Op. Selected and with
   an intro. by Steven Marcus. N.Y.: Random House; 1974.
   xxix, 287p. - U.K. ed.: London: Macmillan; 1974.
   xxix, 287p. pp.ix-xxix.

   repr. In Marcus, Steven. Representations; essays on
   literature and society. N.Y.: Random House; 1975. xvii,
   331p. pp.311-331.

916. Margolies, Edward. "The American detective thriller
and the idea of society." IN Dimensions of detective fiction.
(q.v.) pp.83-87.

917. ... "The thrillers of Chester Himes." IN Studies in
Black Literature v.1 (Summer 1970) pp.1-11.

918. Marill, A. H. "Films on TV [Columbo TV series]."
IN Films in Review v.26 (January 1975 and March 1975)
2 pts. [Jan. 1975: pp.41-44; Mar. 1975: p.178].

919. Marion, Denis. "The detective novel." IN La Nouvelle
Revue Francaise [Paris].

   repr. IN Living Age v.357 (November 1939) pp.283-285.

920. ... La méthode intellectuelle d'Edgar Poe. Paris:
Editions de Minuit; 1952. 127p.

921. Marsch, Edgar. Die Kriminalerzählung; Theorie,
Geschichte, Analyse. Munich: Winkler; 1972. 295p.
(Modelle und Methoden).

922. Marsh, Dame Edith Ngaio (1899-). Black beech and
honeydew; an autobiography. London: Collins; 1966. 287p.,
illus.

923. ... "Entertainments." IN Pacific Quarterly v.3:no.1
(January 1978) pp.27-32.

924. ... "Roderick Alleyn." IN Penzler, O. M. The great
detectives. (q.v.) pp.1-8.

925. ... "Starting with people." IN Mystery and detection
annual; 1973. (q.v.) pp.209-210.

926. Marshall, William Harvey. Wilkie Collins. Boston:
Twayne; 1970. 159p. (Twayne's English Authors series no.94).

927. Marshburn, Joseph H. (jnt. comp.). Blood and knavery;
a collection of English Renaissance pamphlets and ballads of
crime and sin. Comp. by J. H. Marshburn and Alan R. Velie.
Rutherford, N.J.: Fairleigh Dickinson University Press; 1973.
215p., illus.

928. Martin, Bernard. "James Bond; a phenomenon of some
importance." IN Anderson, Donald Stuart (jnt. ed.).
Cunning exiles; studies of modern prose writers. Ed. by
D. S. Anderson and Stephen Knight. Sydney: Angus & Robertson;
1974. 244p. (Contemporary arts series) pp.218-238.

929. Martin, Troy Kennedy. "Four of a kind?" IN Crime
writers. (q.v.) pp.122-133.

*   Marty, Pierre (jnt. auth.). SEE Peske, Antoinette.

930. Mason, Alfred Edward Woodley (1865-1948). "Detective
novels." IN Nation and Athenaeum [London] v.36:no.19
(7 February 1925) pp.645-656.

931. Mason, Bobbie Ann. The girl sleuth; a feminist guide
to Nancy Drew and her sisters. Old Westbury, N.Y.: The
Feminist Press; 1975. 144p., illus.

932. Mason, Michael. "Marlowe, men, and women." IN
Gross, M. (ed.). The world of Raymond Chandler. (q.v.)
pp.89-101.

933. Mason, V. W. "The detective story." IN The writer's
handbook. Ed. by Samuel Gilbert Houghton and Udia Olsen.
Boston: The Writer; 1936. 331p.

934. Matthews, James Brander (1852-1929). "Poe and the
detective story." IN Scribner's Magazine v.42 (September
1907) pp.287-293.

    repr. IN Matthews, James Brander (1852-1929). Inquiries
    and opinions. N.Y.: Scribners; 1907. vii, 305p.

    repr. IN Carlson, E. W. (ed.). The recognition of Edgar
    Allan Poe. (q.v.) pp.82-94.

    repr. in German trans. AS "Edgar Allan Poe und die
    Detektivgeschichte." IN Der Detektiverzählung auf der
    Spur. (q.v.)

935. Maugham, William Somerset (1874-1965). "The decline
and fall of the detective story." IN Maugham, William
Somerset (1874-1965). The vagrant mood; six essays. London:
Heinemann; 1952. 241p. pp.91-122. - U.S. ed.: Garden City,
N.Y.: Doubleday; 1953. - repr.: Port Washington, N.Y.:
Kennikat Press; [n.d.]. (National University Publications
No.0573).

    repr. in German trans. AS "Der Verfall und Untergang
    des Detektivromans." IN Der Detektiverzählung auf der
    Spur. (q.v.)

936. ... "Give me a murder." IN The Saturday Evening Post
v.213 (28 December 1940) pp.27ff.

    - summarized IN Saturday Review of Literature v.23
    (4 January 1941) p.24.

937. ... "[Preface]". IN Maugham, William Somerset
(1874-1965). Ashenden; or, The British agent. London:
Heinemann; 1928. - var. editions and reprints.

938. Mauriac, François. ["A tout âge d'ailleurs, ..."]
IN Figaro Littéraire No.890 (11 May 1963).

  repr. IN Lacassin, F. (jnt. ed.). Simenon. (q.v.)
  pp.283-284.

939. Maurice, Arthur Bartlett. "The detective in fiction."
IN Bookman [N.Y.] v.15 (May 1902) pp.231-236.

940. Maurois, André. Magiciens et logiciens. Paris:
[n.publ.]; 1935. - U.S. (first English) ed. AS Poets and
prophets. N.Y.: Harper; 1935.

  'Poets and prophets' repr. with two new essays AS
  Points of view from Kipling to Graham Greene. N.Y.:
  Ungar; 1968. - U.K. ed.: London: Muller; 1969. xviii,
  409p., illus.

941. May, Clifford D. "Whatever happened to Sam Spade?;
the private eye in fact and fiction." IN Atlantic v.236
(August 1975) pp.27-35.

942. Mealand, Richard. "Hollywoodunit." IN Haycraft,
H. (ed.). The art of the mystery story. (q.v.) pp.298-303.

943. Meet the detective. By Sapper, A. E. W. Mason,
S. Rohmer, Baroness Orczy, R. Grayson, S. Horler, and
others. London: Allen & Unwin; 1935. 142p.

  U.S. ed.: Meet the detective; Bull-dog Drummond, Hanaud,
  Dr. Fu Manchu [and others] ... introduced by "Sapper",
  A. E. W. Mason, Sax Rohmer [and others]. N.Y.: The
  Telegraph Press; 1935. 158p.

  N.B.: Attributed to the editorship of Cecil Madden by
  Tage la Cour (la Cour, T. 'The Murder book' (q.v.),
  p.177).

944. Melling, Philip. "American popular culture in the
Thirties; ideology, myth, genre." IN Bigsby, Christopher
William Edward. Approaches to popular culture. London:
Edw. Arnold; 1976. viii, 280p. pp.241-263.

*   Melvin, Ann Patricia Rothery Skene. SEE Skene
Melvin, A. P. R.

*   Melvin, David Skene. SEE Skene Melvin, L. D. H. St C.

*   Melvin, Lewis David Hillis St Columb Skene. SEE
Skene Melvin, L. D. H. St C.

945. Menguy, Claude. Bibliographie des éditions originales
de Georges Simenon y compris les oeuvres publiées sous des
pseudonymes. Brussels: Le Livre et l'estampe; 1967. 100p.

946. ... Additions et corrections à la bibliographie des
éditions originales de Georges Simenon. Brussels: Le Livre
et l'estampe; 1971. n.pag.

947. Mercier, Vivian. "Defective detectives." IN Nation
v.199 (16 November 1964) pp.362-363.

948. Merry, Bruce. Anatomy of the spy thriller. Montreal:
McGill-Queen's University Press; 1977. [viii], 253p.

949. Mesnet, Marie Béatrice. Graham Greene and the heart
of the matter; an essay. London: Cresset Press; 1954. ix,
116p.

950. Messac, Ralph. "Georges Simenon, romancier-nez."
IN Lacassin, F. (jnt. ed.). Simenon. (q.v.) pp.130-138.

951. Messac, Régis. Le 'detective novel' et l'influence de
la pensée scientifique. Paris: Libraire Ancienne Honoré
Champion; 1929. 698p. (Bibliothèque de la Revue de
littérature comparée) - repr.: Geneva: Slatkine; 1975.
698p.

952. ... Influences françaises dans l'oeuvre d'Edgar Poe.
Paris: Libraire Picart; 1929. 136p.

953. Metropolitan Toronto Central Library. A checklist of
the Arthur Conan Doyle collection in the Metropolitan Toronto
Central Library. Comp. by Donald A. Redmond. Toronto:
Metropolitan Toronto Library Board; 1973. 113p., illus. -
2d ed.: same publ.; 1977. 172p.

954. ... Sherlock Holmes is alive and well at the
Metropolitan Toronto Library; the Arthur Conan Doyle
Collection. Toronto: Metropolitan Toronto Library Board;
[1976?]. 8p.

*   ... SEE also Hollyer, Cameron. The body in the
library.

955. Mierow, Charles Christopher. "Through seas of blood."
IN Sewanee Review v.41 (January 1933) pp.1-22.

956. Millar, A. M. "The detective in literature." IN
Humberside [Manchester, Eng.] (October 1938).

*   Millar, Kenneth (1915-). SEE Macdonald, Ross [pseud.].

957. Miller, Anita. (comp.). Afrikaanse speurverhale
uitgegee tot die einde van 1950; 'n bibliografie.
Johannesburg: Universiteit van die Witwatersrand, Dept.
van bibliografie, biblioteekwese en tipografie; 1967.
iv, 23ℓ.

958. Miller, Donald. "Crime of passion films." IN Films
in Review v.13:no.8 (October 1962) pp.492-494 ("Films
on TV" column).

959. ... "Private eyes; from Sam Spade to J. J. Gittes."
IN Focus on Film No. 22 (Autumn 1975) pp.15-35.

960. Miller, Henry. ["Quel dommage de l'avoir recontré
si tard dans ma vie! ..."]. IN Candide No.4 (May 1961).

  repr. IN Lacassin, F. (jnt. ed.). Simenon. (q.v.)
  pp.268-271.

961. Miller, Joseph Hillis. ["'The secret agent'"] IN
Miller, Joseph Hillis. Poets of reality; six twentieth-century
writers. Harvard U Pr.; 1965. 369p. pp.39-67.

  abridged vers. repr. IN Watt, I. (ed.). Conrad: 'The
  secret agent. (q.v.) pp.179-201.

962. Miller, Robert Henry. "The publication of Raymond
Chandler's 'The long goodbye'." IN Papers of the
Bibliographical Society of America v.63 (1969) pp.279-290.

963. Milliken, Stephen F. Chester Himes; a critical
appraisal. Columbia, Missouri: University of Missouri
Press; 1976. 312p.

964. Milne, Alan Alexander (1882-1956). "Introducing crime."
IN Milne, Alan Alexander (1882-1956). By way of introduction.
London: Methuen; 1929. viii, 208p. - U.S. ed.: N.Y.:
Dutton; 1929. ix, 202p.

965. ... "The Watson touch." IN Milne, Alan Alexander
(1882-1956). If I may. London: Methuen; 1920. viii,
183p. - U.S. ed.: N.Y.: Dutton; 1921. viii, 233p.

966. Mira, Juan José. Biografía de la novela policíaca
(historia y crítica). Barcelona: Editorial AHR; [1955,
c1956]. 254p. (Amanecer).

967. Mirams, Gordon. "Drop that gun!" IN Quarterly of
Film, Radio, and Television v.6:no.1 (Fall 1951) pp.1-19.

968. Moffat, Ivan. "On the fourth floor of Paramount;
interview with Billy Wilder." IN Gross, M. (ed.).
The world of Raymond Chandler. (q.v.) pp.43-51.

*   Mogensen, Harald. (jnt. ed.). SEE Dansk og udenlandsk
kriminallitteratur.

*   ... (jnt. auth.). SEE Also la Cour, T. Mordbogen.

969. Monahan, Anthony. "The uppity private eye as movie
hero." IN Midwest Magazine (4 June 1972) pp.11-15.

*   Montgomery, Robert Bruce. SEE Crispin, Edmund [pseud.].

970. Mooney, Joan M. The American detective story; a study
in popular fiction ... Ph.D. dissertation, University of
Minnesota, 1968.

  - publ. in five installments AS "Best-selling American
  detective fiction" IN The Armchair Detective (January
  1970 through January 1971).

971. Monaco, J. "Notes on 'The big sleep'; thirty years
after." IN Sight and Sound v.44:no.1 (Winter 1974-1975)
pp.34-38.

972. Monod, Sylvère. Dickens romancier; etude sur la
création littéraire dans les romans de Charles Dickens.
Paris: Hachette; 1953. xx, 520p.

973. Morand, Paul. "Preface." IN Sayers, Dorothy Leigh.
Lord Peter devant le cadavre. Paris: Libraire des
Champs-Elysées; 1934. 253p. (Coll. Police sélection, IV).

974. ... "Reflexions sur le roman-policier." IN Revue de
Paris Tome 2 (1 April 1934).

975. Mord Som Hobby; Specialnummer av tidskriften OBS.
No.2 (1955).

   Not verified. Cited in: la Cour, T. 'The murder book'
   (q.v.), p.177.

976. Moré, Marcel. "Simenon et l'enfant de choeur." IN
Dieu vivant No.19 (2e trimestre 1951).

   repr. IN Foudre de Dieu. Paris: Gallimard; 1969.

   repr. IN Lacassin, F. (jnt. ed.). Simenon. (q.v.)
   pp.227-263.

977. Moremans, Victor. "Mon ami Simenon." IN L'Essai
(September 1962).

   repr. IN Lacassin, F. (jnt. ed.). Simenon. (q.v.)
   pp.276-279.

978. Morgan, Bryan. "Introduction." IN Crime on the
lines; an anthology of mystery short stories with a railway
setting. Ed. by Bryan Morgan. London: Routledge & Kegan
Paul; 1975. xiv, 173p. pp.ix-xiv.

979. Morland, Nigel (1905-). How to write detective novels.
London: Allen & Unwin; 1936. 74p. (Practical handbook
series. 32).

980. ... Who's who in crime fiction. London: Hamish
Hamilton; [197?]. (Elm Tree Books).

   Not verified to date. Announced as forthcoming in
   publisher's 'New Books Spring 1977' catalogue, p.47.

981. Morse, Albert Reynolds (1914-). Works of M. P. Shiel;
a study in bibliography: and incl. 'About myself' by M. P.
Shiel (new rev. version). Los Angeles: Fantasy Pub. Co.;
1948. 170p.

982. Morton, Charles W. "The world of Erle Stanley Gardner."
IN Atlantic Monthly v.219 (January 1967) pp.79-86.

983. Moskowitz, Sam. "The sleuth in sci-fi." and "The super-sleuths of sci-fi." IN Worlds of Tomorrow v.3:no.'s 5(whole no.17) and 6(whole no.18) (January and March 1966) pp.66-77 and pp.66-77.

984. Moss, Leonard. "Hammett's heroic operative." IN New Republic v.154 (8 January 1966) pp.32-34.

985. Moss, Sidney Phil. Poe's literary battles; the critic in the context of his literary milieu. Durham, N.C.: Duke University Press/London: Cambridge University Press; 1963. xi, 266p.

986. Ms. mysteries; 19 tales of suspense written by women and featuring female heroines. Ed. by Arthur Liebman. N.Y.: Washington Square Press; 1976. 255p.

*   Muddock, Joyce Emmerson Preston (1843-1934). SEE Preston-Muddock, J. E.

*   Mugar Memorial Library. SEE Bibliography of Dr. R. H. van Gulik.

987. Muhlen, Norbert. "Thinker and the tough guy." IN Commonweal v.51 (25 November 1949) pp.216-217.

  cf. Boucher, A. "Reply to ... ".

988. Mühlenbock, Kjell. "Tung mans liv. [Life of a heavy man] ("Concerning Nero Wolfe")" IN Jury-tidskrift för deckarvänner No.1, and, No.2. pp.18-20 (No.1), and, pp.48-49 (No.2).

989. Mumford, Edward W. "The perfect crime." IN Atlantic Monthly v.149 (March 1932) pp.390-391.

990. Mundell, E. H. A checklist of detective short stories. Portage, Ind.: Mundell Printing; 1968. xii, 337p.

  cf. infra.

991. ... (jnt. comp.). The detective short story; a bibliography and index. By E. H. Mundell and George Jay Rausch. Manhattan, Kansas: Kansas State University Library; 1974. iv, 493p. (Bibliography series - Kansas State University Library; no.14).

  cf. supra.

992. ... Erle Stanley Gardner; a checklist. Kent, Ohio:
Kent State University Press; [c1968], 1969. [xii], 92p.
(The Serif series: bibliographies and checklists. No.6).

993. ... A list of the original appearances of Dashiell
Hammett's magazine work. Portage, Ind.: the author; 1968.
52p. - 2d ed.: Kent, Ohio: Kent State University Press;
[c1968], 1970. [viii], 52p. (The Serif series:
bibliographies and checklists; no. 13).

994. Murch, Alma Elizabeth. The development of the
detective novel. N.Y.: Philosophical Library; 1958. 272p.,
illus. - Cd. ed.: Toronto: Copp Clark; 1958. - U.K. ed.:
London: Peter Owen; 1958. - rev. ed.: Port Washington, N.Y.:
Kennikat Press; 1968. 272p. - U.K. ed.: London: Peter
Owen; 1968. 272p. - repr.: N.Y.: Greenwood Press; [c1958],
1968. 272p., illus.

995. Murder manual; a handbook for mystery story writers.
San Diego, Calif.: The Wight house press; 1936. 120p.

   "Introduction" signed: H. F. Wight, editor.
   Part one and appendix by Irene E. Young.

996. Murdoch, Derrick. The Agatha Christie mystery.
Toronto: Pagurian Press; 1976. 192p.

997. ... "The case of the vanishing hero." IN Pacific
Quarterly v.3:no.1 (January 1978) pp.42-49.

998. Murphy, George D. "A source for ballistics in Poe."
IN American Notes and Queries v.4:no.7 (March 1966) p.99.

999. Murphy, Michael. Vincent Starrett; in memoriam.
Culver City, Calif.: Pontine Press; 1974. 26p., illus.

1000. Murray, Will. The 'Duende' history of 'The Shadow
Magazine'. Greenwood, Ma.: Odyssey Publications; 1980. 128 p.

1001. Musée des Arts Decoratifs, Paris. Exposition Band
Dessinée et Figuration Narrative, 7 avr.-5 juin 1967.
Band dessinée et figuration narrative; histoire, esthétique,
production et sociologie de la band dessinée mondiale,
procédés narratifs et structure de l'image dans la peinture
contamporaine. Paris: Le Musée; 1967. 256p., illus. -
U.S. (first English lang.) ed. AS A history of the comic

strip. By Pierre Couperie, Maurice C. Horn, et al. N.Y.:
Crown; 1968. 256 p., illus.

1002. The mystery and detection annual. Beverly Hills,
Calif.: D. Adams; 1972- .

1003. The mystery story. Ed. by John Ball. San Diego,
Calif.: University Extension, University of California,
San Diego; 1976 - Del Mar, Calif.: Publisher's Inc.; 1976.
xii, 390p. - repr. - Penguin; 1978. xiv, 390p.

1004. Mystery Writers of America. The mystery writer's
handbook; a handbook on the writing of detective, suspense,
mystery and crime stories. Ed. by Herbert Brean. N.Y.:
Harper; 1956. xx, 268p. - repr.: Xerox University
Microfilms.

    rev. ed.: Ed. by Lawrence Treat. Cincinnati, Ohio:
    Writer's Digest; 1976. [xvi], 275p.

N

1005. Nakajima, Kawatarō (1917-). Nihon suiri shōsetsu shi. Tokyo: Tōgensha; [n.d.]. [n.pag.].

1006. Nakauchi, Masatoshi (1903-). Amerika fūbutsushi. Tokyo: Hayakawa Shobō; 1968. 422p.

1007. Nanovic, John L. "I never called him Bill." IN Grant, Maxwell [pseud.]. 'The Crime Oracle' and 'The Teeth of the Dragon'; two adventures of The Shadow. N.Y.: Dover; 1975. xxvi, 163p. pp.xxi-xxv.

1008. Narcejac, Thomas (1908-). Le cas Simenon. Paris: Presses de la Cité; 1950. 191p. - U.K. (first English) ed. AS The art of Simenon. London: Routledge & Kegan Paul; 1952. vii, 178p.

1009. ... Esthétique du roman policier. Paris: Le Portulan; 1947. 208p.

1010. ... La fin d'un bluff; essai sur le roman policier noir américain. Paris: Portulan; 1949. 178p. (La Mauvaise chance).

1011. ... Une machine à lire; le roman policier. Paris: Denoël/Gonthier; 1975. 247p. (Bibliothèque Mediations; 124).

1012. ... "Le point Omega." IN Lacassin, F. (jnt. ed.). Simenon. (q.v.) pp.18-22.

*   ... (jnt. auth.). SEE also Boileau, P. Le roman policier. 1964.

1013. Nash, Ogden. "Don't guess, let me tell you." IN The New Yorker v.16 (20 April 1940) p.26.

   repr. IN Nash, Ogden. The face is familiar; the selected verse of Ogden Nash. Boston: Little Brown; 1940. xxii, 352p. - U.K. ed.: London: Dent; 1942. xxi, 294p.

   repr. IN Haycraft, H. (ed.). The art of the mystery story. (q.v.) pp.319-320.

   repr. IN Writing suspense and mystery fiction (1977). (q.v.) pp.306-307.

   - The definitive statement on the 'HIBK' school within the genre.

*   Nathan, Daniel [pseud.]. SEE Dannay, Frederic (1905-).

1014. National Book League, London. Murder in Albemarle Street; an exhibition of crime books - fact and fiction - first displayed in the National Book League's galleries in Albemarle Street, 7th November, 1962. London: National Book League; 1962. 18p. (Book lists).

1015. ... Paging crime!; [a catalogue from an exhibition of current books of crime fact and fiction]. London: National Book League; 1965. 27p.

*   ... SEE also Great Britain. British Council.

1016. Naumann, Dietrich. "Der Kriminalroman; Ein Literaturbericht." IN Beilage zum DU 1 (1967), Forschungsberichte Literaturwissenschaft 12.

1017. ... "Kriminalroman und Dichtung." IN Vogt, J. (comp.) Der Kriminalroman. (q.v.) pp.473-483.

1018. ... "Zur Typologie des Kriminalromans." IN Žmegač, V. (ed.) Der wohltemperierte Mord. (q.v.) pp.241-260.

1019. "Necrology of R. H. van Gulik (1910-1967)."   IN
T'oung pao v.54 (1968) pp.116-124.

   - attrib. to A. F. P. Hulsewe by Donald F. Lach in
   his "Introduction", (q.v.).

1020. Nelson, Raymond. "Domestic Harlem; the detective
fiction of Chester Himes." IN Virginia Quarterly Review
v.48:no.2 (Spring 1972) pp.260-276.

   repr. IN Dimensions of detective fiction. (q.v.)
   pp.162-173.

1021. Nevins, Francis M. "Cornell Woolrich." IN Armchair
Detective (October 1968, January 1969, April 1969).

   repr. AS "Introduction." IN Woolrich, Cornell.
   Nightwebs; a collection of stories. N.Y.: Harper &
   Row; 1971. - U.K. ed.: London: Gollancz; 1973.
   xxxiv, 403p. pp.ix-xxxiv.

1022. ... "Cornell Woolrich; the years before suspense."
IN Armchair Detective v.12:no.2 (Spring 1979) pp.106-110.

1023. ... "The Drury Lane quartet." IN Nevins, F. M.
(comp.). The mystery writer's art. (q.v.) pp.122-135.

   This is a revision of a section of Part II of the
   author's series "Royal bloodline; the biography of
   the Queen canon" in 'The Queen Canon Bibliophile'
   (January 1969), and re-appeared slightly re-revised
   as Chap.2 (pp.25-34) in the author's Royal bloodline
   (q.v.).

1024. ... (comp.). The mystery writer's art. Bowling
Green, Ohio: Bowling Green University Popular Press; 1970.
xii, 338p.

1025. ... "Name games; mystery writers and their
pseudonyms." IN The mystery story. (q.v.) pp.343-358.

1026. ... "Private eye in an evil time; Mark Sadler's
Paul Shaw." IN Xenophile (q.v.) No.38 (March-April
1978) pp.11.

1027. ... Royal bloodline; Ellery Queen, author and
detective. Bowling Green, Ohio: Bowling Green University
Popular Press; 1974. 288p.

*   ... (jnt. ed.). SEE also Boucher, Anthony [pseud.].
Multiplying villainies.

1028. Newsom, Robert (1944-). Dickens on the romantic
side of familiar things; 'Bleak House' and the novel
tradition. N.Y.: Columbia University Press; 1977.
[xvi], 173p.

1029. Newton, Henry Chance (1854-1931). Crime and the
drama; or, dark deeds dramatized [etc.]. London: Stanley
Paul; 1927. 284p., illus. - repr. - Port Washington, N.Y.:
Kennikat Press; 1970. 284p., illus.

1030. Nicolson, Marjorie H. "The professor and the
detective." IN Atlantic Monthly v.143 (April 1929)
pp.483-493.

   repr. IN MacLean, Malcolm Shaw (jnt. comp.). Men and
   books. Collected and ed. by M. S. MacLean and Elisabeth
   Katz Holmes. N.Y.: R. R. Smith; 1930. xvi, 417p.

   repr. IN Haycraft, H. (ed.). The art of the mystery
   story. (q.v.) pp.110-127.

1031. Nienaber, Petrus Johannes (1910-). Bronnegids by
die studie van die Afrikaanse taal en letterkunde.
Johannesburg: Voortrekkerpers, printer; 1947. [n.pag.].

   Addendum. Johannesburg: [n.publ.]; 1959. [n.pag.].

1032. Nixon, Joan Lowery. Writing mysteries for young
people. Boston: Writer; 1977. xi, 123p.

1033. "The noble art of mystery." IN Nation v.125
(14 September 1927) p.242.

1034. Noel, Mary. Villains galore - the heyday of the
popular story weekly. N.Y. [London]: Macmillan; 1954. xi,
320p., illus.

1035. Nolan, Jack Edmund. "Graham Greene's movies." IN
Films in Review v.15:no.1 (January 1964) pp.23-35.

1036. Nolan, William F. (1928-). "Bogie and the Black
Bird." IN Nolan, William F. (1928-). John Huston; king
rebel. Los Angeles: Sherbourne Press; 1965. 247p., illus.

1037.   ... <u>Dashiell Hammett; a casebook.</u> With an intro. by
Philip Durham. Santa Barbara, Calif.: McNally & Loftin;
1969. 189p.

1038.   ... "Portrait of a tough guy." IN <u>Rogue</u> (1962).

  repr. IN Nolan, William F. <u>Sinners and supermen.</u> 1965.

  rev. and repr. IN <u>Xenophile</u> (q.v.) No.38 (March-
April 1978) pp.13-17.

1039. Nordon, Pierre. <u>Sir Arthur Conan Doyle; l'homme et
l'oeuvre.</u> Paris: Librairie Marcel Didier; 1964. 481p.,
illus. - U.K. (first English) ed.: London: Murray; 1966.
[xi], 370p., illus. - U.S. ed.: N.Y.: Rinehart; 1967.
370p.

1040. Norman, Frank. "Friend and mentor." IN Gross, M.
(ed.). <u>The world of Raymond Chandler.</u> (q.v.) pp.165-170.

1041. Norton, Charles A. <u>Melville Davisson Post; man of
many mysteries.</u> Bowling Green, Ohio: Bowling Green University
Popular Press; 1973. 261p.

1042. <u>Notes for the curious; a John Dickson Carr memorial</u>
journal. Ed. by Larry L. French. Chesterfield, Mo.:
Carrian Press; 1978-

  Vol.1: 1978.

1043. "The novels of Sir Arthur Conan Doyle." IN <u>The
Quarterly Review</u> v.200 (No.399) Article VIII (July 1904)
pp.158-179.

  - De Waal ('The world bibliography of Sherlock Holmes
and Dr. Watson' - q.v.) attributes this item to Andrew
Lang; p.255.

1044. Nye, Russel Blaine (1913-). <u>The unembarassed muse;
the popular arts in America.</u> N.Y.: Dial Press; 1970. 497p.
(Two centuries of American life).

O

1045. Oates, Joyce Carol. "Man under sentence of death;
the novels of James M. Cain." IN Madden D. T. (ed.).
Tough-guy writers of the thirties. (q.v.) pp.110-128.

1046. O'Brien, Frances Blazer. "Faulkner and Wright, alias
S. S. Van Dine." IN Mississippi Quarterly v.14. pp.101-107.

1047. Ocampo, Victoria. "The detective story; an English
institution." IN Books Abroad v.16:no.1 (Winter 1942)
pp.38-39.

1048. O'Connor, John (1870-1952). Father Brown on Chesterton.
London: F. Muller; 1937. 173p. - 2d ed.: London: Burnes
Oates & Washbourne; 1938. 173p.

1049. O'Donnell, Thomas D. "Michael Butor's 'Passing time'
and the detective hero." IN Mystery and detection annual;
1973. (q.v.) pp.211-220.

1050. O'Faoláin, Seán. "Give us back Bill Sykes." IN
Spectator [London] no.5,564 (15 February 1935) pp.242-243.

1051. Olle, James G. "The literature on the detective
story." IN The Library World (July 1960) pp.11-14.

1052. "On intellectual thrillers." IN Bookman [N.Y.]
v.76 (March 1933) pp.253-254.

1053. O'Neill, D. "Too many murders." IN Saturday Review
of Literature v.19 (11 February 1939) p.9.

1054. Orczy, Emmuska, baroness (1865-1947). Links in the
chain of life. London/N.Y.: Hutchinson; 1947. 223p.

1055. Ord om mord; svenska deckarförfattare och kritiker
diskuterar. Ed. by Jan Broberg. Halmstad, Sweden:
Spektra/Solna, Sweden: Seelig; 1974. 269 p., illus.
(Spektras deckar-ess; specialvolym).

1056. Orel, Harold. "Raymond Chandler's last novel; some
observations on the 'private eye' tradition." IN Journal
of the Central Mississippi Valley American Studies
Association (Spring 1961).

1057. O'Riordan, Conal. "The vicious circle." IN New
Statesman [London] v.35:no.896 (28 June 1930) pp.364-365.

*   Orley, I. (jnt. auth.). SEE Holtan, J. (jnt. auth.).

1058. Ormerod, David. (jnt. auth.). The Bond game.
By D. Ormerod and David Ward. IN The London Magazine
v.5 (May 1965) pp.41-55.

1059. Ortiz Vidales, Salvador. Los bandidos en la literatura
mexicana. México: Editorial Tehutle; 1949. 80p.

1060. Orwell, George [pseud.] (1903-1950). "Grandeur et
décadence du roman policier Anglais." Trans. into French
from English by Fernand Auberjonois. IN Fontaine [Algiers]
No.'s 37-40 (1944) pp.213-275.

1061. ... "Raffles and Miss Blandish." IN Horizon
[London] (October 1944).

   also publ. IN Politics [N.Y.].

   repr. IN Orwell, George [pseud.] (1903-1950). Critical
essays. London: Secker and Warburg; 1946. 169p. pp.142-155.
- repr., same publ., 1951, 1954. - repr., same publ.,
1960. 195p. pp.163-178. - repr. - London: Mercury Books;
1961. - U.S. ed. - AS Dickens, Dali and others; studies
in popular culture. N.Y.: Reynal & Hitchcock; 1946. 243p.
pp.202-221. - also publ., N.Y.: Harcourt, Brace & World;
1946. 243p.

repr. IN Orwell, George [pseud.] (1903-1950). A
collection of essays. Garden City, N.Y.: Doubleday;
1957.

repr. IN Rosenberg, Bernard (1923-) (jnt. ed.).
Mass culture; the popular arts in America. Ed. by
B. Rosenberg and David Manning-White. N.Y.: Free Press
of Glencoe; 1957. x, 561p. pp.154-164. - repr., pap.,
same publ., 1964.

repr. IN Fiedler, Leslie Aaron (1917-) (ed.). The
art of the essay. N.Y.: Thomas Y. Crowell; 1958. 640p.
pp.465-476. - 2d ed., same publ., 1969. xii, 593p.

repr. IN Orwell, George [pseud.] (1903-1950). Decline
of the English murder and other essays. London: Penguin;
1972. pp.63-79.

repr. in German trans. AS "Raffles und Miss Blandish."
IN Der Detektiverzählung auf der Spur. (q.v.).

1062. Osborne, Eric A. "Collecting detective fiction."
IN The Bookman [London] v.81:no.485 (February 1932)
pp.287-288. ("The Collector" column).

1063. O'Toole, L. M. "Analytic and synthetic approaches
to narrative structure; Sherlock Holmes and 'The Sussex
vampire'." IN Style and structure in literature; essays
in the new stylistics. Ed. by Roger Fowler. Ithaca, N.Y.:
Cornell University Press; 1975. viii, 262p. pp.143-176 -
U.K. ed.: Oxford: B. Blackwell; 1975. viii, 262p. (Language
and style series; 16).

1064. Ousby, Ian (1947-). Bloodhounds of heaven; the
detective in English fiction from Godwin to Doyle. Cambridge,
Mass.: Harvard University Press; 1976. x, 194p.

1065. ... "My servant Caleb; Godwin's Caleb Williams and
the political trials of the 1790's." IN University of
Toronto Quarterly v.44 (Fall 1974) pp.47-55.

- incorporated in revised form as part of the second
chapter of the author's Bloodhounds of heaven (q.v.).

1066. Overton, Grant Martin (1887-1930). "The art of
Melville Davisson Post." IN Overton, Grant Martin (1887-
1930). Cargoes for Crusoes. N.Y.: Appleton/Geo. H. Doran/
Little Brown; 1924. 416p. - repr.: Freeport, N.Y.: Books
for Libraries Press; 1972. 416p.

1067.   ...   "A breathless chapter."   IN   Overton, Grant
Martin (1887-1930). American nights entertainment.   N.Y."
Appleton; 1923. xi, 414p. pp.51-63.

1068.   ...   "The documents in the case of Arthur Train."
IN   Overton, Grant Martin (1887-1930). American nights
entertainment. N.Y.: D. Appleton/George H. Doran/Doubleday,
Page/Charles Scribner's Sons; 1923. xi, 414p., illus.
pp.91-101.

1069.   ...   "A great impersonation."   IN   Overton, Grant
Martin (1887-1930). Cargoes for Crusoes. N.Y.: Appleton/
Geo. H. Doran/Little Brown; 1924. 416p. - repr.: Freeport,
N.Y.: Books for Libraries Press; 1972. 416p.

P

1070. Pachovsky, George. A brief appreciation of 'The glass key', a novel by Dashiell Hammett. Toronto: the author [unpubl.]; 1974. 5p.

1071. Pacific Quarterly; an international review of arts and ideas. [Hamilton, N.Z.]

   Special number (v.3:no.1 - January 1978) on criminal literature, ed. by David Skene Melvin.

1072. Page, Curtis Hidden (1870-). "Poe in France." IN Nation v.88 (14 January 1909) pp.32-34.

1073. Paiva, Salvyano Cavalcanti de. O gangster no cinema. Revisão Laureano Guimarães. Rio de Janeiro: Editorial Andes; [1954?]. 198p., illus. (Na seara das artes, no.1).

1074. Palance, Leo. "When the private eye was king; nuanced hero in a dark scene." IN Arts Magazine v.42 (September-October 1967) pp.16-17.

1075. Palmer, David. "A last talk with Leslie McFarlane." IN Canadian Children's Literature No.11 (November 1978) pp.5-11.

1076. Palmer, Jerry. "Thrillers; the deviant behind the consensus." IN Politics and deviance. Ed. by Ian and Laurie Taylor. Harmondsworth, Eng.: Penguin; 1973. 217p. (Pelican books) pp.136-156.

1077. ... ... Thrillers; genesis and structure of a
popular genre. London: Edward Arnold; 1978. vi, 232p.

1078. Panek, Leroy Lad. Watteau's shepherds; the detective
novel in Britain 1914-1940. Bowling Green, Ohio: Bowling
Green University Popular Press; 1979. [viii], 232p.

1079. Parinaud, André (1924-). Connaissance de Georges
Simenon. Paris: Presses de la Cité; 1957-   vols.

   Vol.1: Le secret du romancier, suivi des Entretiens
   avec Simenon. 415p. 1957.

1080. Parish, James Robert. (jnt. auth.). The great
gangster pictures. By J. R. Parish and Michael R. Pitts.
Metuchen, N.J.: Scarecrow; 1976. viii, 431p., illus.

1081. ... (jnt. auth.). The great spy pictures. By
J. R. Parish and Michael R. Pitts. Ed. by T. Allan Taylor.
Metuchen, N.J.: Scarecrow Press; 1974. viii, 9-585p.,
illus.

1082. ... The tough guys. New Rochelle, N.Y.: Arlington
House Publ.; 1976. 635p., illus.

1083. Parker, Lyndon. "A word from Dr. Lyndon Parker."
IN Derleth, August. "In re: Sherlock Holmes'; the
adventures of Solar Pons. Sauk City, Wisc.: Mycroft and
Moran; 1945. xvi, 238p. pp.xiii-xv.

1084. Parker, Robert Brown. The violent hero; wilderness
heritage and urban reality: a study of the private eye in
the novels of Dashiell Hammett, Raymond Chandler, and Ross
Macdonald ... Ph.D. dissertation, Boston University, 1971.
188p.

1085. Parrinder, Patrick. "George Orwell and the detective
story." IN Journal of Popular Culture v.6:no.4 (Spring
1973) pp.692-697.

   repr. IN Dimensions of detective fiction (q.v.)
   pp.64-67.

1086. Parrish, Morris Longstreth. Wilkie Collins and
Charles Reade: First editions, with a few exceptions, in
the library at Dormy House, Pine Valley, New Jersey, described
with notes by M. L. Parrish. London: Constable; 1940. x,
354p., illus.

1087. Parsons, Luke. "On the novels of Raymond Chandler."
IN The Fortnightly Review (May 1954) pp.346-351.

1088. ... "Simenon and Chandler." IN The Contemporary
Review v.197 (January 1960) pp.56-58.

1089. Partridge, Ralph. "Detection and thrillers." IN
New Statesman [and Nation] v.47 (9 January 1954) pp.47-48.

1090. "The passing of the detective in literature." IN
Academy [London] (30 December 1905).

  repr. IN Living Age v.246 (7th series:vol.30)
  (17 February 1906) pp.437-439.

  repr. IN Haycraft, H. (ed.). The art of the mystery
  story. (q.v.) pp.511-512.

1091. Pate, Janet. The book of sleuths; an illustrated
history of the detective genre. London: New English
Library/Chicago: Contemporary Books; 1977. 5-124p., illus.
(A Webb & Bower book).

1092. ... The great villains. London: David and Charles/
Indianapolis, Ind.: Bobbs-Merrill; 1975. 120p., illus.

1093. Paterson, John. "A cosmic view of the private eye."
IN Saturday Review of Literature v.36 (22 August 1953)
pp.7-8, 31-33.

  cf. Boucher, A. [pseud.]. "Reply with rejoinder to:
  John Paterson ..."

1094. Patrouch, Joseph F. "... a detailed discussion of
Isaac Asimov's The caves of steel and The naked sun ..."
IN Patrouch, Joseph F. The science fiction of Isaac Asimov.
Garden City, N.Y.: Doubleday; 1974. pp.159-179.

1095. Pattrick, Robert (?-1960). "A chronology of Solar
Pons." IN Derleth, August. The reminiscences of Solar
Pons. Sauk City, Wisc.: Mycroft & Moran; 1961. xii, 199p.
pp.194-199.

1096. Paul, Elliot Harold. "Whodunit; mystery stories in
the making." IN Atlantic Monthly v.168 (July 1941)
pp.36-40.

1097. Paulhan, Jean. "'Les anneaux de Bicetre'." IN
Paulhan, Jean. Les oeuvres complètes. Paris: Tehou; 1963.

   repr. IN Lacassin, F. (jnt. ed.). Simenon. (q.v.)
   pp.280-282.

*   Pavett, Michael (jnt. ed.). SEE Crime writers.

1098. Pearsall, Ronald (1927-). Conan Doyle; a biographical
solution. London: Weidenfeld & Nicolson; 1977. 224p.,
illus. - U.S. ed.: N.Y.: St. Martin's Press; 1977.

1099. Pearson, Edmund Lester (1880-1937). Dime novels; or,
Following an old trail in popular literature. Boston:
Little Brown; 1929. x, 280p., illus. - repr.: Port
Washington, N.Y.: Kennikat Press; [1968, c.1929]. 280p.

1100. ... "Perfect murder." IN Scribner's Magazine
v.102 (July 1937) pp.20-25.

1101. ... "Spring, three one hundred." IN Outlook v.146
(3 August 1927) pp.449-451.

1102. ... "With acknowledgments to Thomas De Quincey."
IN Pearson, Edmund Lester (1880-1937). Books in black or
red. N.Y.: Macmillan; 1923. xii, 213p. - repr.: same
publ.; 1924.

1103. Pearson, Hesketh (1887-). Conan Doyle; his life and
art. London: Methuen; 1943. 193p. - U.S. ed.: N.Y.:
Walker; 1961. 256p. - repr.: London: White Lion; 1974.
256p. - repr.: N.Y.: Taplinger; 1977.

1104. Pearson, John George (1930-). James Bond; the
authorized biography of 007: a fictional biography. London:
Sidgwick & Jackson; 1973. 317p. - U.S. ed.: N.Y.: Morrow;
1973.

1105. ... The life of Ian Fleming; creator of James Bond.
London: Cape; 1966. 352p., illus. - U.S. ed.: N.Y.:
McGraw-Hill; 1966. 338p., illus. - repr.: London: Pan;
1967, [i.e. 1968]. 416p., illus. - repr.: N.Y.: Bantam
Books; 1967. 342p.

1106. Pechter, William S. (1936-). "Anti-Western." and
"Violence, American style." IN Pechter, William S. (1936-).
Twenty-four times a second; films and film-makers. N.Y.:
Harper; 1971. x, 324p. pp.91-96 and pp.85-90, respectively.

1107. Peck, Harry Thurston (1856-1914). "The detective
story." IN Peck, Harry Thurston (1856-1914). Studies in
several literatures. N.Y.: Dodd, Mead; 1909. 296p.

1108. Pederson-Krag, Geraldine. "Detective stories and the
primal scene." IN The Psychoanalytic Quarterly v. 18 (1949)
pp.207-214.

    repr. IN Dimensions of detective fiction. (q.v.)
    pp.58-63.

    cf. Rycroft, Chas. "A detective story".

1109. Peeples, S. A. "Films on 8 & 16 [lost thrillers]."
IN Films in Review v.25 (October 1974) pp.486-487ff.

1110. Pendo, Stephen (1947-). Raymond Chandler on screen;
his novels into film. Metuchen, N.J.: Scarecrow Press; 1976.
240p.

    part of this publ. AS "Raymond Chandler's Philip
    Marlowe; his metamorphoses in film." IN Films in
    Review v.27:no.3 (March 1976) pp.129-136.

1111. The penny dreadful, or, strange, horrid & sensational
tales! Ed. by Peter Haining. London: Gollancz; 1975.
382p., illus.

1112. Pensa, Carlo Maria. "Sua maestà Agatha Christie."
IN Fiera Letteraria v.48:no.2 p.27.

1113. Pentecost, Hugh [pseud.]. "Pierre Chambrun." IN
Penzler, O. M. The great detectives. (q.v.) pp.47-55.

1114. Penzler, Otto. "The amateur detectives." IN The
mystery story. (q.v.) pp.83-109.

1115. ... "Detective fiction; a real fascination with
imagined crime." IN The encyclopedia of collectibles.
v.[5]: "Cookbooks to Detective Fiction". Alexandria, Va.:
Time-Life Books; 1978. 160p., illus. pp.152-160.

1116. ... "The great crooks." IN The mystery story.
(q.v.) pp.321-341.

1117. ... (ed.). The great detectives. Boston: Little
Brown; 1978. xviii, 281p.

1118. ... The private lives of private eyes, spies, crime
fighters & other good guys. N.Y.: Grosset & Dunlap; 1977.
x, 214p., illus.

*   ... (jnt. comp.). SEE also Byrne, E. B.

*   ... (jnt. ed.). SEE also Encyclopedia of mystery
and detection.

1119. Penzoldt, Peter. The supernatural in fiction.
London: Peter Nevill; 1952. xii, 271p.

1120. Peppard, Murray B. Friedrich Dürrenmatt. N.Y.:
Twayne; 1969. 156p. (Twayne's World Authors series 87).

1121. Perry, George. The films of Alfred Hitchcock.
London: Studio Vista/N.Y.: Dutton; 1965. 160p., illus.
(Picturebacks).

1122. Peske, Antoinette. (jnt. auth.). Les terribles;
(Maurice Leblanc, Gaston Leroux, Marcel Allain). By
A. Peske and Pierre Marty. Paris: Chambriand; 1951.
210p., illus. (Coll. Visages).

1123. "The Peter Cheyney legend." IN Cheyney, Reginald
Evelyn Peter Southouse (1896-1951). Calling Mr. Callaghan.
By Peter Cheyney. London: Todd Publishing Group; 1953.
191p. pp.7-16.

1124. Peterson, Spiro (ed.). The counterfeit lady unveiled;
and other criminal fiction of seventeenth-century England.
Garden City, N.Y.: Doubleday; 1961. xv, 380p. (Anchor
Books A232).

1125. Pett, John. "A master of suspense." IN Films
and Filming v.6:no.2 [and] 3 (November [and] December 1959)
pp.9-10, 33-34 [and] pp.9-10, 32.

1126. Pfeiffer, Hans (1925-). Die Mumie im Glassarg;
Bemerkungen zur Kriminalliteratur. Rudolstadt: Greifenverlag;
1960. 315p.

1127. Pfeiffer, John R. "Windows, detectives, and justice
in Dürrenmatt's detective stories." IN Revue des Langues
Vivantes v.33 (1967) pp.451-460.

1128. Phelps, Donald. "Dashiell Hammett's microcosmos."
IN National Review v.18:no.32 (20 September 1966)
pp.941-942.

*   Philips, Judson. SEE Pentecost, Hugh [pseud.].

1129. Phillips, Gene D. Graham Greene; the films of his
fiction. N.Y.: Teachers College Press; 1974. xxviii,
204p., illus. (Studies in Culture & Communication).

1130. Phillips, Walter Clark (1881-). Dickens, Reade, and
Collins, sensation novelists; a study in the conditions and
theories of novel writing in Victorian England ... Ph.D.
thesis, Columbia University, 1918. - first publ., N.Y.:
Columbia University Press; 1919. ix, 230p. (Columbia
University Studies in English and Comparative Literature) -
also publ., N.Y.: Russell and Russell; 1919. 230p. - repr.,
N.Y.: Garland; 1978. 238p.

1131. Phillpotts, Eden. From the angle of 88. London:
Hutchinson; 1951. 128p.

1132. Philmore, R. [pseud.]. (jnt. auth.). "Inquest on
detective stories. By R. Philmore [pseud.] and John Yudkin."
IN Discovery [London] n.s.v.1 (April 1938) pp.28-32.

   Repr. IN Haycraft, H. (Ed.). The art of the mystery
   story. (q.v.) pp.423-429.

1133. ... "Second inquest on detective stories." IN
Discovery [London] n.s.v.1 (September 1938) pp.296-299.

   repr. IN Haycraft, H. (ed.). The art of the mystery
   story. (q.v.) pp.430-435.

*   Pitman, Patricia (jnt. auth.). SEE Wilson, Colin
(1931-). Murder trilogy - vol.1: An encyclopedia of murder.

1134. Pitts, Michael R. <u>Celluloid sleuths; the great movie
detectives</u>.

   Noted as being in preparation in: Parish, J. R. (jnt. auth.)
   <u>The great spy pictures</u> (q.v.), p.585, but not verified
   to date.

*   ... (jnt. auth.). SEE Also Parish, J. R. (jnt.
auth.). <u>The great gangster pictures</u>.

*   ... (jnt. auth.). SEE also Parish, J. R. (jnt.
auth.). <u>The great spy pictures</u>.

1135. Pizer, Donald. <u>The novels of Theodore Dreiser; a
critical study</u>. Minneapolis, Minn.: University of Minnesota
Press; 1976. ix, 382p.

1136. ... (jnt. comp.). <u>Theodore Dreiser; a primary and
secondary bibliography</u>. Comp. by D. Pizer, Richard W.
Dowell, and Frederic E. Rusch. Boston: G. K. Hall; 1975.
x, 515p. (Literature series).

1137. Poe, Edgar Allan. "Charles Dickens." IN Poe, Edgar
Allan. <u>Literary criticism</u>. Boston: Estes; [188?]. vi,
571p. - other eds.

1138. "A poetic investigation of detectives, mystery and
murder" - special issue of <u>Cross Country; [a magazine of
Canadian-U.S. poetry]</u> No.10/11 (1978) 88p.

1139. Pollin, Burton Ralph. <u>Godwin criticism; a synoptic
bibliography</u>. Toronto: University of Toronto Press; 1967.
xlvi, 659p.

1140. ... "Poe and Godwin." IN <u>Nineteenth-century fiction</u>
v.20:no.3 (December 1965) pp.237-253.

1141. Pollock, Wilson. "Man with a toy gun." IN <u>New
Republic</u> v.146 (7 May 1962) pp.21-22.

1142. Pond, James Burton (1838-1903). <u>Eccentricities of
genius; memories of famous men and women of the platform and
stage ... with 91 portraits</u>. N.Y.: G. W. Dillingham Co.;
1900. xxvi, 564p., illus. - U.K. ed.: London: Chatto &
Windus; 1901. xxvi, 564p., illus.

1143. Pope-Hennessy, Dame Una (Birch) (1876-1949). Edgar
Allan Poe, 1809-1849; a critical biography. London:
Macmillan; 1934. xii, 342p.

1144. Popescu, Constantin. "Arta simplă a romanului
poliţist." IN (as Introduction) Hammett, Dashiell
(1894-1961). Şoimul maltez. Bucharest: Minerva; 1970.
pp.vii-x, 323-329.

1145. Portugal, Eustace. "Death to the detectives!" IN
Bookman [London] v.84:no.499 (April 1933) p.28.

   cf. Stone, P. M. "Long life".

1146. Portuondo, José Antonio (1911-). En torno a la
novela detectivesca. Havana: Paginas; 1947, [c1946]. 70p.
(Cuadernos cubanos. Coleccion del siju, 1).

1147. Post, K. D. "Kriminalgeschichte als Heilsgeschichte;
Zu E. T. A. Hoffmans Erzählung 'Das Fraulein von Scuderi'."
IN Zeitschrift für deutsche Philologie; Sonderheft:
E. T. A. Hoffman. Berlin: Erich Schmidt Verlag; 1977.
180p. (Sonderheft zum 95. Band).

1148. Pound, Reginald. The Strand Magazine 1891-1950.
London: Heinemann; 1966. 200p., illus.

1149. Poupart, Jean Marie. Les récréants; essai portant,
entre autres choses, sur le roman policier. Montreal:
Editions duJour (distrib. by Messageries du Jour ...
Montreal); 1972. 123p. (Collection Littérature du jour,
Y-4).

1150. Pouplier, Erik (ed.). Ti kriminelle minutter.
Copenhagn: [n.publ.]; 1966. 47p.

   Not verified. Cited in: la Cour, T. "The murder
   book" (q.v.), p.177.

1151. Powell, Dilys. "Ray and Cissy." IN Gross, M. (ed.).
The world of Raymond Chandler. (q.v.) pp.81-87.

1152. Powell, Lawrence Clark (1906-). "Farewell, my
lovely." IN Powell, Lawrence Clark (1906-). California
classics; the creative literature of the Golden State. Los
Angeles: Ward Ritchie Press; 1971. xviii, 393p. pp.371-381.

1153. Powers, Richard Gid. "J. Edgar Hoover and the
detective hero." IN Journal of Popular Culture v.9:no.2
(Fall 1975) pp.257-278.

   repr. IN Dimensions of detective fiction. (q.v.)
   pp.203-227.

1154. Prager, Arthur. Rascals at large; or, The clue in
the old nostalgia. Garden City, N.Y.: Doubleday; 1971.
334p.

   Note: Chapter on Nancy Drew is a revision of his
   article: "The secret of Nancy Drew; pushing forty
   and going strong." orig. publ. IN Saturday Review
   of Literature v.52 (25 January 1969) pp.18-19ff.

1155. Praz, Mario (1896-). The hero in eclipse in
Victorian fiction. London/N.Y.: Oxford University Press;
1956. 478p. (Oxford paperbacks 175).

1156. Preston-Muddock, Joyce Emmerson (1843-1934). Pages
from an adventurous life; [autobiography]. by "Dick Donovan"
[pseud.]. London: T. Werner Laurie; 1907. xvi, 351p.,
illus. - U.S. ed.: N.Y.: M. Kennerley; 1907. xvi,
351p., illus.

1157. Price, Alan (1921-). Brighton Rock (Graham Greene).
Oxford: Blackwell; 1969. 107p. (Notes on English
literature, 40).

1158. Priestley, John Boynton (1894-). "Close-up of
Chandler." IN New Statesman v.63 (16 March 1962)
pp.379-380.

1159. ... "On holiday with the bodies." IN Saturday
Review [London] v.142:no.3688 (3 July 1926) pp.8-10.

   cf. Rendall, V. "Reply to ..."

1160. Pritchett, Victor Sawdon (1900-). "An émigré."
IN Pritchett, Victor Sawdon (1900-). Books in general.
London: Chatto & Windus; 1953. 258p. pp.216-222. -
U.S. ed. - N.Y.: Harcourt Brace; 1953. 258p.

   repr. IN Watt, I. (ed.). Conrad; 'The secret agent'.
   (q.v.) pp.133-139.

1161. ... "The Poe centenary." and "The roots of
detection." Both IN Pritchett, Victor Sawson (1900-).
Books in general. London: Chatto & Windus; 1953. viii,
258p. pp.185-190 and pp.179-184, respectively.

Note: "The roots of detection." orig. appeared
untitled as part of the author's "Books in general"
column IN New Statesman and Nation v.41:no.1,058
(16 June 1951) pp.684-685.

1162. "Private eye" - chapter. IN Hollywood and the great
stars; the stars, the sex symbols, the legend, the movies,
how it all began. Ed. by Jeremy Pascall. Comp. by Mundy
Ellis. London: Phoebus; 1976. 256p., illus. pp.198-203.

1163. Pronzini, Bill. "Bibliography; [mystery stories
dealing with trains]." IN Pronzini, Bill (ed.). Midnight
specials; an anthology for train buffs and suspense
aficionados. N.Y.: Bobbs-Merrill; 1977. - repr. N.Y.:
Avon; 1978. 262p. pp.249-261.

1164. Pry, Elmer. Lew Archer's "moral landscape". ...
presented at the Popular Culture Association convention,
May 1974.

repr., slightly rev. IN Armchair Detective v.8:no.2
(February 1975) pp.104-107.

repr. IN Dimensions of detective fiction. (q.v.)
pp.174-181.

1165. Pryce-Jones, David (1936-). Graham Greene.
Edinburgh: Oliver & Boyd; 1963. 119p. (Writers and
Critics ser.) - U.S. ed.: N.Y.: Barnes & Noble; 1963.
119p. - repr.: same publ.; 1968. 119p. - 2d ed.:
Edinburgh: Oliver & Boyd; 1973. 126p. (Writers & critics).

Q

1166.   Quayle, Eric.   "Detective fiction."   IN   Quayle, Eric.
The collector's book of books.   London: Studio Vista; 1971.
144p., illus.   pp.98-104.

1167.   ...   The collector's book of detective fiction.
London: Studio Vista; 1972.   143p., illus.

1168.   Queen, Ellery [pseud.].   The detective short story;
a bibliography.   Ltd. ed.   Boston: Little Brown/Toronto:
McClelland & Stewart; 1942.   146p.   -   repr.: With a new
intro. by the author.   N.Y.: Biblo & Tannen; 1969, [1942].
146p.

1169.   ...   Erle Stanley Gardner; an unorthodox introduction."
IN   Gardner, Erle Stanley (1889-1970).   The case of the
murderer's bride and other stories.   Ed. and with intro.
by Ellery Queen [pseud.].   N.Y.: Davis Publications; 1974.
188p.   (Ellery Queen presents, no.5).

*   ...   (jnt. comp.).   The Haycraft-Queen definitive
library of detective-crime-mystery fiction.   SEE   Haycraft, H.
From Poe to Hammett.

1170.   ...   In the Queen's parlor; and other leaves from the
editors' notebook.   N.Y.: Simon & Schuster; 1957.   195p.   -
U.K. ed.: London: Gollancz; 1957.   195p.   -   repr.: N.Y.:
Biblo & Tannen; 1969.   195p.

1171.   ...   "Introduction."   IN   Derleth, August.   The memoirs
of Solar Pons.   Sauk City, Wisc.: Mycroft & Moran; 1951.
xxii, 245p.   pp.ix-xii.

1172.   ... "Introduction [and] afterwords." IN Queen,
Ellery [pseud.].(ed.). Ellery Queen's challenge to the reader;
an anthology. N.Y.: Frederick A. Stokes; 1936. vii, 502p. -
repr.: N.Y.: Blue Ribbon Books; 1940. 502p.

1173.   ... "Introduction." IN Queen, Ellery [pseud.].
(ed.). Ellery Queen's Japanese golden dozen; the detective
story world in Japan. Rutland, Vt.: Charles E. Tuttle; 1978.
288p. pp.7-12.

1174.   ... "Introduction." IN Queen, Ellery [pseud.].
(ed.). The female of the species; the great women detectives
and criminals. Boston: Little Brown; 1943. xii, 422p. -
U.K. ed. AS Ladies in crime; a collection of detective
stories by English and American writers. London: Faber;
1947. 416p.

1175.   ... "Introduction." IN Queen, Ellery [pseud.].
(ed.). 101 years entertainment; the great detective stories
1841-1941. Boston: Little Brown; 1941. xxii, 999p. - also
publ.: N.Y.: Modern Library; 1941. xviii, 995p. (A Modern
Library giant, G69) pp.v-xviii.

   rev. (1946) and repr. AS "The detective short story;
   the first hundred years." IN Haycraft, H. (ed.).
   The art of the mystery story. (q.v.) pp.476-491.

1176.   ... "Leaves from the editors' notebook; [seven critical
commentaries from 'Ellery Queen's Mystery Magazine']." IN
Ellery Queen's Mystery Magazine. [var. dates].

   repr. IN Haycraft, H. (ed.). The art of the mystery
   story. (q.v.) pp.406-414.

   repr., with rev., IN Queen, E. [pseud.]. In the
   Queen's parlor. (q.v.)

1177.   ... "Letter to the reader." IN Hammett, Dashiell
(1894-1961). Hammett homicides. Collected and ed., with
intro. and critical notes, by Ellery Queen. N.Y.: L. E. Spivak;
1946. 128p.

1178.   ,.. Med Hälsningar; från Ellery Queen och Tage la
Cour. Översättning av Carl Olof Nyman. Teckningar av Leo
Estvad. Stockholm: Sällskapet bokvännerna; 1958. 58p.,
illus. (Bokvännens bibliotek, nr.38).

1179. ... Med venlig hilsen fra Ellery Queen. By E. Queen
and Tage la Cour. Copenhagn: [n.publ.]; 1958.

  Not verified. Cited in: la Cour, T. 'The murder book'
  (q.v.), p.177.

1180. ... "Meet Sam Spade." IN Hammett, Dashiell (1894-
1961). A man called Spade; and other stories. N.Y.: Dell;
1944, [1945?]. 192p. (Private detective mystery stories).

1181. ... Queen's quorum; a history of the detective-crime
short story as revealed by the 106 most important books
published in this field since 1845. Boston: Little Brown;
1951. ix, 132p. - U.K. ed.: London: Gollancz; 1953. -
Cdn. ed.: Toronto: McClelland & Stewart; 1951. - engl. and
repr. AS ... : supplements through 1967. N.Y.: Biblo and
Tannen; 1969. ix, 146p.

1182. ... ""Who shall ever forget" ... [from first section
of Introduction]". IN Queen, Ellery [pseud.]. (ed.).
The misadventures of Sherlock Holmes. Boston: Little Brown;
1944. xxii, 363p., illus. pp.v-ix.

  repr. IN Queen, E. [pseud.]. In the Queen's parlor.
  (q.v.) pp.125-129.

  repr. IN Nevins, F. M. (comp.). The mystery writer's
  art. (q.v.) pp.37-41.

1183. Quennell, Peter. "'The Thin Man'." IN New Statesman
and Nation [London] v.7 (26 May 1934) pp.800-801.

1184. Quinn, Arthur Hobson (1875-1944). Edgar Allan Poe;
a critical biography. N.Y./London: D. Appleton-Century Co.,
inc.; 1941. xvi, 804p., illus. - repr.: N.Y.: Cooper
Square; 1969, [c.1941]. 804p.

1185. Quinn, Patrick Francis (1918-). The French face of
Edgar Poe. Carbondale, Ill.: Southern Illinois University
Press; 1957. 310p. - repr.: same publ.; 1971. 310p.

1186. Quintano Ripollés, Antonio. La criminología en la
literatura universal. Barcelona: [n.publ.]; 1951. 204p.

  2d ed.: ... ; ensayo de propedéutica biológico-criminal
  sobre fuentes literarias. Buenos Aires: [n.publ.]; 1963.
  188p. (Biblioteca policial, año 29, no.220-221).

1187.   Quinton, Anthony.   "The decadence of detection."   IN Encounter   v.4:no.5(issue 20) (May 1955)   pp.81-84.

1188.   Quiz, Quintus [pseud.].   "Mental holidays."   IN Christian Century   v.51:no.30   (25 July 1934)   p.968.

1189.   ...   "A resolution and a protest."   IN Christian Century   v.56:no.6   (8 February 1939)   pp.177-178.

   cf. Steel, Kurt.   "A literary crisis".

R

1190. Race, Herbert. _Joseph Conrad: "The secret agent"_. London: Brodie; 1960. 71p. (Notes on chosen English Texts).

1191. Radine, Serge. _Quelques aspects du roman policier psychologique_. Geneva: Éditions du Mont-Blanc; 1960. 293p.

1192. Ramsey, Gordon C. _Agatha Christie; mistress of mystery_. N.Y.: Dodd, Mead; 1967. 124p. - U.K. ed.: London: Collins; 1968. 127p.

* Randall, David A. (comp.). SEE Indiana. University. Lilly Library.

* ... (jnt. comp.). SEE also Scribner, firm, publishers, New York.

1193. Rans, Geoffrey. _Edgar Allan Poe_. Edinburgh: Oliver & Boyd; 1965. 119p. (Writers and critics ser.).

1194. Ransome, Arthur Michell. _Edgar Allan Poe; a critical study_. London: Martin Secker; 1910. xiii, 236p.

1195. Rauber, D. F. "Sherlock Holmes and Nero Wolfe; the role of the 'great detective' in intellectual history." IN _Journal of Popular Culture_ v.6:no.3 (Spring 1973) pp.483-495.

  repr. IN _Dimensions of detective fiction_. (q.v.) pp.89-96.

*   Rausch, George Jay (1930-). (jnt. auth.). SEE
Mundell, E. H. The detective short story.

*   Rawlings, E. (jnt. auth.). SEE Berkowitz, L.
(jnt. auth.).

1196. Rawson, Clayton (1906-). "... critical discussion of
locked-room theory ..." IN Rawson, Clayton (1906-).
Death from a top hat; a Merlini mystery. N.Y.: G. P. Putnam's
sons; 1938. 256p. Chap.13: "Designs for escape." - U.K.
ed. - London: Collins; 1938. 284p./repr. - London: Tom
Stacey; 1971. 284p. pp.130-137.

1197. Ray, Laura Krugman. "The mysteries of 'Gaudy Night';
feminism, faith, and the depth of character." IN Mystery
and Detection Annual; 1973. (q.v.) pp.272-284.

1198. Raymond, John (1923-). Simenon in court. London:
Hamish Hamilton; 1968. 193p. - U.S. ed.: N.Y.: Harcourt,
Brace & World; c1968, 1969. 178p.

1199. Raynor, Henry. "Decline and fall of the detective
story." IN Fortnightly Review v.179 (ns173) (February 1953)
pp.125-133.

1200. Reaves, R. B. "Crime and punishment in the detective
fiction of Dorothy L. Sayers." IN As her whimsey took her.
(q.v.) pp.1-13.

1201. Reck, T. S. "Raymond Chandler's Los Angeles." IN
Nation v.221 (20 December 1975) pp.661-663.

1202. Reclams Kriminalromanführer. Ed. by Armin Arnold and
Josef Schmidt. Stuttgart: Reclam; 1978. 455p.

1203. Redman, Ben Ray. "Decline and fall of the whodunit."
IN Saturday Review v.35 (31 May 1952) pp.8-9, 31-32.

*   Redmond, Donald Aitcheson (1922-). (ed.). SEE
Metropolitan Toronto Central Library.

1204. Reed, Ishmael. ["Essay on Chester Himes."] IN
Reed, Ishmael. Shrovetide in old New Orleans. Garden City,
N.Y.: Doubleday; 1978. viii, 292p.

1205. Reed, John R. "English imperialism and the unacknowledged crime of 'The moonstone'." IN Clio v.2 (1973) pp.281-290.

1206. Reeve, Arthur Benjamin (1880-). "In defense of the detective story." IN Independent v.75 (10 July 1913) pp.91-94.

1207. Rein, David M. Edgar A. Poe; the inner pattern. N.Y.: Philosophical Library; 1960. 134p. - U.K. ed.: London: Peter Owen; 1962. 134p.

1208. Reinert, Claus (1942-). Detektivliteratur bei Sophokles, Schiller und Kleist; oder, Das Rätsel der Warheit und die Abenteuer des Erkennens. Kronberg/Ts.: Scriptor Verlag; 1975. 142p. (Theorie, Kritik, Geschichte; Bd.8).

1209. ... Das Unheimliche und die Detektivliteratur; Entwurf einer poetologischen Theorie über Entstehung, Entfaltung und Problematik der Detektivliteratur. Bonn: Bouvier Verlag/Herbert Grundmann; 1973. 158p. (Abhandlungen zur Kunst-, Musik-, und Literaturwissenschaft; Bd. 139).

1210. Rendall, Vernon. "The genesis of the detective story; reply to: J. B. Priestley. "On holiday with the bodies.", 'Saturday Review', 3 july 1926." IN Saturday Review [London] v.142:no.3,689 (10 July 1926) p.43 ("Letters to the Editor" column).

1211. Reynolds, Barbara. "The origin of Lord Peter Wimsey." IN T.L.S.; The Times Literary Supplement No.3,919 (Friday 22 April 1977) p.429.

    " ... condensed version of lecture given to the Dorothy L. Sayers Historical and Literary Society in November, 1976."

1212. Reynolds, Quentin James (1902-). The fiction factory; or, From Pulp Row to Quality Street: the story of 100 years of publishing at Street & Smith. N.Y.: Random House; 1955. 233p.

1213. Rexroth, Kenneth. "Disengagement; the art of the Beat Generation." IN New World Writing [New York] No.11 (1957) pp.28-41.

1214.   Rhode, John [pseud.]. (ed.).   Detection medley.
London: Hutchinson, 1939. 528p. - U.S. ed. AS Line-up;
a collection of crime stories by famous mystery writers.
Intro. by A. A. Milne. Stories by E. C. Bentley, J. Dickson
Carr, G. K. Chesterton et al. N.Y.: Dodd Mead; 1940. ix,
378p.

1215.   Rhodes, Henry Taylor Fowkes. "The detective in
fiction - and in fact." IN Cornhill Magazine [London]
v.157 (January 1938) pp.53-67.

   repr. IN Rhodes, Henry Taylor Fowkes. The tracks of
crime; [a week-end book for the amateur criminologist].
London: Turnstile Press; 1952. xii, 337p. pp.57-68.

1216.   Rice, Craig. "Murder makes merry." IN Haycraft, H.
(ed.). The art of the mystery story. (q.v.) pp.238-244.

1217.   Richards, Franklin Thomas Grant (1872-1948). Author
hunting; memories of years spent mainly in publishing
[1897-1925] ..., [by an old literary sportsman] ... London:
H. Hamilton; 1934. xiv, 295p., illus. - repr.: London:
Unicorn Press; 1960. xix, 238p., illus.

1218.   Richardson, Maurice. "Simenon and Highsmith; into the
criminal's head." IN Crime writers. (q.v.) pp.100-117.

1219.   Richardson, Maurice Lane. "Introduction." IN
Richardson, Maurice Lane (ed.). Novels of mystery from the
Victorian age; four complete unabridged novels by J. Sheridan
Le Fanu (Carmilla), Anon. (The Notting Hill mystery), Wilkie
Collins (The woman in white), R. L. Stevenson (Dr. Jekyll and
Mr. Hyde). Selected with an intro. by M. Richardson. London:
Pilot Press/N.Y.: Duell, Sloan and Pearce; 1945. xviii, 678p.
(Pilot Omnibus) - repr.: same publ.; 1946. xviii, 678p.

1220.   Richert, J. Gustaf. Detektiven i romanen och i
verkligheten. Stockholm: Åhlen & Åkerlund; 1928. 209p.

   Not verified. Cited in: la Cour, T. 'The murder book'
   (q.v.), p.177.

1221.   Richie, Donald (1924-). "'High and low'." IN Richie,
Donald (1924-). The films of Akira Kurosawa. Berkeley,
Calif.: University of California Press; 1965. 218p. - 2d
ed.: same publ.: 1970. 223p.

   repr. IN Nevins, F. M. (comp.). The mystery writer's
art. (q.v.) pp.162-179.

1222. Richler, Mordecai. "James Bond unmasked." IN
Commentary v.46 (july 1968) pp.74-81.

  repr. IN Rosenberg, Bernard. (jnt. ed.). Mass culture
  revisited. Ed. by B. Rosenberg and David Manning-White.
  N.Y.: Van Nostrand Reinhold; 1971. xii, 473p. pp.341-355.

1223. Richter, Anne. Georges Simenon et l'homme desintegre.
Bruxelles: Renaissance du livre; 1964. 115p. (Collection
anthologique).

1224. Rickmann, H. P. "From detection to theology; (the
work of Dorothy Sayers)." IN Hibbert Journal v.60:no.4
(no.239) (July 1962) pp.290-296.

1225. ... "Die metaphysische Bedeutung des Detektivromans."
IN Eckart, Jg.29,4. (hier zitiert nach, Literatur, 2.
Analytische Texte. Frankfurt, 1970).

1226. Ridley, Maurice Roy (1890-). "A misrated author?"
IN Ridley, Maurice Roy (1890-). Second thoughts; more
studies in literature. London: Dent; 1965. ix, 175p.

1227. ... "Sherlock Holmes and the detective story." IN
The Listener v.51:no.1298 (14 January 1954) pp.65-66.

*   Rietzlen, Conrad. SEE Ritzen, Quentin [pseud.].

1228. Rinehart, Mary Roberts (1876-?). My story. N.Y.:
Farrar & Rinehart; 1931. vi, 432p., illus.

*   Ripollés, Antonio Quintano. SEE Quintano Ripollés, A.

1229. Ritchie, John. "Agatha Christie's England 1918-39;
sickness in the heart and sickness in society as seen in the
detective thriller." IN Australian National University
Historical Journal v.9 (December 1972) pp.3-9.

1230. Ritzen, Quentin [pseud.]. Simenon; avocat des hommes.
Pref. de Gilbert Sigaux. Paris: Le Livre contemporain; 1961.
208p., illus.

  Attributed by T. la Cour ('The murder book' (q.v.), p.177)
  to a "Conrad Rietzlen", but this is not supported by any
  of the accepted standard bibliographical reference sources.

*   Rix, Walter T. (jnt. auth.). SEE Wulff, Antje.

1231. Robbins, Frank E. "The firm of Cool and Lam." IN
The Michigan Alumnus Quarterly Review v.59 (Spring 1953)
pp.222-228.

    repr. IN Nevins, F. M. (comp.). The mystery writer's
    art. (q.v.) pp.136-148.

1232. ... "The world of Perry Mason." IN The Michigan
Alumnus Quarterly Review (Summer 1950). n.v.

1233. Roberts, Daisy Mae. "'The Red-headed League' and
'The Rue Morgue'." IN Scholastic v.32 (26 February 1938)
pp.19E-20E.

1234. Roberts, Kenneth Lewis (1885-). "For authors only;
mysteries easily solved in English detective stories."
IN Saturday Evening Post v.205 (24 September 1932)
pp.14-15.

    repr. IN Roberts, Kenneth Lewis (1885-). For authors
    only; and other gloomy essays. Garden City, N.Y.:
    Doubleday, Doran; 1935. 446p., illus.

1235. Robinson, E. Arthur. "Poe's 'The Tell-tale heart'."
IN Nineteenth-century Fiction v.19:no.4 (March 1965)
pp.369-378.

1236. Robinson, Kenneth. Wilkie Collins; a biography.
London: J. Lane; 1951. 348p., illus. - U.S. ed. - N.Y.:
Macmillan; 1952. 348p., illus., col. frontis.

1237. Robson, W. W. "G. K. Chesterton's 'Father Brown'
stories." IN Southern Review v.5 (Summer 1969)
pp.611-629.

1238. Robyns, Gwen. The mystery of Agatha Christie; [an
intimate biography of the first lady of crime]. Garden City,
N.Y.: Doubleday; 1978. xvi, 247p., illus. - repr. -
Penguin; 1979. 320p., illus.

1239. Rockwell, Joan. "Normative attitudes of spies in
fiction." IN Rosenberg, Bernard (1923-). (jnt. comp.).
Mass culture revisited. Comp. by B. Rosenberg and David
Manning-White. N.Y.: Van Nostrand-Reinhold; 1971. xii,
473p. pp.325-340.

1240. Rodell, Marie (Freid) (1912-). <u>Mystery fiction;</u>
<u>theory and technique</u>. Boston: The Writer; 1943. x, 230p.
(Bloodhound mystery) - also publ. N.Y.: Duell, Sloan &
Pearce; 1943. x, 230p. - Cdn. ed. - Toronto: Collins;
1943. x, 230p.

    2d (rev.) ed. - N.Y.: Hermitage House; 1952. 230p.
    (Professional writers library) - Cdn. ed. - Toronto:
    George J. McLeod; 1952. 230p. - U.K. ed. - Intro. by
    Maurice Richardson. London: Hammond, Hammond; 1954.
    xviii, 171p.

    Note: Chapter on clues repr. IN Haycraft, H. (ed.).
    <u>The art of the mystery story</u>. (q.v.) pp.264-272.

1241. Rodríguez Joulia Saint-Cyr, Carlos. <u>La novela de</u>
<u>intriga</u>. Madrid: Asociación Nacional de Bibliotecarios,
Archiveros y Arqueólogos; 1970. 126p. (Biblioteca
Profesional de ANABA. 3. Cuadernos, 2).

    2d ed.: ... (Diccionario de autores, obras y personajes).
    Ediciones en castellano. Madrid: Asociación Nacional de
    Bibliotecarios, Archiveros y Arqueólogos; 1972. xii,
    154p. (Biblioteca profesional de Anaba. 2. Bibliografias,
    2).

*   Rohmer, Elizabeth Sax. (jnt. auth.). SEE Van Ash, Cay.

1242. Rolleke, H. "Erzähltes Mysterium; Studie zur
"Judenbuche" der Annette von Drost-Hülshoff." IN <u>DVjs.</u>
v.42 (1968) pp.399-426.

1243. Rolo, Charles J. "Simenon and Spillane; metaphysics
for the millions." IN <u>New World Writing</u>. [N.Y.: New
American Library] No. 1. (1952) pp.234-245.

    repr. IN Rosenberg, Bernard (1923-). (jnt. ed.).
    <u>Mass culture; the popular arts in America</u>. Ed. by
    B. Rosenberg and David Manning-White. N.Y.: Free Press
    of Glencoe; 1957. x, 561p. pp.165-175. - repr. pap.:
    same publ.; 1964.

1244. Rosenbach, Abraham Simon Wolf (1876-). "Old mystery
books." IN <u>Saturday Evening Post</u> v.204 (5 September 1931)
pp.23ff.

1245. ... "The trail of scarlet." IN <u>Saturday Evening Post</u>
v.205 (1 October 1932) pp.8-9.

repr. IN Rosenbach, Abraham Simon Wolf (1876-). A book
hunter's holiday; adventures with books and manuscripts.
Boston: Houghton Mifflin; 1936. xiv, 259p., illus.

1246. Rosow, Eugene. Born to lose; the gangster film in
America. N.Y.: Oxford University Press; 1978. xvi, 422p.,
illus.

1247. Ross Macdonald; in the first person. [I] [Motion
picture]   Made by Davidson Films; released by Silver Burdett
Co., 1971. 23 min., sd., col., 16mm (Writers on film)
(Ross Macdonald, using the detective story genre, demonstrates
writing about what you know and gives an example of how a
writer re-writes a four-line paragraph).

1248. Ross Macdonald; in the first person. [II] [Motion
picture]   Made by Davidson Films; released by Silver Burdett
Co., 1971. 23 min., sd., sol., 16mm (Writers on writing)
(Presents the detective-story writer Ross Macdonald discussing
his work, his philosophy, and his feelings about writing).

1249. Roth, Martin. The detective, the clue, and the corpse
in Freud and Einstein.

   - unpublished paper presented at the 1973 meeting of
   the Midwest Modern Language Association. Cited in:
   Cawleti, J. G. "Adventure, mystery, and romance"
   (q.v.), p.326.

1250. ... "The poet's purloined letter." IN Mystery and
Detection Annual; 1973. (q.v.) pp.113-128.

1251. Rothstein, Eric. "Allusion and analogy in the romance
of 'Caleb Williams'." IN University of Toronto Quarterly
v.37 (1967) pp.18-30.

   Expanded vers. repr. AS "Caleb Williams". IN Rothstein,
   Eric. Systems of order and inquiry in later eighteenth-
   century fiction. Berkeley, Calif.: University of California
   Press; 1975. 274p. pp.208-242.

*   Rottenburg, Ger. (Diocese). Akademie. SEE
Katholische Akademie Stuttgart-Hohenheim.

1252. Routley, Erik. The puritan pleasures of the detective
story [from Sherlock Holmes to Van der Valk]; a personal
monograph [on the excellences & limitations of detective
fiction]. London: Victor Gollancz; 1972. 253p.

1253. Roux, Fernand (Substitut du Procureur-general de la
Cour d'Appel de Riom). Balzac; jurisconsulte et criminaliste.
Paris: [n.publ.]; 1906. vii, 380p.

1254. Rowland, John. "Phillpotts's detective fiction."
IN Girvan, W. (ed.). 'Eden Phillpotts' (q.v.) Chap.8.
pp.135-151.

1255. Ruber, Peter A. (jnt. comp.). The detective short
story (a bibliography). Ed. by P. A. Ruber and William Swift
Dalliba. N.Y.: the author; 1961. 15p.

1256. Ruehlmann, William (1946-). Saint with a gun; the
unlawful American private eye. N.Y.: New York University
Press; 1974. xvi, 155p.

1257. Ruhm, Herbert. "In Rats' Alley." IN Carleton
Miscellany v.8:no.1 (Winter 1967) pp.118-122.

1258. ... "Introduction". IN Ruhm, Herbert (ed.).
The hard-boiled detective; stories from 'Black Mask'
magazine (1920-1951). N.Y.: Random House; 1977. xviii,
397p. (Vintage Books). pp.viii-xviii.

1259. ... "Raymond Chandler; from Bloomsbury to the
jungle - and beyond." IN Madden, D. T. (ed.). Tough-guy
writers of the Thirties. (q.v.) pp.171-185.

*   Runnquist, Åke. (jnt. auth.). SEE Elgström, J.
Mord i biblioteket.

   SEE also Elgström, J. Svensk mordbok.

1260. Russell, D. C. "The Chandler books." IN The
Atlantic v.175 (March 1945) pp.123-124.

1261. Rutter, Frank. "Detectives in fiction." IN Bookman
[London] v.48:no.406 (July 1925) pp.212-213.

1262. Rycroft, Charles. "A detective story; psychoanalytic
observations." IN The Psychoanalytic Quarterly v.26 (1957)
pp.229-245.

   repr. AS "Analysis of a detective story." IN Rycroft,
   Charles. Imagination and reality. London: Hogarth

Press; 1968.   (International Psychoanalytical Library,
no.75).

cf.   Pederson-Krag, G.   "Detective stories and the
primal scene."

S

1263. Sachs, Hanns. "Edgar Allan Poe." IN The Psychoanalytic Quarterly v.4 (1935).

1264. Sacks, Arthur. "An analysis of gangster movies of the early thirties." IN The Velvet Light Trap No.1 (June 1971).

1265. Sadleir, Michael Thomas Harvey (1888-1957). XIX century fiction; a bibliographical record based on his own collection. London: Constable; 1951. 2 vols., illus. - U.S. ed.: Berkeley, Calif.: University of California Press; 1951. 2 vols., illus. - repr.: N.Y.: Cooper Square Publishers; 1969. 2 vols., illus.

1266. ... "Wilkie Collins; essay and bibliography." IN Sadleir, Michael Thomas Harvey (1888-1957). Excursions in Victorian bibliography. London: Chaundy & Cox; 1922. vii, 240p. - repr.: Folcroft, Pa.: Folcroft Press; 1969. vii, 240p.

1267. Sage, L. "Kojak and co." IN Sight and Sound v.44 (Summer 1975) pp.183-185.

1268. Saintsbury, George Edward Bateman (1845-1933). "Preface." IN Balzac, Honore de (1799-1850). The thirteen; [histoire des treize]. Trans. by Ellen Marriage, with a preface by George Saintsbury. London: Dent; 1898. 308p. - U.S. ed.: N.Y.: De Fau; 1901. - also publ.: N.Y.: Macmillan; 1901. - London: Society of English Bibliophiles; 1901. - N.Y.: Groscup & Sterling; 1901; - Philadelphia: Avil Pub. Co.; 1901. repr.: [n.pl.]: McKinlay Stone & Mackenzie; 1915.

1269. Sanderson, Elizabeth. "Ex-detective Hammett." IN
Bookman [N.Y.] v.74 (January-February 1932) pp.516-518.

1270. Sandison, Alan. "John Buchan; the church of empire."
IN Sandison, Alan. The wheel of empire; a study of the
imperial idea in some late nineteenth and early twentieth-
century fiction. London: Macmillan; 1967. viii, 213p.
pp.149-194 (Chap.6).

1271. Sandoe, James (1912-). "Criminal clef; tales and
plays based on real crime." IN Wilson Library Bulletin
v.21 (December 1946) pp.299-307.

    repr. IN Sandoe, James (1912-) (ed.). Murder: plain
and fanciful; with some milder malefactions, written by
divers hands. N.Y.: Sheridan House; 1948. xii, 628p.
pp.591-624.

1272. ... "Dagger of the mind." IN Poetry Magazine v.68
(June 1946) pp.146-163.

    repr. IN Haycraft, H. (ed.). The art of the mystery
story. (q.v.) pp.250-263.

1273. ... "The detective story and academe." IN Wilson
Library Bulletin v.18 (April 1944) pp.619-623.

    rev. and repr. AS "Readers' guide to crime" IN
Haycraft, H. (ed.). The art of the mystery story.
(q.v.) pp.492-507.

1274. ... The hard-boiled dick, a personal checklist.
Chicago: A. Lovell; 1952. 10p.

    - privately-printed pamphlet.

    This could not be verified in any of the accepted standard
bibliographical reference sources. It is cited in: Barzun,
J., & Taylor, W. (A Catalogue of crime - q.v.), p.610;
Nolan, W. F. (Dashiell Hammett - q.v.), p.178; la Cour, T.
(The murder book - q.v.), p.178; and the 'Encyclopedia of
mystery and detection' - q.v. - p.352. This last merely
quotes its appearance in Barzun & Taylor (op. cit.).
According to Nolan (op. cit.) and the 'Encyclopedia of
mystery and detection' (op. cit.), this item was reprinted
IN The Armchair Detective v.1:no.2 (January 1968).

1275. ... "Introduction." IN Sayers, Dorothy Leigh
(1893-1957). Lord Peter; a collection of all the Lord Peter
Wimsey stories. Comp. and with an intro. by James Sandoe.
Coda by Carolyn Heilbrun. Codetta by E. C. Bentley. N.Y.:
Harper & Row: [1971, c1972]. xii, 464p. pp.vii-xii. -
repr.: N.Y.: Harper & Row; [c1972]. xiv, 487p. - repr.:
N.Y.: Avon; 1972.

1276. ... "The private eye." IN The mystery story.
(q.v.) pp.111-123.

1277. Santesson, Hans Stefan. "Introduction." IN
Santesson, Hans Stefan (comp.). The locked room reader;
stories of impossible crimes and escapes. N.Y.: Random
House; 1968. xi, 464p.

1278. Sarjeant, William Antony S. "The great Australian
detective." IN Armchair Detective v.12:no.2 (Spring 1979)
pp.99-105.

1279. Savey-Casard, Paul. Le crime et la peine dans l'oeuvre
de Victor Hugo. Paris: Presses universitaires de France;
1956. 424p.

1280. Sayers, Dorothy Leigh (1893-1957). "Aristotle on
detective fiction." IN English [London] v.1:no.1
(Spring 1936) pp.23-35.

   repr. IN Sayers, D. L. 'Unpopular opinions' (q.v.)
   pp.178-190.

1281. ... "Detective stories for the screen." IN Sight
and Sound v.7:no.26 (Summer 1938) pp.49-50.

1282. ... "Emile Gaboriau 1835-1873; the detective
novelist's dilemma." IN Times Literary Supplement No.1,761
(2 November 1935) p.678.

1283. ... "Gaudy night." IN Roberts, Denys Kilham Harry
(ed.). Titles to fame; [essays by various novelists, each
describing the inception and composition of a particular
novel]. London: Thomas Nelson; 1937. xviii, 242p., illus.

   repr. IN Haycraft, H. (ed.). The art of the mystery
   story. (q.v.) pp.208-221.

1284. ... "Introduction." IN Collins, Wilkie. The
moonstone. London: Dent; 1944. xviii, 430p. (Everyman's
Library. No. 979 - Fiction) - repr.: same publ.; 1967.

1285. ... "Introduction." IN Sayers, Dorothy Leigh
(1893-1957) (ed.). Great short stories of detection,
mystery, and horror. London: Gollancz; 1928. - U.S. ed.
AS The omnibus of crime. N.Y.: Payson & Clarke; 1929. -
repr. - Garden City, N.Y.: Garden City Publishing Company;
[n.d.]. 1177p. pp.9-47.

    repr. AS "Detective fiction; origins and development."
    IN Burack, A. S. (ed.). Writing detective and mystery
    fiction. (q.v.)

    repr. IN Writing suspense and mystery fiction (1977).
    (q.v.) pp.221-266.

    repr. AS "The omnibus of crime." IN Haycraft, H. (ed.).
    The art of the mystery story. (q.v.) pp.71-109.

    repr. IN Sayers, Dorothy Leigh (1893-1957) (ed.). Tales
    of detection and mystery; from 'The omnibus of crime.'.
    N.Y.: Macfadden Books; 1962, repr. 1967. 159p. pp.7-40.

    repr. IN Allen, R. S. (jnt. ed.). Detective fiction.
    (q.v.) pp.351-383.

    repr. in German trans. AS "Einleitung zu 'Great short
    stories of detection, mystery, and horror.'." IN Der
    Detektiverzählung auf der Spur. (q.v.)

1286. ... "Introduction." IN Sayers, Dorothy Leigh
(1893-1957). (ed.). Great short stories of detection,
mystery, and horror; second series. London: Gollancz;
1931. - U.S. ed. AS The second omnibus of crime. N.Y.:
Doubleday; 1932.

1287. ... "Introduction." IN Sayers, Dorothy Leigh
(1893-1957). (ed.). Great short stories of detection,
mystery, and horror; third series. London: Gollancz;
1934. - U.S. ed. AS The third omnibus of crime. N.Y.:
Coward, McCann; 1934.

1288. ... "Introduction." IN Tales of detection. Ed. by
Dorothy L. Sayers. London: Dent; 1936. xvi, 382p.
(Everyman's Library: Fiction, No.928) pp.vii,xiv.

1289. ... "The present status of the mystery story." IN
London Mercury v.23 (November 1930) pp.47-52.

cf. MacDonald, A. G. "The present conventions of the
mystery story."

1290. ... "The sport of noble minds." IN Saturday Review
of Literature v.6 (3 August 1929) pp.22-23.

1291. ... Unpopular opinions. London: Gollancz; 1946.
190p. - U.S. ed.: N.Y.: Harcourt Brace; 1947.

1292. ... Wilkie Collins; a biographical and critical
survey. Toledo, Ohio: The Friends of the University of
Toledo Libraries; 1977. 120p.

1293. Schickel, Richard. "Raymond Chandler, private eye."
IN Commentary v.35 (February 1963) pp.158-161.

1294. Schimmelpfenning, Arthur. Beiträge zur Geschichte
des Kriminalromans. Dresden: [n.publ.]; 1908. 16p.

Not verified. Cited in: la Cour, T. 'The murder
book' (q.v.), p.178.

*   Schmidt, Josef (jnt. ed.). SEE Reclams
Kriminalromanfuhrer.

1295. Schmidt-Henkel, G. "Kriminalroman und Trivialliteratur." IN Žmegač, V. (ed.). Der wohltemperierte
Mord. (q.v.)

1296. Schönhaar, Rainer. Novelle und Kriminalschema; Ein
Strukurmodell deutscher Erzählkunst um 1800. Bad Homburg
v.d.H./Berlin/Zurich: Gehlen; 1969. 220p.

1297. "School of detective yarns needed." IN Literary
Digest v.74 (23 September 1922) p.33.

1298. Schraiber, Eléonore. "Georges Simenon et la
littérature russe." IN Lacassin, F. (jnt. ed.). Simenon
(q.v.) pp.184-189.

1299. Schubert, Leland. "Almost real reality; John Buchan's
visible world." IN The Serif; Kent State University Library
Quarterly [Kent, Ohio: Kent State University] v.2:no.3
(September 1965) pp.5-14.

1300. Schulz-Buschhaus, Ulrich. Formen und Ideologien des
Kriminalromans; ein gattungsgeschichtl. Essays. Frankfurt
(M): Athenaion; 1975. xii, 244p. (Schwerpunkte Romanistik
14).

1301. Schwartz, Saul. (ed.). The detective story; an
introduction to the Whodunit. Skokie, Ill.: National
Textbook Company; 1975. iv, 442p.

*   Scott, Helen G. (jnt. auth.). SEE Truffaut, François.

1302. Scott, Mark. "An introduction to the private eye
novel." IN Anderson, Donald Stuart. (jnt. ed.). Cunning
exiles; studies of modern prose writers. Ed. by D. S. Anderson
and Stephen Knight. Sydney: Angus & Robertson; 1974. 244p.
(Contemporary arts series) pp.198-217.

1303. Scott, Sutherland. Blood in their ink; the march of
the modern mystery novel. London/N.Y.: Stanley Paul; 1953.
200p. - Cdn. ed.: Toronto: McGraw-Hill; 1953. - repr.:
Folcroft, Penn.; Folcroft Library Editions; 1953, 1973. 200p.

1304. Scott-Giles, C. W. The Wimsey family; a fragmentary
history compiled from correspondence with Dorothy L. Sayers.
London: Victor Gollancz; 1977. 88p., illus.

1305. Scott-James, Rolfe Arnold. "Detective novels." IN
London Mercury v.39:no.232 (February 1939) pp.377-379.

1306. Scribner, firm, publishers, New York. (1935. Charles
Scribner's sons). Detective fiction; a collection (really a
catalogue) of first and a few early editions. N.Y.: The
Scribner bookstore; 1935. 79p. (Catalogue number 98).

   Barzun and Taylor (A catalogue of crime - q.v. - p.585)
   and Steinbrunner and Penzler (Encyclopedia of mystery
   and detection - q.v. - p.94) both attribute this catalogue
   to John Carter (1905-), and Ellery Queen (In the Queen's
   parlor - q.v. - p.41) attributes it to both Carter and
   David A. Randall, but none of these sources offer any
   documentation for their contentions, and neither gentleman
   is mentioned in connexion with this item in any of the
   accepted standard bibliographical reference sources.

1307. Seaborne, E. A. "Introduction." IN Seaborne, E. A.
(ed.). The detective in fiction; a posse of eight. London:
G. Bell; 1931. 239p. (Bell's English Language and Literature
series) pp.1-36. - repr.: same publ.; 1954.

1308. Seagle, W. "Murder, Marx, and McCarthy; a reply to
Mary McCarthy." IN Nation v.142 (15 April 1936) pp.494-
495.

   cf. McCarthy, M. "Murder and Karl Marx."

1309. See, Carolyn. "The Hollywood novel; the American
dream cheat." IN Madden, D. T. (ed.). Tough-guy writers
of the Thirties. (q.v.) pp.199-217.

1310. Seelye, John. "Buckskin and ballistics; William
Leggett and the American detective story." IN Journal
of Popular Culture v.1:no.1 (Summer 1967) pp.52-57.

1311. Sehlbach, Hans (1901-). Untersuchungen über die
Romankunst von Wilkie Collins. Zelle-Mehlis: M. v.
Nordheimsche Buchdruckerei; 1930. xii, 35, [3]p. -
repr. Jena: Verlag der Frommannschen Buchhandlung; 1931.
xiv, 184p. (Forschungen zur englischen Philologie. no.2) -
repr. N.Y.: Garland; 1978. 198p.

1312. Seldes, Gilbert Vivian. "Diplomat's delight." IN
Bookman [N.Y.] v.66 (September 1927) pp.91-93.

1313. ... "Van Dine and his public." IN New Republic
v.59 (19 June 1929) pp.125-126.

1314. Shadbolt, Maurice. "Ngaio Marsh." IN Shadbolt,
Maurice. Love and legend; some 20th century New Zealanders.
Auckland: Hodder and Stoughton; 1976. 194p., illus. pp.51-61.

1315. Shadoian, Jack. Dreams and dead ends; the American
gangster/crime film. Cambridge, Mass.: MIT Press; 1977.
366p., illus.

1316. Shannon, Dell [pseud.]. "Lieutenant Luis Mendoza."
IN Penzler, O. M. The great detectives. (q.v.) pp.147-153.

1317. Shapiro, Charles. "'Nightmare Alley'; geeks, cons,
tips, and marks." IN Madden, D. (ed.). Tough guy writers
of the Thirties. (q.v.) pp.218-224.

1318. Shaw, Joseph Thompson (1874-). "Introduction." IN
Black Mask (periodical. The hard-boiled omnibus; early
stories from 'Black Mask'. Ed. and with an intro. by
Joseph T. Shaw. N.Y.: Simon & Schuster; 1946. xii, 468p. -
repr., abridged: N.Y.: Pocket Books; 1952.

1319. Shawen, E. "Social interaction in John O'Hara's 'The
gangster'." IN Studies in Short Fiction v.11 (Fall 1974)
pp.367-370.

1320. Shearer, Lawrence. "Crime certainly pays on the
screen." IN New York Times Magazine (5 August 1945)
pp.17ff.

*   Sheppard, Judith. (jnt. ed.). SEE Sheppard, Roger.

1321. Sheppard, Roger. (jnt. ed.). Crime and detective
fiction; handbook of dealers and collectors in Britain and
America. Ed. by R. and Judith Sheppard. London: Trigon
Press; 1977. 160p.

1322. "Sherlock Holmes and after." IN Saturday Review of
Literature v.6:no.52 (19 July 1930) p.1201.

   Attributed by De Waal (q.v.) to Henry Seidel Canby.

1323. Sherry, Norman. "The Greenwich bomb outrage and
'The secret agent'." IN Review of English studies n.s.v.18
(November 1967) pp.412-428.

   repr. IN Watt, I. (ed.). Conrad; 'The secret agent'.
   (q.v.) pp.202-227.

1324. Shibuk, Charles. "Cyril Hare." IN Armchair Detective
v.3:no.1 (October 1969) pp.28-30.

1325. ... "Henry Wade." IN Nevins, F. M. (comp.). The
mystery writer's art. (q.v.) pp.88-97.

   This essay is an amalgamation and revision of two articles:
   'Henry Wade' and 'Henry Wade revisited', that appeared in The
   Armchair Detective in July and October 1968 respectively.

1326. ... (comp.). A preliminary checklist of the detective
novel and its variants. Bronx, N.Y.: the author; 1966. 5p.

   Supplement. Bronx, N.Y.: the author; 1967. [n.pag.].

1327. Shiel, Matthew Phipps (1865-1947). "About myself."
IN Morse, A. R. 'Works of M. P. Shiel'. (q.v.)

1328. ... Science, life and literature. London: Williams &
Norgate; 1950. 217p.

1329. "Shifting the apology." IN Saturday Review of
Literature v.3 (11 September 1926) p.97.

1330. Shishkina, T. "[Foreword]." IN Christie, Dame
Agatha Mary Clarissa Miller (1890-1976). Sbornik rasskazov.
Moscow: Progress; 1969. 334p.

1331. Shrapnel, N. "Die Literatur der Gewalttätigkeit und
der Verfolgung." - orig. publ. 1961.

   repr. IN Der Detektiverzählung auf der Spur. (q.v.)

1332. Shroyer, Frederick. "Introduction." IN Le Fanu,
Joseph Sheridan (1814-1873). Uncle Silas; a tale of
Bartram-Haugh. N.Y.: Dover; 1966. xxii, 436p. pp.v-xiii.

1333. Sigaux, Gilbert. "Lire Simenon." IN Lacassin, F.
(jnt. ed.). Simenon. (q.v.) pp.13-17.

*   ... (jnt. ed.). SEE also Lacassin, F. (jnt. ed.).
Simenon.

1334. Silver, A. "'Kiss me deadly'; evidence of a style."
IN Film Comment v.11 (March 1975) pp.24-30.

1335. A silver anniversary tribute to Ellery Queen from the
author's critics, editors, and famous fans. Boston: Little
Brown; 1954. 31p.

   Not verified. Cited in: Nevins, F. M. Royal bloodline.
   (q.v.), p.263.

1336. Simenon, Georges Joseph Christian (1903-). Le Paris
de Simenon. Paris: Tchou; 1969. 191p., illus.

   U.K. (first English) ed. AS Simenon's Paris. London:
   Ebury Press; 1970. 192p., illus.

1337. ... Pedigree. Paris: Presses de la Cité; 1948.
500p. - U.S./U.K. (first English) ed.: N.Y./London: Random
House; 1963, [c1962]. 543p.

1338. ... Quand j'etais vieux. Paris: Presses de la Cité;
1970. 407p. - U.K. (first English) ed. AS When I was old;
[Simenon on Simenon]. London: Hamish Hamilton; 1972. 343p.

1339. Simenon; special number [of] Adam International Review.
[Rochester University Press] No.'s 328-330 (1969) Ed. by
Miron Grindea.

   - contains essay by George Grella on Maigret, and
   bibliography by Claude Menguy.

1340. Simenon; special number [of] Magazine Littéraire
No.20 (August 1968).

1341. Simmel, Georg (1858-1918). "The adventure." IN
Wolff, Kurt H. (1912-) (ed.). Georg Simmel, 1858-1918; a
collection of essays, with translations and a bibliography.
Contributors: Howard Becker et al. Columbus, Ohio: Ohio
State University Press; 1959. xv, 396p.

   repr. AS Essays on sociology, philosophy and aesthetics.
   N.Y.: Harper & Row; c1959 , 1965. xiii, 392p. (Harper
   Torchbooks) (The Academy Library, TB1234K) (Researches
   in the social, cultural, and behavioural sciences).

1342. Simpson, Louis Aston Marantz (1923-). James Hogg;
a critical study. N.Y.: St. Martin's; 1962. vi, 222p.
(Biography and criticism, 11).

1343. Sington, Derrick. "Raymond Chandler on crime and
punishment." IN 20th Century v.165:no.987 (May 1959)
pp.502-504. ("Out and about" column).

1344. Siodmak, Robert. "Hoodlums; the myth." IN Films
and Filming v.5:no.9 (June 1959) pp.10, 35.

   cf. Wilson, R. "Hoodlums".

1345. Sipper, Ralph Bruno. "An interview with Ross
Macdonald." IN Mystery and Detection Annual; 1973.
(q.v.) pp.53-58.

1346. Sir Arthur Conan Doyle: centenary, 1859-1959; some
aspects of his works and personality. Ed. by Adrian M.
Conan Doyle and P. Weil-Nordon. London: John Murray; 1959.
137p., illus.

1347. Sisk, J. P. "Crime and criticism." IN Commonweal
v.64 (20 April 1956) pp.72-74.

1348. ... "Rejoinder (to G. Cashman)." IN Commonweal
v.64 (15 June 1956) pp.275.

   cf. Cashman, G. "Reply to ..."

1349. Sissman, L. E. "Raymond Chandler thirteen years
after." IN New Yorker v.48 (11 March 1972) pp.123-125.

1350. Sister, M. Carol. A. C. G. K. Chesterton; the
dynamic classicist. New Delhi: Motilal Banarsidass; 1971.
378p.

*   Skene Melvin, Ann Patricia Rothery (jnt. comp.).
SEE Skene Melvin, L. D. H. St C. Crime, detective,
espionage, mystery and thriller fiction and film.

*   Skene Melvin, David. SEE Skene Melvin, L. D. H. St C.

1351. Skene Melvin, Lewis David Hillis St Columb (1936-)
(jnt. comp.). Crime, detective, espionage, mystery, and
thriller fiction and film; a comprehensive bibliography of
critical writing through 1979. Comp. by David and Ann Skene
Melvin. Westport, Ct.: Greenwood Press; 1980. (A Greenwood
Press original reference book).

1352. ... "The secret eye: the spy in literature; the
evolution of espionage literature - a survey of the history
and development of the spy and espionage novel." IN
Pacific Quarterly v.3:no.1 (January 1978) pp.11-26.

*   ... (ed.). SEE also Pacific Quarterly.

1353. Škreb, Zdenko. "Die neue Gattung; Zur Geschichte und
Poetik des Detektivromans." IN Žmegač, V. (ed.). Der
wohltemperierte Mord. (q.v.) pp.35-95.

1354. Skvoreckỳ, Josef. Nápady čtenáře detektivek. Prague:
Ceskoslovenskỳ spisovatel; 1965. 163p., illus. (Otázky a
názory, sv.55).

1355. Sladen, Norman St. Barbe. The real Le Queux; the
official biography of William Le Queux. London: Nicholson &
Watson; 1938. xx, 239p., illus.

1356. Slopen, Beverley. "The most private eye; the man
behind Lew Archer - and the woman behind Ross Macdonald."
IN The Canadian (20 August 1977) pp.9-10.

1357. Slung, Michele B. (1947-). (ed.). Crime on her mind;
fifteen stories of female sleuths from the Victorian era to
the Forties: with a descriptive catalogue of over 100 women
detectives, 1861-1974. Ed. and with intro.'s by Michele B.
Slung. N.Y.: Pantheon/Random House; 1975. xxx, 381p. -
U.K. ed.: London: Michael Joseph; 1976. 381p.

     Contains: Introduction, pp.xv-xxx; and, The women
     detectives; a chronological survey, pp.357-357; as
     well as individual biographical introductions to
     each story.

1358. ... "Women in detective fiction." IN The mystery
story. (q.v.) pp.125-140.

1359. Smith, David R. "S. S. Van Dine at 20th Century-Fox."
IN Tuska, J. Philo Vance. (q.v.) pp.48-58.

1360. Smith, Edgar W. "Introduction." IN Derleth, August.
The return of Solar Pons. Sauk City, Wisc.: Mycroft & Moran;
1958. xiii, 261p. pp.vii-xiii.

1361. Smith, Grahame. Charles Dickens; 'Bleak House'.
London: Edw. Arnold; 1974. 64p. (Studies in English
Literature no.54).

1362. Smith, Janet Buchanan Adam. John Buchan; a biography.
London: Rupert Hart-Davis; 1965. 524p., illus.

1363. Smith, Myron J. Cloak-and-dagger bibliography; an
annotated guide to spy fiction, 1937-1975. Metuchen, N.J.:
Scarecrow Press; 1976. xi, 225p.

1364. Smith, Wilbur Jordan. "Mystery fiction in the
nineteenth century." IN Mystery and Detection Annual; 1973.
(q.v.) pp.193-206.

1365. Smuda, Manfred. "Variation und Innovation; Modelle
literarischer Möglichkeiten der Prosa in der Nachfolge
Edgar Allan Poes." IN Vogt, J. (comp.). Der Kriminalroman.
(q.v.) pp.33-63.

1366. Smyth, Frank (jnt. auth.). The detectives; crime and
detection in fact and fiction. By F. Smyth and Miles Ludwig.
Philadelphia: J. B. Lippincott; 1978. 191p., illus.

1367. Snelling, Oswald Frederick. Double 0 Seven: James
Bond; a report. London: Neville Spearman-Holland Press;
1964. 160p. - U.S. ed.: N.Y.: Signet; 1965.

   repr. AS 007 James Bond; a report. London: Panther;
   1965. 192p.

1368. Snodgrass, William DeWitt (1926-). "Crime for
punishment; the tenor of part one." IN Snodgrass, William
De Witt (1926-). In radical pursuit; critical essays and
lectures. N.Y.: Harper; 1975. xiii, 364p. pp.141-200.

1369. Spanos, William V. "The detective and the boundary;
some notes on the postmodern literary imagination." IN
Boundary 2 v.1:no.1 (Fall 1972) pp.147-168.

1370. Sparne, K. "Reply to "Cops" by P. French." (q.v.)
IN Sight and Sound v.43:no.3 (Summer 1974) pp.185-186.

1371. Spector, Robert D. "Irony as theme; Conrad's 'The
secret agent'." IN Nineteenth-century Fiction v.13:no.1
(1958) pp.69-71.

   repr. IN Watt, I. (ed.). Conrad; 'The secret agent'.
   (q.v.) pp.166-169.

1372. Speir, Jerry. Ross Macdonald. N.Y.: Frederick Ungar;
1978. x, 182p. (Recognitions - detective/suspense: science
fiction. No.1).

1373. Spender, Natasha. "His own long goodbye." IN
Gross, M. (ed.). The world of Raymond Chandler. (q.v.)
pp.127-158.

1374. Spiller, Robert E. "The world of the detective story."
IN The Times Literary Supplement [London] (17 September
1954).

repr. IN The Times Literary Supplement. American
writing today; its independence and vigour. London:
The Times; 1954. - U.S. ed.: ... Ed. by Allan Angoff.
N.Y.: New York University Press; 1957. 433p. - repr.:
Freeport, N.Y.: Books for Libraries Press; 1971. xx,
433p. (Essay index reprint series).

1375. Spoto, Donald (1941-). The art of Alfred Hitchcock;
fifty years of his motion pictures. N.Y.: Hopkinson & Blake;
1976. 523p., illus. (Cinema studies series).

1376. Sprague, Paul W. "A plea for mystery relief." IN
Atlantic Monthly v.151 (June 1933) pp.765-766.

1377. Squires, Paul Chatham. "Charles Dickens as
criminologist." IN Journal of Criminal Law v.29
(July 1938) pp.170-201.

1378. Stade, George. "I've been reading thrillers." IN
Columbia Forum: quarterly journal of fact and opinion
v.13:no.1 (Spring 1970) pp.34-37.

1379. Standish, Robert [pseud.]. The prince of storytellers;
the life of E. Phillips Oppenheim. London: P. Davies; 1957.
253p.

*   Starrett, Charles Vincent Emerson. SEE Starrett,
Vincent.

1380. Starrett, Vincent. "From Poe to Poirot." IN
Starrett, Vincent. Books alive, by Vincent Starrett; a
profane chronicle of literary endeavour and literary
misdemeanor, with an informal index by Christopher Morley.
N.Y.: Random House; 1940. 360p.

1381. ... "In re: Solar Pons." IN Derleth, August.
"In re: Sherlock Holmes"; the adventures of Solar Pons.
Sauk City, Wisc.: Mycroft & Moran; 1945. xvi, 238p.
pp.ix-xii.

1382. ... "Introduction." IN Starrett, Vincent. (ed.).
World's great spy stories. Cleveland: World; 1944. 445p.

1383. ... "Of detective literature [introduction]." IN
Fourteen great detective stories. Ed., with an intro. by
Vincent Starrett. N.Y.: Random House; [c1928]. xv, 400p.
(The Modern Library). pp.ix-xv.

1384. ... "Some Chinese detective stories." IN Starrett,
Vincent. Bookman's holiday; the private satisfactions of an
incurable collector. N.Y.: Random House; 1942. 312p.
pp.3-26.

*   ... (jnt. auth.). SEE also Boucher, A. Sincerely,
Tony/Faithfully, Vincent.

1385. Stauffer, Donald Barlow. "Poe as phrenologist; the
example of Monsieur Dupin." IN Veler, R. P. (ed.). Papers
on Poe. (q.v.) pp.113-125.

1386. Steel, Kurt. "A literary crisis; reply to Quintus
Quiz." IN Christian Century v.56:no.20 (17 May 1939)
p.646.

   cf. Quiz, Q. [pseud.]. "A resolution and a protest."

1387. Steeves, Harrison Ross. "A sober word on the detective
story." IN Harper's v.182 (April 1941) pp.485-492.

   repr. IN Haycraft, H. (ed.). The art of the mystery
   story. (q.v.) pp.513-526.

1388. Stein, Aaron Marc. "The mystery story in cultural
perspective." IN The mystery story. (q.v.) pp.29-59.

*   Stein, Aaron Marc. SEE also Bagby, George [pseud.].

*   Steinbrunner, Chris. (jnt. ed.). SEE Detectionary.

*   ... SEE also Encyclopedia of mystery and detection.

1389. Steinem, Gloria. "Introduction." IN Wonder Woman.
(q.v.) [unpag.].

1390. Stéphane, Roger. Le dossier Simenon. Paris: Robert
Laffont; 1961. 142p., illus.

1391. Stern, Madeleine Bettina. "Introductions." IN
respectively, Alcott, Louisa May (1832-1888). Behind a mask;
the unknown thrillers of Louisa May Alcott. Ed. and with an
intro. by Madeleine Stern. N.Y.: Wm. Morrow; 1975. xxxiii,
277p. pp.vii-xxxiii.

   AND

      ... Plots and counterplots; more unknown thrillers
of Louisa May Alcott. Ed. and with an intro. by Madeleine
Stern. N.Y.: Wm. Morrow; 1976. 315p.

1392. Stern, Philip Van Doren. "The case of the corpse in
the blind alley." IN Virginia Quarterly Review v.17:no.2
(Spring [April] 1941) pp.227-236.

   repr. IN Haycraft, H. (ed.). The art of the mystery
   story. (q.v.) pp.527-535.

1393. Stevens, George. "Death by misadventure; centennial
of the detective story." IN Saturday Review of Literature
v.24 (18 October 1941) pp.6-7.

1394. Stevenson, Burton Egbert. "Supreme moments in
detective fiction." IN Bookman [N.Y.] (March 1913)
pp.49-54.

1395. Stevenson, William Bruce (1906-) (comp.). Detective
fiction; a reader's guide. London: Published for the National
Book League by the Cambridge University Press; 1949. 19p.
(The Reader's guides).

   rev. ed.: Cambridge: Cambridge University Press for the
   National Book League; 1958. 32p. (Reader's Guide; third
   series).

1396. Stewart, Alfred Walter (1880-). Alias J. J. Connington.
London: Hollis & Carter; 1947. xi, 279p.

1397. Stewart, Douglas Galloway (1914-). "Graham Greene."
IN Stewart, Douglas Galloway (1914-). The ark of God;
studies in five modern novelists. London: Carey Kingsgate;
1961. 158p. (W. T. Whitley Lectures - 1960).

1398. Stewart, G. "'The long goodbye' from 'Chinatown'."
IN Film Quarterly v.28:no.2 (Winter 1974-1975) pp.25-32.

*   Stewart, John Innes Mackintosh (1906-). SEE   Innes,
Michael [pseud.].

1399. Stewart, Lawrence D. "The dust jackets of 'The great
Gatsby' and 'The long goodbye'." IN Mystery and Detection
Annual; 1973. (q.v.) pp.331-334.

1400. ... "Gertrude Stein and the vital dead." IN
Mystery and Detection Annual; 1972. (q.v.).

1401. ... "Paul Bowles; 'Up above the world' so high."
IN Mystery and Detection Annual; 1973. (q.v.) pp.245-270.

1402. Stewart, Seumas. "Adventure, detection and children's
books." IN Stewart, Seumas. Book collecting; a beginner's
guide. Wellington: A. H. & A. W. Reed; 1972. pp.117-134
(Chap.6).

*   Stock, Barbara (jnt. auth.). SEE Stock, Robert D.
(jnt. auth.).

1403. Stock, Robert J. (jnt. auth.). "The agents of evil
and justice in the novels of Dorothy L. Sayers." By R. D.
and Barbara Stock. IN As her whimsey took her. (q.v.)
pp.14-22.

1404. Stoddard, Roger E. "Some uncollected authors, XXXI;
Dashiell Hammett, 1894-1961." IN Book Collector [London]
v.11 (Spring 1962) pp.71-78.

1405. Stolper, Benjamin John Reeman. "Who done it?" IN
Scholastic v.33 (22 October 1938) pp.29-31.

1406. Stone, Edward. "Caleb Williams and Martin Faber; a
contrast." IN Modern Language Notes v.62 (November 1947)
pp.480-483.

1407. Stone, P. M. "Long life; to some detectives." IN
Bookman [London] v.84:no.501 (June 1933) pp.150-151.

   cf. Portugal, E. "Death to the detectives!"

*   ... SEE also Freeman, R. A. Thorndykiana.

1408. Stout, Rex. "These grapes need sugar." IN Vogue.
Vogue's first reader. N.Y.: J. Messner; 1942. xvi, 557p.
pp.421-425. - repr. - Garden City, N.Y.: Halcyon House;
1949.

U.K. ed. AS Vogue's fireside book. London: Hammond,
Hammond; 1944. 423p. pp.323-327. - repr. 1948.

1409. ... "Why Nero Wolfe likes orchids." By Archie
Goodwin [pseud.]. IN Life v.54 (19 April 1963) pp.108.

repr. In Corsage. (q.v.) pp.155-160.

1410. Stovall, Floyd. "Poe." IN Stovall, Floyd (ed.).
Eight American authors; a review of research and criticism.
N.Y.: Modern Language Association of America; 1956. xv,
418p. (Modern Language Association of America Revolving
Fund series no.19) - U.K. ed.: London: Oxford University
Press; 1956.

1411. Strachey, Evelyn John St. Loe (1901-1963). "The
golden age of English detection." IN The Saturday Review
of Literature v.19 (7 January 1939) pp.12-14.

*   Street, Cecil John Charles (1884-1964). SEE Rhode,
John [pseud.].

1412. Strong, L. A. G. (?-1958). "The crime Short story."
IN Gilbert, M. (ed.). Crime in good company. (q.v.)
pp.149-162.

1413. Strunsky, Simeon. "Cold chills of 1928." IN Forbes,
Anita Prentice (ed.). Essays for discussion. N.Y.: Harper;
1931. xi, 471p.

1414. ... "On the floor of the library." IN Strunsky,
Simeon. Sinbad and his friends. N.Y.: H. Holt; 1921. vii,
261p.

repr. IN Pence, Raymond Woodburn (1885-). (ed.).
Essays by present-day writers. N.Y.: Macmillan; 1924.
xiv, 360p. - sev. reprs.

repr. IN Leonard, Sterling Andrews (1881-1931) (comp.).
Introducing essays. Comp. by S. A. Leonard and completed
by Robert Cecil Pooley. Chicago: Scott Foresman; 1933.
295p.

1415. Sturak, John Thomas (1931-). "A foreword to 'Death in Hollywood'." IN Mystery and Detection Annual; 1973. (q.v.) pp.16-19.

1416. ... "Horace McCoy, Captain Shaw, and the 'Black Mask'." IN Mystery and Detection Annual; 1972. (q.v.)

1417. ... "Horace McCoy's objective lyricism." IN Madden, D. (ed.). Tough guy writers of the Thirties. (q.v.) pp.137-162.

1418. ... The life and writings of Horace McCoy, 1897-1955 ... Ph.D. thesis, University of California at Los Angeles, 1966. xviii, 590p./Ann Arbor, Mich.: University Microfilms; 1967. microfilm - 1 reel.

1419. Suerbaum, Ulrich. "Der gefesselte Detektivromans." IN Žmegač, V. (ed.). Der wohltemperierte Mord. (q.v.)

   also publ. IN Vogt, J. (comp.). Der Kriminalroman. (q.v.) pp.437-456.

1420. Sullerot, Evelyne. "Les hommes, les hommes ..." IN Lacassin, F. (jnt. ed.). Simenon. (q.v.) pp.89-98.

1421. Sullivan, John (1904-). G. K. Chesterton; a bibliography. London: University of London Press; 1958-1968. 2 vols. - U.S. ed.: N.Y.: Barnes & Noble; 1958-1969. 2 vols.

   Vol.1: G. K. Chesterton; a bibliography. 1958. 208p. - U.S. ed.: 1958. - repr.: Westport, Conn.: Greenwood Press; 1974, [c.1958].

   Vol.2: Chesterton continued; a bibliographical supplement. 1968. xiv, 120p. - U.S. ed.: ... : together with some uncollected prose and verse. 1969, [c1968]. xiv, 120p.

1422. ... G. K. Chesterton; a centenary appraisal. London: Paul Elek; 1974. xi, 243p., illus. - U.S. ed.: N.Y.: Barnes & Noble; 1974. xi, 243p., illus.

1423. ... G. K. Chesterton, 1874-1974; an exhibition of books, manuscripts, drawings, and other material relating to G. K. Chesterton [held at the National Book League], 14-31 May, 1974. London: National Book League; 1974. 27p.

1424. Summers, Alphonsus Joseph-Mary Augustus Montague
(1880-1948). A Gothic bibliography. London: Fortune Press;
1940. xx, 621p., illus. - U.S. ed.: N.Y.: Russell &
Russell; 1964. xx, 620p.

*   Summers, Montague. SEE Summers, A. J.-M. A. M.

1425. The Sunday Times (London). The hundred best crime
stories. Comp. by Julian Symons. London: The Sunday Times;
1959. 21p.

1426. Swann, Thomas Burnett (1928-). A. A. Milne. N.Y.:
Twayne; 1971. 153p. (Twayne's English Authors series
no.113).

1427. Swiggett, Howard. "Introduction." IN Buchan, John
(1875-1940). Mountain meadow. Boston: Houghton Mifflin;
1941. , 277p. pp.v-xlix.

   N.B.: 'Mountain meadow' is the U.S. title of Buchan's
   'Sick Heart River'; Swiggett's introduction appears
   only in this edition.

1428. Swinburne, Algernon Charles (1837-1909). "Wilkie
Collins." IN Swinburne, Algernon Charles (1837-1909).
Studies in prose and poetry. London: Chatto & Windus;
1894. 298p.

1429. Swinnerton, Frank Arthur (1884-). "A postwar
symptom." IN Swinnerton, Frank Arthur (1884-). The
Georgian literary scene; a panorama. London: Hutchinson;
1935. x, 548p. - U.S. ed. AS The Georgian scene; a
literary panorama. N.Y.: Farrar & Rinehart; 1934. x,
522p.

1430. Sykes, Marjorie. "The imaginative world of John
Buchan." IN Library Review v.25:no.3/4 (Autumn/Winter
1975/1976) pp.104-106.

1431. Symons, Julian (1912-). "An aesthete discovers the
pulps." IN Gross, M. (ed.). The world of Raymond Chandler.
(q.v.). pp.19-29.

1432.   ... Bloody murder; from the detective story to the
crime novel: a history. London: Faber and Faber; 1972. 254p.

   U.S. ed. AS Mortal consequences; a history - from the
   detective story to the crime novel. N.Y.: Harper & Row;
   1972. x, 269p. - repr. pap.: N.Y.: Schocken Books;
   1973.

1433.   ... "The crime novel; the face in the mirror." IN
Gilbert, M. (ed.). Crime in good company. (q.v.) pp.126-133.

1434.   ... "Dashiell Hammett; the onlie begetter." IN
Crime writers. (q.v.) pp.80-93.

1435.   ... The detective story in Britain. London:
Published for the British Council and the National Book
League by Longmans, Green; 1962. 48p., illus. (British
Book News Bibliographical series of supplements on writers
and their work, no.145).

1436.   ... "The great detective." IN The Saturday Book: 14.
London: Hutchinson; 1954. 288p., illus. pp.47-53.

1437.   ... "Introduction." IN Bardin, John Franklin.
The John Franklin Bardin omnibus. With an introd. by Julian
Symons. Harmondsworth, Eng./N.Y.: Penguin; 1976. 601p.

1438.   ... "Marlowe's victim." IN Times Literary Supplement
no.3,134 (23 March 1962) p.200.

   repr. IN Symons, Julian (1912-). Critical occasions.
   London: Hamish Hamilton; 1966. 213p. pp.174-180.

1439.   ... "The mistress of complication." IN Agatha
Christie. (q.v.) pp.25-38.

1440.   ... "The new wave in crime; crime novels and detective
stories." IN The London Magazine n.s.v.1:no.2 (May 1961)
pp.76-81.

1441.   ... "Progress of a crime writer." IN Mystery and
Detection Annual; 1973. (q.v.) pp.238-243.

*   ... (comp.). SEE also The Sunday Times (London).

T

1442. Tallack, Douglas G. "William Faulkner and the tradition of tough-guy fiction." IN Dimensions of detective fiction. (q.v.) pp.247-264.

1443. Tanner, William [pseud.]. The book of Bond; or, Every man his own 007. By Lt.-Col. William ("Bill") Tanner. London: Jonathan Cape; 1965. 111p., illus. - repr.: London: Pan Books; 1966. [117]p., illus.

1444. Tarantino, M. "Movement as metaphor; 'The long goodbye'." IN Sight and Sound v.44 (Spring 1975) pp.98-102.

1445. Taylor, Frank Sherwood. "The crux of a murder; disposal of the body." IN Spectator no.5,676 (9 April 1937) pp.658-659.

   repr. AS "Corpus delicti; secret disposal of the body." IN Living Age v.352 (July 1937) pp.445-448.

   repr. (orig. title) IN Haycraft H. (ed.). The art of the mystery story. (q.v.) pp.447-450.

1446. Taylor, Isabelle. "Mystery midwife; the crime editor's job." IN Haycraft, H. (ed.). The art of the mystery story. (q.v.) pp.292-297.

1447. Taylor, Robert Lewis. "Two authors in an attic; [John Dickson Carr]." IN New Yorker v.27 (8 and 15 September 1951) pp.39-44, 47-48, and pp.36-40, 43-44, 46, 48.

*   Taylor, T. Allan. (ed.). SEE Parish, J. R. (jnt.
auth.). The great spy pictures.

*   Taylor, Wendell Hertig (1905-). (jnt. auth.). SEE
Barzun, J. A book of prefaces.

*   ... (jnt. auth.). SEE also Barzun, J. A catalogue
of crime.

1448. Texas. University. Humanities Research Center.
An exhibition on the occasion of the opening of the Ellery
Queen collection. Austin, Texas: Research Center, University
of Texas; 1959. 27p., illus.

1449. Thalmann, M. "E. T. A. Hoffmans "Fraulein von
Scuderi"." IN MDU v.41 (1949) pp.107-116.

1450. Thiede, Karl. "S. S. Van Dine filmography." IN
Tuska, J. (ed.). Philo Vance. (q.v.) pp.59-62.

1451. Thomas, Gilbert Oliver (1891-). How to enjoy
detective fiction. London: Rockliff; 1947. [vi], 108p.
(The How to enjoy series).

1452. Thompson, Don (jnt. ed.). The comic-book book.
Ed. by D. Thompson and Dick Lupoff. New Rochelle, N.Y.:
Arlington House; 1973. 360p., illus.

1453. Thompson, G. R. "Is Poe's 'A tale of the Ragged
Mountains' a hoax?" IN Studies in Short Fiction v.6:no.4
(Summer 1969) pp.454-460.

1454. Thompson, George J. The problem of moral vision in
Dashiell Hammett's detective novels ... Ph.D. dissertation,
University of Connecticut, 1972. 222p.

   repr. IN Armchair Detective vol.6 (1973) - vol.7
   (1974).

1455. Thomson, Henry Douglas. "Detective films." IN
Sight and Sound v.4:no.13 (Spring 1935) pp.10-11.

1456.   ...   Masters of mystery; a study of the detective
story. London: Collins; 1931. 288p. - repr. - Folcroft,
Pa.: Folcroft Library Editions; [1931], 1973. 288p. -
repr. - N.Y.: Dover; 1978. 288p.

    Note: Selection from the opening chapter repr. AS
    "Masters of mystery." IN Haycraft, H. (ed.). The
    art of the mystery story. (q.v.) pp.128-145.

1457. Thoorens, Leon. [Qui êtes-vous,] Georges Simenon?
Verviers, Belgium: Éditions Gérard; 1959. 159p., illus.
(Coll. Marabout-Flesh, 21).

1458. Thurber, James (1894-). "The wings of Henry James."
IN Thurber, James (1894-). Lanterns and lances. N.Y.:
Harper; 1961. 215p. - repr.: N.Y.: Time, Inc.; 1962.
179p.

1459. The Times Literary Supplement. Crime, detection, and
society; [special number]. no.3095 (23 June 1961) pp.i-xii.

1460. ... Detective fiction; [special number]. (25 February
1955).

*   The Times, London. Literary Supplement. SEE The
Times Literary Supplement.

1461. Tompkins, Joyce Marjorie Sanxter. The popular novel
in England, 1770-1800. London: Constable; 1932. - repr.:
London: Methuen; 1962. ix, 389p. - repr.: same publ.;
1969. ix, 389p. - U.S. ed.: Lincoln, Neb.: University
of Nebraska Press; 1961. (A Bison book) - repr.: Westport,
Conn.: Greenwood Press; 1976.

1462. "Too many corpses in detective fiction." IN Literary
Digest v.112 (27 February 1932) p.18.

*   Torge, Martha (jnt. comp.). SEE Chertok, Harvey.

1463. Tourteau, Jean-Jacques. D'Arsène Lupin à San-Antonio;
le roman policier français de 1900 à 1970. Paris: Mame;
1970. 326p.

1464. Trahair, Richard C. S. "A contribution to the
psychoanalytic study of the modern hero; the case of James
Bond." IN Australian and New Zealand Journal of Psychiatry
(September 1974).

   repr. IN Festschrift Jean Martin. Bundoora, Vic.:
La Trobe University [priv. pr.]; 1974.

   rev. ed., exp. pr. as separate - Bundoora, Vic.: Dept.
of Sociology, School of Social Sciences, La Trobe
University; 1976. 39p. (La Trobe Sociology Papers
No.28).

*   Traz, Georges de (1881-). SEE de Traz, Georges
(1881-).

*   Treat, Lawrence (ed.). SEE Mystery Writers of
America. The mystery writer's handbook. 1975.

1465. Trengove, Alan. "In the tracks of Detective-Inspector
"Bony"." IN The Reader's Digest; [New Zealand (i.e.
Australian) edition]. [Surry Hills, N.S.W.: Reader's
Digest Services Pty. Limited] v.107:no.646 (February 1976)
pp.32-37.

1466. Treves, Sir Frederick, bart. The country of 'The Ring
and the Book'. London: Cassell; 1913. xv, 303p., illus.

*   Trevor, Elleston. SEE Hall, Adam [pseud.].

1467. Trewin, J. C. "A midas gift to the theatre." IN
Agatha Christie. (q.v.) pp.131-154.

1468. Triviallitteratur; Aufsätze herausgegeben von Gerhard
Schmidt-Henkel u.a.m. Berlin: [n.publ.]; 1964.

   Not verified. Cited in: la, Cour, T. 'The murder book'
   (q.v.), p.178.

1469. Truffaut, François. Le cinema selon Hitchcock. By
F. Truffaut with the collaboration of Helen G. Scott. Paris:
Laffont; 1966. 256p., illus. - U.S. (first English) ed.:
N.Y.: Simon & Schuster; 1967. 256p., illus. - U.K. ed.:
London: Secker & Warburg; 1968. 280p., illus. - repr.:
London: Pantheon; 1969. 423p., illus.

1470. Tschimmel, Ira. Kriminalroman und Gesellschaftsdarstellung; Eine vergleichende Untersuchung zu Werken von
Christie, Simenon, Dürrenmatt, Capote. Bonn: Bouvier; 1979.
276p. (Stud. z. Germanistik Anglistik u. Komparat. 69).

1471. Tsuzuki, Michio (1929-). Shitai o buji ni kesu made.
Tokyo: Shōbunsha; 1973. 357p.

1472. Tullberg, Sigurd. O och A; handledning för
deckarvänner: Förteckning över detektivromaner på svenska
språket utgivna 1901-1954 med titel- och pseudonymregister.
Stockholm: Bibliotekens bokförmedling; 1954. 95p.

*   Turgeon, Charlotte Snyder (1912-). (jnt. auth.).
SEE   Larmoth, Jeanine.

1473. Turner, Arthur Campbell. Mr. Buchan, writer; a life
of the first Lord Tweedsmuir. London: SCM Press; 1949.
114p. (The Torch biographies).

1474. Turner, Darwin T.   "The Rocky Steele novels of
John B. West." IN The Armchair Detective v.6:no.4
(August 1973)   pp.226-231.

   repr. IN Dimensions of detective fiction. (q.v.)
   pp.140-148.

1475. Turner, Ernest Sackville (1909-). Boys will be boys;
the story of Sweeney Todd, Deadwood Dick, Sexton Blake, Billy
Bunter, Dick Barton, et al. London: Michael Joseph; 1948.
269p., illus.   - rev. ed.: London: Michael Joseph; 1975.
280p.

1476. Turner, Robert. "The not so literary digests."   IN
Xenophile (q.v.) No.38 (March-April 1978)   pp.19.

1477. Tuska, Jon. The detective in Hollywood. Garden City,
N.Y.: Doubleday; 1978. xxiv, 436p., illus.

1478. ... (et al.). Philo Vance; the life and times of
S. S. Van Dine. Bowling Green, Ohio: Bowling Green University
Popular Press; 1971, [c1969, 1970]. 63p.

   - Title essay orig. appeared IN Views & Reviews
   Magazine (1969).

1479. Tuska, Jon. "Rex Stout and the detective story." IN
Views and Reviews (Spring 1974) pp.28-35.

1480. Tutunjian, Jerry. "A conversation with Ross Macdonald."
IN Tamarack Review No.62 (1st quarter, 1974) pp.67-85.

*   Tweedsmuir, John Buchan, 1st baron (1875-1940). SEE
Buchan, John.

1481. Tyler, R. "Curtains for Poirot." IN Saturday Review
v.3 (4 October 1975) pp.24ff.

1482. Tynan, Kathleen. Agatha; [a novel of mystery].
N.Y.: Ballantine Books; 1978. [vi], 247p.

1483. Tynan, Kenneth. "Cagney and the Mob." IN Sight
and Sound v.20:no.1 (May 1951) pp.12-16.

U

1484. Uekusa, Jin'ichi (1908-). Amefuri dakara misuterī de mo benkyōshiyō. Tokyo: Shōbunsha; 1972. 437, 8p.

1485. Ulanov, Barry. "The mystery story." IN Ulanov, Barry. The two worlds of American art; the private and the popular. N.Y.: Macmillan; 1965. 528p. pp.284-297.

1486. "The ultimate source of Sherlock Holmes." IN Bookman v.27 (April 1908) pp.113-114.

  - attrib. by De Waal (q.v.) to Arthur Bartlett Maurice.

*   University of California, Los Angeles. SEE California. University. University at Los Angeles.

*   University of California, San Diego. SEE California. University. University at San Diego.

*   University of Texas. SEE Texas. University.

1487. "Upright-men and walking morts; low life under Elizabeth." IN Times Literary Supplement. TLS; essays and reviews from the 'Times Literary Supplement', 1965 [vol.4]. London: Oxford University Press, 1966. ix, 260p.

1488. Usborne, Richard. Clubland heroes; a nostalgic study of some recurrent characters in the romantic fiction of Dornford Yates, John Buchan, and Sapper. London: Constable; 1953. ix, 217p. - rev. ed. London: Barrie & Jenkins; 1974. 186p.

V

1489. Valentine, B. B. "The original of Hortense and the trial of Marcia [sic] Manning for murder." IN _Dickensian_ v.19 (January 1923) pp.21-22.

1490. Van Ash, Cay (jnt. auth.). _Master of villainy; a biography of Sax Rohmer._ By C. Van Ash and Elizabeth Sax Rohmer. Ed. with foreword, notes and bibliography by Robert E. Briney. Bowling Green, Ohio: Bowling Green University Popular Press; 1972. ix, 312p.

*   Van Dine, S. S. [pseud.]. SEE Wright, Willard Huntington.

1491. van Gulik, Robert Hans (1910-1968). "[Introduction]." IN Wu tsê t'ien ssŭ ta ch'i an. English selections. _Dee goong an; Three murder cases solved by Judge Dee, an old Chinese detective novel translated from the original Chinese with an introd. and notes by R. H. van Gulik._ Tokyo: [n.publ.]; 1949. xxiii, 237p., illus.   - repr.: N.Y.: Arno Press; 1976. (Literature of mystery and detection).

1492. ... "Introductions and postscripts in the author's Judge Dee series of novels." - Var. publ.; var. d.

1493. ... "Judge Dee chronology." IN van Gulik, Robert Hans (1910-1968). _Judge Dee at work; eight Chinese detective stories._ London: Heinemann; 1967. 178p. pp.[175-178].

*   van Gulik, Robert Hans (1910-1968). SEE also
Bibliography of Dr. R. H. van Gulik.

*   Van Hecke, B. C. (jnt. auth.). SEE Lee, R. (jnt.
auth.).

1494. Van Meter, Jan R. "Sophocles and the rest of the boys
in the pulps; myth and the detective novel." IN Dimensions
of detective fiction. (q.v.) pp.12-21.

1495. Vann, Jerry Don. Graham Greene; a checklist of
criticism. Kent, Ohio: Kent State University Press; 1970.
vii, 69p. (Serif series: bibliographies and checklists;
no.14).

1496. Van Selms, A. "Aristotle en die speurverhaal." IN
Standpunte v.41:no.1 (October 1960) pp.45-59.

1497. Veler, Richard P. (ed.). Papers on Poe; essays in
honor of John Ward Ostrom. Springfield, Ohio: Chantry Music
Press; 1972. 234p.

*   Velie, Alan R. (1937-). (jnt. comp.). SEE
Marshburn, J. H. Blood and knavery.

1498. Véry, Pierre. "Murder on Parnassus; the literature
of the future." IN Marianne [Paris].

   repr. (trans.) IN Living Age v.348 (April 1935)
   pp.163-166.

   repr. IN Haycraft, H. (ed.). The art of the mystery
   story. (q.v.) pp.355-359.

1499. Ves Losada, Alfredo E. En torno al género policial.
La Plata: n.publ. ; 1956, [i.e. 1957]. 96p. (Provincia de
Buenos Aires. Ediciones del Ministerio de Educación. Serie
de ensayos).

1500. Vesselo, Arthur. "Crime over the world." IN Sight
and Sound v.6:no.23 (Autumn 1937) pp.135-137.

1501. Vickers, Roy. "Crime on the stage; the criminological
illusion." IN Gilbert, M. (ed.). Crime in good company.
(q.v.) pp.178-191.

*   Vidales, Salvador Ortiz. SEE   Ortiz Vidales, S.

1502. Vidocq, Francois Eugene (1775-1857). Mémoires; chef
de la police de sûreté jusqu'en 1827. Paris: Tenon; 1828-1829.
4 vols. - U.K. (first English) ed.: London: Hunt and Clarke;
1828. - U.S. ed.: Philadelphia: E. L. Carey & A. Hart;
1834. - Var. other ed's. and reprints.

1503. Vigniel, D. Sherlock Holmes; [Thesis for the Diploma
of Advanced Studies of the University of Paris, 1959 ...
unpublished]. 81p.

*   Viking Press, Inc., New York. SEE   Barzun, J.
A birthday tribute to Rex Stout.

1504. Visser, Ab (1913-). Kaïn sloeg Abel; een handleiding
voor de detective-lezer. Utrecht: Bruna; 1963. 155p.
(Zwarte beertjes, 687).

1505. ... Onder de gordel, Erotiek en geweld in de
misdaadroman. Utrecht: A. W. Bruna; 1968. 152p., illus.
(Bruna boeken).

1506. Vogt, Jochen (comp.). Der Kriminalroman; zur Theorie
und Geschichte einer Gattung. Munich: W. Fink; 1971. 2 vol.
(595p.) (Uni-Taschenbücher, 81-82. Literaturwissenschaft).

1507. Voorhees, Richard J. "Flashman and Richard Hannay."
IN Dalhousie Review v.53 (1973) pp.113-120.

1508. Vries, Paulus Henri de. Poe and after; the detective-
story investigated. Amsterdam: Drukkerij Bakker; 1956. 172p.

W

1509. Wagner, Geoffrey. Parade of pleasure; a study of popular iconography in the USA. London: Derek Verschoyle; 1954. 192p., illus.

1510. Waite, John Barker. "If judges wrote detective stories." IN Scribner's Magazine v.95 (April 1934) pp.275-277.

   cf. Denbie, R. "Reply to ..."

1511. ... (jnt. auth.). "The lawyer looks at detective fiction." By J. Waite and Miles W. Kimball. IN Bookman [N.Y.] v.69 (August 1929) pp.616-621.

   repr., abridged, with reply by S. S. Van Dine [pseud.] IN Literary Digest v.103:no.4(whole no.2,062) (26 October 1929) pp.47-49.

   repr. IN Haycraft, H. (ed.). The art of the mystery story. (q.v.) pp.436-446.

1512. Walker, Hugh (1855-1939). The literature of the Victorian era. London: Cambridge University Press; 1910. viii, 1067p. - repr.: New Delhi: S. Chand; 1964. 756p.

*   Walker, Kathrine Sorley (jnt. ed.). SEE Chandler, R. Raymond Chandler speaking.

1513. Wallace, Edgar (1875-1932). "The mystery story today and yesterday." IN Bookman [London] v.77:no.459 (December 1929) pp.175-177.

1514. Wallace, Irving (1916-). The fabulous originals;
lives of extraordinary people who inspired memorable
characters in fiction. N.Y.: Knopf; 1955. 316p. -
U.K. ed.: London: Longmans Green; 1956. xv, 296p.

   Of peripheral interest: contains background material
   on the real people behind the fictional characters of
   Sherlock Holmes, Marie Rogêt, and Collins's Sgt Cuff.

1515. Wallace, Penelope. "A man and his books." IN
Mystery and Detection Annual; 1972. (q.v.) pp.93-97.

*   Wallace, Richard Horatio Edgar (1875-1932). SEE
Wallace, Edgar.

1516. Wallace, Violet King. Edgar Wallace. By his wife,
in collaboration with Haydon Talbot. London: Hutchinson;
1932. 217p.

1517. Walpole, Sir Hugh Seymour. ["'The secret agent'."]
IN Keating, George T. (1892-). A Conrad memorial library;
the collection of George T. Keating. N.Y.: Doubleday, Doran;
1929. xvi, 448p., illus. pp.159-163.

   repr. IN Watt, I. (ed.). Conrad; 'The secret agent'.
   (q.v.) pp.113-117.

1518. Walsh, John Evangelist (1927-). Poe the detective;
the curious circumstances behind the mystery of Marie Rogêt.
New Brunswick, N.J.: Rutgers University Press; 1967. 154p.

1519. Walter, Elizabeth. "The case of the escalating sales."
IN Agatha Christie. (q.v.) pp.11-24.

*   Ward, David. SEE Ormerod, D.

1520. Ward, Richard Heron. William Somerset Maugham.
London: Geoffrey Bles; 1937. 208p.

1521. Warner, Alan. "Gangster heroes." IN Films and
Filming v.18:no.2 (November 1971) pp.16-25, illus.
(Part 2 of "Yesterdays Hollywood").

1522. Warshow, Robert (1917-1955). "The gangster as tragic
hero." IN Partisan Review v.15 (February 1948) pp.240-244.

   repr. IN Warshow, Robert (1917-1955). The immediate
experience; movies, comics, theatre, and other aspects
of popular culture. Garden City, N.Y.: Doubleday; 1962.
282p. pp.127-133. - repr., same publ., 1964. 212p.
(Anchor Books) - repr., N.Y.: Atheneum; 1970, 1975.
282p. pp.127-133.

   repr. IN Endleman, Shalom (comp.). Violence in the
streets. Chicago: Quadrangle Books; 1968. 471p.
pp.161-166.

   repr. IN Deer, Irving (jnt. ed.). The popular arts;
a critical reader. Ed. by I. and Harriet A. Deer.
N.Y.: Scribner; 1967. xi, 356p. pp.155-161.

1523. Wasiolek, E. "Raskolnikov's motives; love and murder."
IN American Imago v.31 (Fall 1974) pp.252-269.

1524. Watson, Colin. "Mayhem Parva and wicked Belgravia."
IN Crime writers (q.v.) pp.48-63.

1525. ... The message of Mayhem Parva. IN Agatha Christie.
(q.v.) pp.95-110.

1526. ... Snobbery with violence; crime stories and their
audience. London: Eyre & Spottiswoode; 1971. 256p., illus.
- U.S. ed.: N.Y.: St. Martin's Press; 1972. 256p.

1527. Watt, Ian Pierre (ed.). Conrad: 'The secret agent';
a casebook. London: Macmillan; 1973. 258p. (Casebook
series).

1528. ... "The political and social background of 'The
secret agent'." IN Watt, I. (ed.). Conrad: 'The secret
agent'. (q.v.) pp.229-251.

1529. Waugh, Coulton (1896-). The comics. N.Y.: Macmillan;
1947. xiii, 360p., illus.

1530. Waugh, Evelyn (1903-1966). The life of the Right
Reverend Ronald Knox. London: Chapman & Hall; 1959.

   U.S. ed. AS Monsignor Ronald Knox, fellow of Trinity
College, Oxford, and Protonotary Apostolic to His Holiness
Pope Pius XII. Boston: Little Brown; 1959. 357p.

1531. Waugh, Hillary. "Fred Fellows." IN Penzler, O. M.
The great detectives. (q.v.) pp.99-108.

1532. ... "The mystery versus the novel." IN The mystery
story. (q.v.) pp.61-80.

1533. ... "The police procedural." IN The mystery story.
(q.v.) pp.163-187.

1534. Weaver, William. "Music and mystery." IN Agatha
Christie. (q.v.) pp.183-192.

  repr. IN T.L.S.; The Times Literary Supplement
  No.3,919 (Friday 22 April 1977) p.493.

1535. Weibel, Kay. "Mickey Spillane as a fifties phenomenon."
IN Dimensions of detective fiction. (q.v.) pp.114-123.

*   Weil-Nordon, P. SEE Nordon, Pierre.

1536. Weinberg, Robert (jnt. auth.). The hero pulp index.
By R. Weinberg and Lohr McKinstry. 2d printing. Chicago:
Robert Weinberg; [1971], 1973. [iv], 48p., illus.

1537. ... (ed.). The man behind Doc Savage; a tribute to
Lester Dent. Oak Lawn, Ill.: Robert Weinberg; 1974.

1538. Welcome, John. "Introduction." IN Best secret
service stories 2. Ed. and with an intro. by John Welcome.
London: Faber and Faber, 1965. 223p. pp.9-18.

1539. Wells, Carolyn (1869-1942). "The detective story's
place in literature." IN World Review v.7 (21 January 1929)
p.247.

1540. ... The technique of the mystery story. Springfield,
Mass.: The Home Correspondence School; 1913. 336p. (The
Writer's Library) - rev. ed.: same publ.; 1929. 435p. -
repr. (1913 [orig.] ed.): Folcroft, Pa.: Folcroft Library
Editions; 1973, [c1913]. xiv, 336p.

1541. Wells, Walter (1937-). "Grey Knight in the Great Wrong Place." IN Wells, Walter (1937-). Tycoons and locusts; a regional look at Hollywood fiction of the 1930s. Carbondale, Illinois: Southern Illinois University Press/ London: Feffer & Simons; 1973. xvi, 139p. (Crosscurrents/ Modern critiques) pp.71-85.

1542. ... "The Postman and the Marathon." IN Wells, Walter (1937-). Tycoons and locusts; a regional look at Hollywood fiction of the 1930s. Carbondale, Illinois: Southern Illinois University Press/London: Feffer & Simons; 1973. xvi, 139p. (Crosscurrents/Modern critiques) pp.14-35.

1543. Wertham, Frederic. A sign for Cain; an exploration of human violence. N.Y.: Macmillan; 1966. 391p. - repr. - N.Y.: Warner Books; 1973. - U.K. ed. - London: R. Hale; 1968. 391p.

1544. West, Nathaniel. "Some notes on violence." IN Contact v.1:no.3 (1932) pp.132-133.

1545. Wexman, Virginia. " ... Ph.D. dissertation on the hard-boiled detective film ..." [in prep.]

  Not verified. Cited in: Cawelti, J. G. 'Adventure, mystery, and romance'. (q.v.), p.327.

*   Whanel, Paddy (jnt. auth.). SEE Hall, S. (jnt. auth.).

1546. Wheatley, Dennis. The time has come -: the memories of Dennis Wheatley. London: Hutchinson; 1977-   vols.

  Vol.1: The young man said; 1897-1914. 1977. 255p., illus.

1547. Whipple, Leon. "Nirvana for two dollars." IN Survey v.62 (1 May 1929) pp.191-192.

1548. White, Trentwell Mason (1901-). "The detective story." IN White, Trentwell Mason (1901-). How to write for a living. N.Y.: Reynal & Hitchcock; 1937. xvii, 327p.

1549. White, William. "About Dashiell." and "Hammett; postscript." Both IN Armchair Detective v.3 (1970) pp.171-172, and p.175, respectively.

1550. ... "Bramah; a footnote to Carrados." IN Mystery
Lover's Newsletter v.2 (April 1969) pp.19-20.

*   White, William Anthony Parker (1911-1968). SEE
Boucher, Anthony [pseud.].

1551. Whitehall, Richard. "Crime, Inc.; a three-part dossier
on the American gangster film." IN Films and Filming
v.10:no's.4,5,6 (January through March 1964) pp.7-12,
17-22, 39-44, respectively.

1552. Whitehall, Richard. "Some thoughts on fifties gangster
films." IN The Velvet Light Trap No.11 (Winter 1974)
pp.17-19.

1553. Whitehead, J. "'Whodunit' and Somerset Maugham."
IN Notes and Queries v.21 (October 1974) pp.370.

1554. Whiteley, J. Stuart. "Simenon; the shadow and the
self: an interview with Georges Simenon." IN Mystery and
Detection Annual; 1973. (q.v.) pp.221-236.

1555. Whiteside, Thomas. "Murder a minute." IN Collier's
v.123:no.10 (5 February 1949) pp.28-29ff.

1556. Whitley, John S. F. Scott Fitzgerald; 'The great
Gatsby'. London: Edw. Arnold; 1976. 64p. (Studies in
English Literature no.60).

1557. Whitley, John. "Raymond Chandler and the traditions."
IN The London Review v.2 (1967) pp.34-36.

1558. Whitney, Phyllis A. "Gothic mysteries." IN The
mystery story. (q.v.) pp.223-232.

1559. Whitt, J. F. 'The Strand Magazine' 1891-1950; a
selective checklist: listing all material relating to Arthur
Conan Doyle, all stories by P. G. Wodehouse, and a selection
of detective, mystery, or fantasy fiction. London:
J. F. Whitt; 1979. 48p.

1560. "Who done it as Dickens did it." IN Collier's v.131
(14 March 1953) p.74.

*   Wibberley, Leonard. SEE Holton, Leonard [pseud.].

*   Wight, Harley Franklin (1891-). SEE Murder manual.

1561. Wilkinson, Burke (1913-). The zeal of the convert;
the life of Erskine Childers. Washington, D.C.: R. B. Luce
Co.; 1976. viii, 256p., illus.

1562. Williams, George Valentine (1883-). "Detective
fiction." IN Bookman [N.Y.] v.67 (July 1928) pp.521-524.

1563. ... "The detective in fiction." IN Fortnightly
Review [London] v.134 (September 1930) pp.381-392.

1564. ... "Gaboriau; father of the detective novel."
IN National Review [London] v.82 (December 1923)
p.611-622.

1565. ... "On crime fiction." IN Warren, Frank Dale
(1897-). (ed.). What is a book?: Thoughts about writing
by Frances Lester Warner, Ellen Glasgow, Rafael Sabatini,
et al. Ed. by Dale Warren. Boston: Houghton, Mifflin;
1935. 298p. - U.K. ed.: London: Allen & Unwin; 1936.

1566. ... "Putting the shock into shockers." IN Bookman
[N.Y.] v.66 (November 1927) pp.270-272.

1567. Williams, H. L. "The germ of the detective novel."
IN Book-Buyer v.21 (November 1900) pp.268-274.

*   Williams, J. E. Hodder. SEE Hodder Williams, J. E.

*   Williams, Valentine. SEE Williams, George V.

1568. Williamson, J. N. A critical history and analysis of
the 'whodunit'. Indianapolis, Ind.: [n.publ.]; 1951. 26p.

   Not verified. Cited in: la Cour, T. 'The murder book'.
   (q.v.), p.178.

1569. Wilson, Colin (1931-). Murder trilogy. 1961-1972.
3 vols.

　Vol.1: An encyclopedia of murder. By C. Wilson and
　Patricia Pitman. London: A. Barker; 1961. 576p.,
　illus. - U.S. ed. - N.Y.: Putnam; 1962.

　Vol.2: A casebook of murder; [a compelling study of the
　world's most macabre murder cases]. London: Leslie
　Frewin; 1969. 288p. - U.S. ed. - N.Y.: Cowles; 1970.
　288p. - repr. - London: Mayflower Books; 1971. 253p.
　(A Mayflower Paperback).

　Vol.3: Order of assassins; the psychology of murder.
　London: Rupert Hart-Davis; 1972. [12], 242p. - repr. -
　London: Panther Books; 1975. 266p.

1570. Wilson, Edmund G. (1895-). "The boys in the back
room; James M. Cain and John O'Hara." IN New Republic
v.108 (11 November 1940) pp.665-666.

　repr., with commentary on other writers added IN
　Wilson, Edmund G. (1895-). Classics and commercials;
　a literary chronicle of the Forties. N.Y.: Farrar,
　Straus; 1950, repr. 1958. x, 534p. pp.19-56. -
　repr. - N.Y.: Vintage Books; 1962. - U.K. ed. -
　London: W. H. Allen; 1951. 534p.

1571. ... "Mr. Holmes, they were the footprints of a
gigantic hound!" IN New Yorker v.21 (17 February 1945)
pp.73-78.

　repr. IN Wilson, E. G. Classics and commercials
　(v. supra) pp.266-274.

　repr. IN Wilson, Edmund G. (1895-). A literary
　chronicle, 1920-1950; selections from 'Classics and
　commercials' and 'The shores of light'. Garden City,
　N.Y.: Doubleday; 1956. 442p. (Anchor books, A85).

1572. ... "Who cares who killed Roger Ackroyd?; a second
report on detective fiction." IN New Yorker v.20
(20 January 1945) pp.52-54, 57-58.

　- for "first report", v. infra.

　repr. IN Wilson, E. G. Classics and commercials.
　(v. supra) pp.257-265.

　repr. IN Wilson, E. G. A literary chronicle.
　(v. supra) pp.338-345.

repr. IN Haycraft, H. (ed.). The art of the mystery
story. (q.v.) pp.390-397.

repr. IN Rosenberg, Bernard (1923-) (jnt. ed.).
Mass culture; the popular arts in America. Ed. by
B. Rosenberg and David Manning-White. N.Y.: Free
Press of Glencoe; 1957, repr. pap. 1964. x, 561p.
pp.149-153.

repr. in German trans. AS "Wen interessiert es
schon wer Roger Ackroyd ermordete?" IN Der
Detektiverzählung auf der Spur. (q.v.)

1573. ... "Why do people read detective stories?; [a first
report on detective fiction]." IN New Yorker v.20
(14 October 1944) pp.73-74, 76.

- for "second report", v. supra.

repr. IN Wilson, E. G. Classics and commercials.
(v. supra) pp.231-237.

repr. IN Wilson, E. G. A literary chronicle.
(v. supra) pp.323-327.

repr. in German trans. AS "Warum werden Detektivromane
gelesen?" IN Žmegač, V. (ed.). Der wohltemperierte
Mord. (q.v.)

1574. Wilson, Richard. "Hoodlums; the myth or reality."
IN Films and Filming v.5:no.9 (June 1959) pp.10ff.

cf. Siodmak, R. "Hoodlums."

1575. Wimsatt, William Kurtz. "Mary Rogers, John Anderson,
and others." IN American Literature v.21:no.4 (January
1950) pp.482-484.

1576. ... "Poe and the mystery of Mary Rogers." IN
Publications of the Modern Language Association of America
v.56:no.1 (March 1941) pp.230-248.

1577. Wingate, Nancy. "Getting away with murder; an
analysis." IN Journal of Popular Culture v.12:no.4
(Spring 1979) pp.581-603.

1578. Winks, Robin W. (ed.). The historian as detective;
essays on evidence. N.Y.: Harper & Row; 1969. xxiv, 543p.

1579. Wodehouse, Pelham Grenville. "About these mystery stories." IN Saturday Evening Post v.201 (25 May 1929) p.33.

1580. Wohlgelernter, Maurice. Israel Zangwill; a study. N.Y./London: Columbia University Press; 1964. xvi, 364p.

1581. Wölcken, Fritz (1903-). Der literarische Mord; Eine Untersuchung über die englische und amerikanische Detektivliteratur. Nürnberg: Nest Verlag; 1953. 347p. - repr. - N.Y.: Garland; 1978. 348p.

1582. Wolfe, Peter (1933-). Beams falling; the art of Dashiell Hammett. Bowling Green, Ohio: Bowling Green University Popular Press; 1979.

   - announced as forthcoming in Xenophile (q.v.) No.38 (March-April 1978) [special issue on hard-boiled detectives] p.21.

1583. ... Dreamers who live their dreams; the world of Ross Macdonald's novels. Bowling Green, Ohio: Bowling Green University Popular Press; 1976. [x], 1-346p.

1584. ... Graham Greene; the entertainer. Carbondale, Ill.: Southern Illinois University Press; 1972. ix, 181p. (Crosscurrents: modern critiques).

1585. ... "Sam Spade, lover." - speech presented at Popular Culture Association Conference, Baltimore, April 1977.

   repr. IN Xenophile (q.v.) No.38 (March-April 1978) pp.21-26.

1586. Wolfe, Tom. "Introduction." IN Cain, James Mallahan (1892-). Cain X 3: The postman always rings twice; Mildred Pierce; Double indemnity. N.Y.: Alfred A. Knopf; 1969. viii, 465p. pp.v-viii.

1587. Wolfenstein, Martha (1911-). (jnt. auth.). "Crime patterns in today's movies." By M. Wolfenstein and Nathan Leites. IN Films in Review v.1:no.2 (March 1950) pp.11-15.

1588. <u>Wonder Woman</u>. Intro. by Gloria Steinem [and]
interpretive [sic] essay by Phyllis Chesler. N.Y.: Holt,
Rinehart and Winston/Warner Books; 1972. unpag., illus.
(A Ms. Book) - repr.: N.Y.: Paperback Library; 1974.
unpag.

1589. Wood, Grace A. "Crime and contrition in literature."
IN <u>Contemporary Review</u> v.198 (July 1960) pp.391-397.

1590. Wood, James Playsted (1905-). "Scotland Yard in
fiction." IN Wood, James Playsted (1905-). <u>Scotland Yard</u>.
N.Y.: Hawthorn Books; 1970. xii, 211p. pp.153-171 (Chaps.
13 & 14).

1591. Wood, Robin (1931-). <u>Hitchcock's films</u>. London:
A. Zwemmer/N.Y.: Barnes; 1965. 193p., illus. - rev. ed. -
London: Tantivy Press; 1969.

    Note: section on "Hitchcock's 'Psycho'" repr. from
    rev. ed. IN Nevins, F. M. (comp.). <u>The mystery</u>
    <u>writer's art</u>. (q.v.) pp.149-161.

1592. Wood, Warren. "Melville Davisson Post." IN Wood,
Warren. <u>Representative authors of West Virginia</u>. Ravenwood,
W. Va.: Worth-While Book Co.; 1926. xvii, 322p., illus.

1593. Woods, Katharine Pearson. "Renaissance of wonder."
IN <u>Bookman</u> [N.Y.] v.10:pt.4 (December 1899) pp.340-343.

1594. <u>The world encyclopedia of comics</u>. N.Y.: Chelsea
House; 1976. 2 vols. [i.e. 898p.].

1595. Worthen, S. C. "Poe and the beautiful cigar girl."
IN <u>American Literature</u> v.20:no.3 (November 1948)
pp.305-312.

1596. Wren-Lewis, J. "Adam, Eve, and Agatha Christie."
IN <u>New Christian</u> (16 April 1970) pp.9-10.

1597. Wright, Lee. "Command performance." IN Haycraft, H.
(ed.). <u>The art of the mystery story</u>. (q.v.) pp.287-291.

1598. Wright, Lyle Henry (1903-). American fiction; a contribution toward a bibliography. San Marino, Calif.: Huntington Library; 1939-1966. 3 vols. (Huntington Library Publications).

   Vol.1: 1774-1850. xviii, 246p., illus. - rev. ed.: 1948. xviii, 355p. - 2d rev. ed.: 1969. xviii, 411p.

   Vol.2: 1851-1875. 1957. 413p. - 2d ed.: 1965. 438p.

   Vol.3: 1876-1900. 1966. xix, 883p.

1599. Wright, Richardson Little. "Forgotten dentures; molars and murders in Old New York." IN Saturday Review of Literature v.27 (1 January 1944) pp.8ff.

1600. Wright, Willard Huntington (1888-1939). "The detective novel." IN Scribner's Magazine v.80 (November 1926) pp.532-539.

1601. ... "I used to be a highbrow but look at me now." IN American Magazine v.106 (September 1928) pp.14-15, 118, 122, 124-129.

   repr. IN Wright, Willard Huntington (1888-1939). Philo Vance murder cases: The Scarab murder case, The kennel murder case, The dragon murder case. By S. S. Van Dine [pseud.]. N.Y.: C. Scribner's sons; 1936. 1037p., illus.

1602. ... "Introduction; "The detective story"." IN Wright, Willard Huntington (1888-1939). (ed.). The great detective stories; a chronological anthology. N.Y.: Scribners; 1927. pp.3-40. - repr.: N.Y.: Blue Ribbon Books; 1931. - repr.: N.Y.: Scribner; 1939.

   repr. AS "The great detective stories." IN Haycraft, H. (ed.). The art of the mystery story. (q.v.) pp.33-70.

1603. ... "Introduction." IN Wright, W. H. 'Philo Vance murder cases'. (v. supra) pp.1-28.

1604. ... "Twenty rules for writing detective stories." IN American Magazine v.106 (September 1928) pp.129-131.

   repr. IN Wright, W. H. Philo Vance murder cases. (v. supra) pp.74-81.

   repr. IN Haycraft, H. (ed.). The art of the mystery story. (q.v.) pp.189-193.

repr. IN Writing suspense and mystery fiction (1977).
(q.v.) pp.267-272.

1605. Writing suspense and mystery fiction. Ed. by A. S.
Burack. Boston: Writer; 1977. x, 341p.

1606. Wrong, Edward Murray (1889-1928). "Introduction."
IN Wrong, Edward Murray (1889-1928) (ed.). Crime and
detection. London: Oxford University Press; 1926. xxx,
394, 16p. (World Classic ser. no.301) pp.ix-xxx.

   repr. IN Haycraft, H. (ed.). The art of the mystery
   story. (q.v.) pp.18-32.

   repr. in German trans. IN Der Detektiverzählung auf
   der Spur. (q.v.)

1607. Wulff, Antje. (jnt. auth.). "Beiträgen." By
A. Wulff and Walter T. Rix. IN Buchloh, P. G. (jnt. auth.).
Der Detektivroman. (q.v.)

1608. Würtenberger, Thomas. Die deutsche Kriminalerzählung.
Erlangen: [n.publ.]; 1941. 40p. - repr. - N.Y.: Garland;
1978.

1609. Wyndham, Francis. Graham Greene. London: for the
British Council and The National Book League by Longmans,
Green; 1955. 31p. (British Book News. Biographical series
of supplements no.67).

1610. Wyndham, Horace. "The lure of the "crime book"."
IN Saturday Review [London] v.156:no.4,054 (8 July 1933)
p.41.

1611. Wynne, Nancy Blue. An Agatha Christie chronology.
N.Y.: Ace; 1976. 266p.

X

1612. <u>Xenophile</u> [St. Louis, Mo.]   No.38   (1978) – special
issue on hard-boiled detectives.

Y

1613. Yamamura, Masao (1931-). _Suiri bundan sengo shi._
Tokyo: Futabasha; 1973. 293p.

1614. Yates, Donald A. _The Argentine detective story_ ...
Ph.D. dissertation, University of Michigan, Ann Arbor, Mich.,
1960. xiii, 274ℓ.

1615. ... Detectives in fiction; [an anthology of crime-
fiction scholarship].

- announced as being in prep. IN Nevins, F. M. (ed.).
The mystery writer's art. (q.v.) p.283. Not verified
to date.

1616. ... "Introduction." IN Yates, Donald A. (comp.).
_Latin blood; the best crime and detective stories of South
America._ N.Y.: Herder and Herder; 1972. xv, 224p.

1617. ... "The locked room." IN _The Michigan Alumnus
Quarterly Review_ (Spring 1957) n.v.

rev. and repr. AS "The locked house; an essay on
locked rooms." IN _Armchair Detective_ v.3:no.2
(January 1970) pp.81-84.

repr. from _Armchair Detective_ AS "An essay on locked
rooms." IN Nevins, F. M. (ed.). _The mystery writer's
art._ (q.v.) pp.272-284.

1618. ... "Locked rooms and puzzles; a critical memoir."
IN _The mystery story._ (q.v.) pp.189-203.

*   Young, Irene E. SEE Murder manual.

1619. Young, Trudee. Georges Simenon; a checklist of his
"Maigret" and other mystery novels and short stories in
French and in English translations. Metuchen, N.J.:
Scarecrow Press; 1976. iii, 153p. (The Scarecrow author
bibliographies, no.29).

*   Yudkin, John. (jnt. auth.). SEE Philmore, R. [pseud.].
Inquest on detective stories.

Z

1620. Zacharias, Lee. "Nancy Drew, ballbuster." IN
Journal of Popular Culture v.9:no.4 (Spring 1976)
pp.1027-1038.

1621. Zamorano, Manuel. Crimen y literatura; ensayo de una
antología criminológico-literaria de Chile. Santiago:
Facultad de Filosofía y Educación, Universidad de Chile;
1967, [c1966]. 468p., illus.

1622. Zegel, Sylvain. "A l'est du nouveau dans le roman
policier; les Sovietiques ont leur commissaire Maigret et
les Polonais leur inspecteur Bourel." IN Le Figaro
Litteraire no.970 (19-25 November 1964) p.4.

   repr. AS "Whodunit - Soviet style." IN Atlas [N.Y.]
   v.9:no.5 (May 1965) pp.309-310.

1623. Zeiger, Henry A. Ian Fleming; the spy who came in
with the gold. N.Y.: Duell, Sloane, & Pearce; 1965. 150p.

1624. Zeltner, Gerda. "Robert Pinget et le roman policier."
IN Marche Romane No.21 (1971).

1625. Ziolkowski, Theodore. "A portrait of the artist as a
criminal." IN Ziolkowski, Theodore. Dimensions of the
modern novel; German texts and European contexts. Princeton,
N.J.: Princeton University Press; 1969. xi, 378p. pp.289-331.

1626. Žmegač, Viktor. "Aspekte des Detektivromans." IN
Žmegač, V. (ed.). Der wohltemperierte Mord. (q.v.)

1627.   ... Der wohltemperierte Mord.   Zur Theorie und
Geschichte des Detektivromans.   Frankfurt am Main:
Athenäum-Verlag; 1971.   278p.   (Schwerpunkte Germanistik, 4).

1628.   Zulliger, Hans.   "Der Abenteurer-Schundroman."   IN
Ztschr. f. psa. Pädagogik   v.7   (1933).

TITLE INDEX

Afrikaanse speurverhale uitgegee tot die einde van 1950.
Miller, A., comp.

After a century, will anyone care whodunit? Graves, R.

"Afterword: Raymond Chandler and Hollywood". Bruccoli, M. J.

"Afterword" (The private memoirs). Gide, A.

Agatha; a novel of mystery. Tynan, K.

Agatha Christie. Christie, A.

"Agatha Christie". Ercoli, E.

Agatha Christie. Ramsey, G.

An Agatha Christie chronology. Wynne, N.

"The Agatha Christie films". Jenkinson, P.

The Agatha Christie mystery. Murdoch, D.

Agatha Christie quizzbook. East, A. R.

"Agatha Christie's England, 1918-39". Ritchie, J.

L'âge du roman américain. Magny, C.-E.

The age of the American novel. Magny, C.-E.

"Age of the great detective". Lejeune, A.

"The agents of evil and justice in the novels of Dorothy L.
Sayers". Stock, R. D.

"Alan Resnais; the quest for Harry Dickson". Lacassin, F.

"A l'est du nouveau dans le roman policier". Zegel, S.

Alias J. J. Connington. Stewart, A.

"Alias Nero Wolfe". De Voto, B.

Alistair MacLean; the key is fear. Lee, R.

"Allusion and analogy in the romance of 'Caleb Williams'".
Rothstein, E.

"Almost real reality". Schubert, R.

"The amateur detectives". Penzler, O.

"The amazon legacy". Chesler, P.

Amefuri dakara misuterí de mo benkyōshiyō. Uekusa, J.

The American boys' book series bibliography 1895-1935.
Dikty, A. S.

The American detective story. Mooney, J.

"The American detective thriller and the idea of society".
Margolies, E.

American fiction. Wright, L.

American film genres. Kaminsky, S.

Amerika fūbutsushi. Nakauchi, M.

"American popular culture in the Thirties". Melling, P.

The American rivals of Sherlock Holmes. Greene, Sir H., (ed.)

America's secret service ace. Carr, N.

"Analysis of a detective story". Rycroft, C.

"An analysis of gangster movies of the early thirties".
Sacks, A.

"Analytic and synthetic approaches to narrative structure".
O'Toole, L.

"Anatomie des Detektivromans". Alewyn, R.

Anatomy of the spy thriller. Merry, B.

The androgynous orchid. Carnillon, J.

"Die Anfänge des Detektivromans". Alewyn, R.

"Les anneaux de Bicetre". Paulhan, J.

An annotated guide to the works of Dorothy L. Sayers.
Harmon, R. B. (jnt. comp.).

"Anti-professionalism in the works of Mickey Spillane".
Banks, R. J.

"Anti-Western". Pechter, W.

"À propos du roman policier". Chesterton, G.

The Argentine detective story. Yates, D.

An aristocrat of intellect. Dorset, G.

"Aristotle en die speurverhaal". Van Selms, A.

Band dessinée et figuration narrative. Musée des Arts Decoratifs. Paris.

Los bandidos en la literatura mexicana. Ortiz Vidales. S.

"The barbarians are within the gates". Gardiner, H. C.

Basil Rathbone. Druxman, M. B.

Batman. SEE Encyclopedia of comic book heroes.

"Battle of the sexes". Lynch, J. [pseud.].

Beams falling. Wolfe, P.

Beiträge zur Geschichte des Kriminalromans. Schimmelpfenning, A.

"Beiträgen". Wulff, A.

Best detective fiction. Barnes, M. P.

"Best detective story in the world". Dane, C. [pseud.].

"Best-selling American detective fiction". Mooney, J.

Bibliographic des éditions originales de Georges Simenson. Menguy, C.

A bibliographical catalogue of the writings of Sir Arthur Conan Doyle. Locke, H.

"Bibliography". Pronzini, B.

The bibliography of crime fiction 1749-1975. Hubin, A.

Bibliography of Dime novels. Bragin, C.

"Bigger and better murders". Benét, S.

Biografiá de la novels policíaca. Mira, J.

A birthday tribute to Rex Stout. Barzun, J. M.

Blå briller og løssjegg i Kristiania. Dahl, W.

Black beech and honeydew; an autobiography. Marsh, Dame N.

"'Black Mask'". Borneman, E.

"The 'Black Mask' school". Durham, P.

Bleak House. Daniel, P.

Blodige fotspor. Degn, P.

Blood and knavery. Marshburn, J., jnt. comp.

Blood and Thunder. Disher, M. W.

Blood in their ink. Scott, S.

"Blood marks in the sylvan glade". Arlen, M. J.

Bloodhounds of heaven. Ousby, I.

"The bloody movies". Farber, S.

Bloody murder. Symons, J.

"The bloody pulps". Beaumont, C.

The body in the library. Hollyer, C.

"Bogie and The Black Bird". Nolan, W.

The Bond affair. SEE Il caso Bond.

"The Bond game". Ormerod, D., jt. author.

The book of Bond. Tanner, W. [pseud.]

A book of prefaces. Barzun, J. M. (jt. auth.)

The book of sleuths. Pate, J.

"The book, the bibliographer, and the absence of mind".
Barzun, J.

Born to lose. Rosow, E.

Bound and gagged. Lahue, K.

"The boys in the back room". Wilson, E.

The boys in the Black mask. California University, University
at Los Angeles, Library.

Boys will be boys. Turner, E.

"Bramah; a footnote to Carrados". White, T.

"A breathless chapter". Overton, G.

Breve storia del romanzo poliziesco. Del Monte, A.

"A brief appreciation of 'The glass Key'". Pachovsky, G.

"A brief history of the early years of the locked room".
Adey, R.

"A briefbag of felonies". Barzun, J.

Brighton Rock (Graham Greene). Price, A.

The British bibliography of Edgar Wallace. Lofts, W., jt.
author.

British crime fiction. Great Britain, British Council.

Broads. Cameron, I. A. and E. Cameron

Bronnegids by die studie van die Afrikaanse taal en letterkunde.
Nienaber, P.

Browning's Roman murder story. Altick, R. D.

"Buckskin and ballistics". Seelye, J.

The buried day. Day Lewis, C.

"Cagney and the Mob". Tynan, K.

Le cahier de recettes de Madame Maigret. Courtine, R.

"Cain in the movies". Lerner, M.

"Cain X 3". Macdonald, R. [pseud.].

"Cain's movietone realism". Farrell, J. T.

"Cain's 'The postman always rings twice' and Camus'
'L'Étranger'". Madden, D.

"Caleb Williams". Rothstein, E.

"Caleb Williams and Martin Faber". Stone, E.

"Captain José Da Silva". Fish, R. L.

["A careful analysis of Curme Gray's 'Murder in Millenium
VI'"]. Knight, D.

Le cas Simenon. Narcejac, T.

"The case of Erle Stanley Gardner". Johnston, A.

"The case of Miss Dorothy Sayers". Leavis, Q. D.

"The case of Mr. Fleming". Bergonzi, B.

"The case of the corpse in the blind alley". Stern, P.

"The case of the early beginning". Gardner, E. S.

"The case of the escalating sales". Walter, E.

"The case of the vanishing hero". Murdoch, D.

"The case of the versatile A. Conan Doyle". SEE "Arthur Conan Doyle".

A casebook of murder. Wilson, C.

Il caso Bond. Buono, O. D. (jt. auth.).

A catalogue of crime. Barzun, J. M. (jnt. comp.).

Catalogue the seventh of rare and interesting books. Bates, G.

"A Cato to the cruelties". Flint, R. W.

Celluloid sleuths. Pitts, M.

"Chandler and Hammett". McLaren, J.

"The Chandler books". Russell, D.

"Charles Dickens". Poe, E.

"Charles Dickens as criminologist". Squires, P.

Charles Dickens; 'Bleak House'. Smith, G.

Cheap thrills. Goulart, R.

A checklist of detective short stories. Mundell, E.

A checklist of the Arthur Conan Doyle collection in the Metropolitan Toronto Central Library. Redmond, D.

Chester Himes. Lundquist, J.

Chester Himes. Milliken, S.

"Chester Himes, interview". Cullaz, M.

"Chicago letter". Kaminsky, S.

"The Christie everybody knew". Fremlin, C.

"The Christie nobody knew". Hughes, D. B. F.

"A chronology of Solar Pons". Pattrick, R.

The cinema of Alfred Hitchcock. Bogdanovich, P.

Le cinéma selon Hitchcock. Truffaut, F.

"The classic form". Hare, C.

"The cliché of the mystery writers". McElroy, C.

"The climate of violence". Gossett, L. Y.

Cloak-and-dagger bibliography. Smith, M.

"Close-up of Chandler". Priestley, J.

Clubland heroes. Usborne, R.

"Cold chills of 1928". Strunsky, S.

"Collecting detective fiction". Carter, J.

"Collecting detective fiction". Osborne, E.

The collector's book of detective fiction. Quayle, E.

Comic art in America. Becker, S. D.

The comic-book book. Thompson, D., jt. ed.

The comics. Waugh, C.

Comix. Daniels, L.

"Command performance". Wright, L.

Commissaire Maigret, qui êtes-vous? Henry, G.

Conan Doyle. Brown, I. J. C.

Conan Doyle; a biographical solution. Pearsall, R.

Conan Doyle; his life and art. Pearson, H.

Connaissance de Georges Simenon. Parinaud, A.

Conrad; 'The secret agent'. Watt, I., ed.

"A contribution to the psychoanalytic study of the modern hero". Trahair, R.

"The contributions of Edgar Allan Poe". Lowndes, R.

"A conversation with Ross Macdonald". Tutunjian, J.

"Cops". French, P.

"Cops and robbers". Ferguson, O.

"Cops, robbers, and citizens". Ferkiss, V.

"Cops, robbers, heroes and anti-heroes". Jones, A. H.

"Cornell Woolrich". Nevins, M.

"Cornwallis's revenge". Lathen, E. [pseud.].

"Corpus delicti". Taylor, F.

Corpus delicti of mystery fiction. Herman, L.

"A cosmic view of the private eye". Paterson, J.

Cosmopolitan crimes. SEE More rivals of Sherlock Holmes.

The counterfeit lady unveiled. Peterson, S. ed.

"The counterworld of Victorian fiction and 'The woman in white'". Knoepflmacher, U. C.

"The country behind the hill". James, C.

"Country full of blondes". Elliott, G.

The country of 'The Ring and the Book'. Treves, Sir F., bart.

"Courtroom plays of the Yüan and early Ming periods". Hayden, G. A.

"Crime and contrition in literature". Wood, A.

"Crime and criticism". Sisk, J.

"Crime and detection in the novels of Marguerite Duras". Eisinger, E. M.

Crime and detective fiction. Sheppard, R., jt. ed.

"Crime and punishment in the detective fiction of Dorothy L. Sayers". Reaves, R. B.

Crime and the drama. Newton, H.

"Crime and the stage". Wilson, A.

"Crime certainly pays on the screen". Shearer, L.

Crime, detection, and society. The Times Literary Supplement.

Crime, detective, espionage, mystery, and thriller fiction
and film; a comprehensive bibliography. Skene Melvin, L.,
jt. comp.

O crime e os criminosos na literatura brasileira. Lemos
Britto, J.

Le crime et la peine dans l'oeuvre de Victor Hugo. Savey-
Casard, P.

"Le crime et le mysterè d'Edgar Poe à Geo. London".
Campinchi, C.

"Crime fiction". Cruse, A.

"Crime fiction for intellectuals". Bremner, M.

"Crime films and social criticism". Henry, C.

"Crime for punishment". Snodgrass, W.

Crime in good company. Gilbert, M. F.

"Crime in modern literature". Langbaum, R.

"Crime, Inc.". Whitehall, R.

"The crime novel". Symons, J.

"Crime of passion films". Miller, D.

Crime on her mind. Slung, M., ed.

"Crime on the radio". Fitt, M.

"Crime on the stage". Vickers, R.

"Crime over the world". Vesselo, A.

"Crime patterns in today's movies". Wolfenstein, J., jt.
author.

"The crime short story". Ellin, S.

"The crime short story". Strong, L.

Crimen y literatura. Zamorano, M.

"Criminal clef". Sandoe, J.

Criminal types in Shakespeare. Goll, A.

La criminalistique. Locard, E.

La criminalogía en la literatura universal. Quintano Ripollés, A.

"A critical biography of Hammett". Godshalk, W.

"'Critical discussion of locked room theory'". Boucher, A. [pseud.].

"Critical discussion of locked-room theory". Rawson, C.

A critical history and analysis of the 'whodunit'. Williamson, J.

The crooked counties. Greene, Sir H., (ed.).

"Cruel devourer of the world's light". Gose, E.

"The crux of a murder". Taylor, F.

Curious annals. Cortona Codex.

"Curtains for Poirot". Tyler, R.

"Cyril Hare". Shibuk, C.

"Dagger of the mind". Sandoe, J.

"Damer på den litteraere forbryderbane". La Cour, T.

"'The damned'". Hoyt, C.

The dangerous edge. Lambert, G.

"Dashiell Hammett". Blair, W.

"Dashiell Hammett". Symons, J.

Dashiell Hammett; a casebook. Nolan, W.

"Dashiell Hammett; a memoir". Hellman, L.

"Dashiell Hammett's microcosmos". Phelps, D.

"Dashiell Hammett's 'Private Eye'". Bazelon, D. T.

"Dashiell Hammett and the Continental Op". Marcus, S.

The Dashiell Hammett tradition... Kenney, W. P.

"Death as a game". Innes, M. [pseud.].

"Death by misadventure". Stevens, G.

"Death rays, demons, and worms unknown to science". Briney, R.

"Death to the detectives". Portugal, E.

"Death Valley, U.S.A.". Hofsess, J.

"The decadence of detection". Quinton, A.

"A decennial detective digest". SEE   "From Poe to Hammett".

Deckare och thrillers på svenska 1864-1973. SEE Svensk deckare- thrillerbibliografi.

"The decline and fall of the detective story". Maugham, W.

"Decline and fall of the detective story". Raynor, H.

"Decline and fall of the whodunit". Redman, B.

"Defective detectives". Mercier, V.

"A defense of detective stories". Chesterton, G.

I delinquenti nell'arte. Ferri, E.

"The design of Conrad's 'The secret agent'". Hagan, J.

"Desipere in loco". Gass, S. B.

"A detailed discussion of Isaac Asimov's The caves of steel and The naked sun". Patrouch, J.

"Detection and the literary art". Barzun, J.

"Detection and thrillers". Partridge, R.

"Detection in extremis". Barzun, J.

Detection medley. Rhode, J. [pseud.].

"Detective and mystery novels". Landrum, L.

"The detective and the boundary". Spanos, W.

"The detective as metaphor in the nineteenth century". Gilbert, E. G.

"Detective detected". Byrd, M.

Detective fiction. Allen, R. S. (jnt. comp.).

"Detective fiction". Brophy, B.

"Detective fiction". Carter, J.

"Detective fiction". Hutchinson, H. G.

"Detective fiction". Penzler, O.

"Detective fiction".   Quayle, E.

Detective fiction.   Scribner, firm, publishers, New York.

Detective fiction.   Stevenson, W., comp.

"Detective fiction".   Williams, G.

"Detective fiction; origins and development".   Sayers, D.

Detective fiction [special number].   The Times Literary
Supplement.

"Detective films".   Thomson, H.

"The detective in fact and fiction".   Harrison, R.

"The detective in fact and fiction".   Hughes, R.

"The detective in fiction".   Maurice, A.

"The detective in fiction".   Williams, G.

"The detective in fiction - and in fact".   Rhodes, H.

The detective in film.   Everson, W. K.

The detective in Hollywood.   Tuska, J.

"The detective in literature".   Millar, A.

"The detective novel".   Marion, D.

"The detective novel".   Wright, W.

Le "detective novel" et l'influence de la pensée scientifique.
Messac, R.

"Detective novels".   Ilyina, N.

"Detective novels".   Mason, A.

"Detective novels".   Scott-James, R.

The detective short story.   Mundell, E., jt. comp.

The detective short story.   Queen, E. [pseud.].

The detective short story.   Ruber, P., jt. comp.

"Detective stories".   Chesterton, G.

"Detective stories".   Cummings, J. C.

"Detective stories and the primal scene".   Peterson-Krag, G.

"Detective stories as literature". Honce, C. E.

"Detective stories for the screen". Sayers, D.

"The detective story". Barzun, J. M.

"The detective story". Harwood, H. C.

"The detective story". Mason, V.

"The detective story". Peck, H.

The detective story. Schwartz, S., ed.

"The detective story". White, T.

"The detective story; an English institution". Ocampo, V.

"The detective story and academe". Sandoe, J.

"The detective story as a historical source". Aydelotte, W. O.

"The detective story as an art form". Chandler, R.

The detective story in Britain. Symons, J.

"Detective story in Germany and Scandinavia". Colbron, G.

"A detective story; psychoanalytical observations". Rycroft, C.

"The detective story - why?" SEE "Introduction" (Murder for pleasure)

"The detective story's origin". Johnston, C.

"The detective story's place in literature". Wells, C.

The detective, the clue, and the corpse in Freud and Einstein. Roth, M.

Detektive. Gerteis, W.

Detektiven i romanen och i verkligheten. Richert, J.

Die Detektivgeschichte für junge Leser. Hasubek, P.

Detektivliteratur bei Sophokles, Schiller and Kleist. Reinert, C.

Der Detektivroman (Boileau-Narcejac). SEE Le roman policier.

Der Detektivroman. Buchloh, P. G., jt. author.

Der detektivroman der Unterschicht. Epstein, H.

"Detektivroman in Unterricht". Bien, G.

"Dr Jekyll og Mr Brodie". La Cour, T.

"The documents in the case of Arthur Train". Overton, G.

"Domestic Harlem". Nelson, R.

"The domesticity of detectives". Chesterton, G. K.

"Don't guess, let me tell you". Nash, O.

Dorothy L. Sayers. Hone, R.

"Dorothy L. Sayers and the tidy art of detective fiction". Harrison, B. G.

"Dorothy L. Sayers; from puzzle to novel". James, P.

Le dossier Simenon. Stéphane, R.

"'Double Indemnity'". Allyn, J.

Double O Seven. Snelling, O.

Down these mean streets. Durham, P. C.

"Down these streets a mean man must go". Macdonald, R. [pseud.].

Dreamers who live their dreams. Wolfe, P.

Dreams and dead ends. Shadoian, J.

"Drop that gun!" Mirams, G.

"The Drury Lane quartet". Nevins, F.

The 'Duende' history of 'The Shadow Magazine'. Murray, W.

"Duncan Maclain". Kenrick, B. H.

"Dupin; the reality behind the fictions". Harrison, M.

The durable desperadoes. Butler, W. V.

"Durrenmatt's detective stories". Ashbrook, B.

"Durrenmatt's detective stories". Leah, G.

"The dust jackets of 'The great Gatsby' and 'The Long Goodbye'". Stewart, L.

E. C. Bentley. Baker, I. L.

Eccentricities of genius. Pond, J.

Eden Phillpotts. Girvan, W.

Edgar A. Poe. Rein, D.

Edgar A. Poe as a detective. Locard, E.

Edgar Allan Poe. Asselineau, R.

Edgar Allan Poe. Buranelli, V.

Edgar Allan Poe. Dameron, J. L.

Edgar Allan Poe. Hyneman, E. F.

Edgar Allan Poe. Quinn, A.

Edgar Allan Poe. Rans, G.

Edgar Allan Poe. Ransome, A.

"Edgar Allan Poe". Sachs, H.

Edgar Allan Poe, 1809-1849. Pope-Hennessy, Dame U.

Edgar Allan Poe in Selbstzeug-nissen and Bilddokumenten.
Lennig, W.

"Edgar Allan Poe and die Folgen". Just, K. G.

Edgar Poe. Bonaparte, M., Princess.

Edgar Poe et les conteurs français. Lemonnier, L.

Edgar Wallace. Wallace, V.

Edgar Wallace; the biography of a phenomenon. Lane, M.

"The effects of film violence". Berkowitz, L., (jt. auth.)

"The 87th Precinct". McBain, E.

"Elementary, my dear Watson". McInnes, G.

"Elements of the detective story in William Faulkner's fiction".
Gidley, M.

Ellery Queen. Boucher, A. [pseud.].

"An Émigré". Pritchett, V.

"Émile Gaboriau". Sayers, D. L.

En torno a la novela detectivesca. Portuondo, J.

En torno al género policial. Ves Losada, A.

An encyclopedia of murder. Wilson, C.

Der englische Spionageroman. Becker, J.-P.

"English imperialism and the unacknowledged crime of 'The moonstone'". Reed, J.

The English novel, 1740-1850. Block, A.

"L'Enquête policière dans le nouveau roman". Alter, J.

"Entertainments". Marsh, Dame N.

"Epitaph for a tough guy; Humphrey Bogart". Cooke, A.

"Eric Ambler". James, C.

Erle Stanley Gardner. Hughes, D. B. F.

Erle Stanley Gardner. Mundell, E.

"Erle Stanley Gardner". Queen, E. [pseud.].

"Erzähltes Mysterium". Rolleke, H.

["Essay on Chester Himes"]. Reed, I.

Esthétique du roman policier. Narcejac, T.

"E.T.A. Hoffmans Erzählung 'Das Fraulein von Scuderi' als Kriminalgeschichte". Kanzog, K.

"E.T.A. Hoffmans 'Fraulein von Scuderi'". Thalmann, M.

"The ethics of the mystery. Boucher, A. [pseud.].

"The ethnic detective". Ball, J. D.

"Evelyn Waugh and Erle Stanley Gardner". Borrello, A.

"Evil plots". Grella, G.

"The evolution of the great American detective". Kittredge, W.

"Ex-detective Hammett". Sanderson, E.

An exhibition on the occasion of the opening of the Ellery Queen collection. Texas University. Humanities Research Centre.

The fabulour originals. Wallace, I.

"The face in the mirror". Symons, J.

"Farewell, my lovely. Powell, L.

"Father Bredder". Holton, L.

For Bond lovers only. Lane, S., (comp.)

"Foreword". (The golden violet). Lewis, S.

"Foreword". (Sbornik rasskazov). Shishkina, T.

"A foreword to 'Death in Hollywood'". Sturak, T.

"Forgotten dentures". Wright, R.

Formen und Ideologien des Kriminalromans. Schulz-Buschhaus, U.

"The four Ellery Queens". Connor, E.

"Four of a kind?". Martin, T.

"Fred Fellows". Waugh, Hillary.

"Freeman Wills Crofts". Keddie, J.

French crime in the Romantic age. Heppenstall, R.

The French face of Edgar Poe. Quinn, P.

Friedrich Dürrenmatt. Arnold, A.

Friedrich Dürrenmatt. Knopf, J.

Friedrich Dürrenmatt. Peppard, M.

"Friederich Schiller und die Kriminalliteratur". Haslinger, A.

"Friend and mentor". Norman, F.

Fritz Lang. Eisner, L.

Fritz Lang in America. Bogdanovich, P.

"From detection to theology; the work of Dorothy Sayers".
Rickmann, H.

"From 'Phèdre' to Sherlock Holmes". Barzun, J. M.

"From Poe to Hammett". Haycraft, H.

"From Poe to Poirot". Starrett, V.

From the angle of 88. Phillpotts, E.

F. Scott Fitzgerald: 'The Great Gatsby'. Whitley, J.

Für und wider den krimi. Katholische Akademie Stuttgart-
Hohenheim.

Fyra decennier med Dennis Wheatley. Hedman, I.

"Gaboriau". Williams, G.

A gallery of rogues. Maggs Brothers, London, booksellers.

"Gallows literature of the streets". McDade, T.

"Den gamle mästaren". Lundin, B.

Gangster and crime movies. Grogg, S. L.

"The gangster as tragic hero". Warshow, R.

The gangster film. Baxter, J.

The gangster film. Karpf, S. L.

"Gangster heroes". Warner, A.

Gangster movies. Hossent, H.

O gangster no cinema. Paiva, S.

"The gangster novel; the urban pastoral". Grella, G.

Gangsters. Gabree, J.

Gangsters and hoodlums. Lee, R., (jt. auth.).

Gangsters on the screen. Manchel, F.

"Gaudy night". Sayers, D.

"Der gefesselte Detektivromans". Suerbaum, U.

"Geistes' Blitze aus Kriminal-Romanen". Langenbrucher, E., (et al.).

"The genesis of the detective story". Rendall, V.

"Géographie de Simenon". Dubourg, M.

"George Orwell and the detective story". Parrinder, P.

Georges Simenon. Becker, L.

"Georges Simenon". Bishop, J.

Georges Simenon; a checklist. Young, T.

"Georges Simenon clinicien de l'âme". Deniker, Professeur.

"Georges Simenon, écrivain liegeois". Boverie, D.

"Georges Simenon et la littérature russe". Schraiber, E.

Georges Simenon et l'homme desintegre. Richter, A.

"George Simenon, romancier-nez". Messac, R.

"The germ of the detective novel". Williams, H.

"Gertrude Stein and the vital dead". Stewart, L.

Get, come, and go. Behre, F.

"Getting away with murder". Gardner, E. S.

"Getting away with murder". Wingate, N.

"The Greenwich bomb outrage and 'The secret agent'".
Sherry, N.

Ghost of the Hardy Boys. McFarlane, L.

The girl in the pictorial wrapper. Breen, J. L.

The girl sleuth. Mason, B.

"Give me a murder". Maugham, W.

"Give us back Bill Sykes". O'Faolain, S.

G. K. Chesterton. Barker, D.

G. K. Chesterton. Clipper, L. J.

G. K. Chesterton. Conlon, D.

G. K. Chesterton. Hollis, C.

G. K. Chesterton. Sister, M.

G. K. Chesterton; a bibliography. Sullivan, J.

G. K. Chesterton; a centenary appraisal. Sullivan, J.

G. K. Chesterton, 1874-1974. Sullivan, J.

"G. K. Chesterton's 'Father Brown' stories". Robson, W.

Glorious incense. Bradly, H.

Godwin criticism. Pollin, B.

"The golden age of English detection". Strachey, E.

The golden summer. Dannay, F.

A gothic bibliography. Summers, A.

"Gothic mysteries". Whitney, P.

Graham Greene. Atkins, J. A.

Graham Greene. Lodge, D.

"Graham Greene". McCann, J.

Graham Greene. Phillips, G.

Graham Greene. Pryce-Jones, D.

"Graham Greene". Stewart, D.

Graham Greene. Vann, J.

Graham Greene. Wolfe, P.

Graham Greene. Wyndham, F.

Graham Greene and the heart of the matter. Mesnet, M.

"Graham Greene's movies". Nolan, J.

"A grammar of assassination". Maloney, M.

Grande dames of detection. Manley, S., (jt. comp.).

"The grandest game in the world". Carr, J. D.

"Grandeur et décadence du roman policier Anglais". Orwell, G.,
[pseud].

"The great Australian detective". Sarjeant, W.

The great Canadian comic books. Hirsh, M.

The great comic book heroes. Feiffer, J.

"The great crooks". Penzler, O.

"The great detective". Symons, J.

The great detectives. Penzler, O.

"The great detective team". Leithead, J.

"Great films of the century: 'The Maltese Falcon'". Eyles, A.

The great gangster pictures. Parish, J.

"A great impersonation". Overton, G.

The great radio heroes. Harmon, J.

The great spy pictures. Parish, J., (jt. auth.).

The great villains. Pate, J.

"Grey Knight in the Great Wrong Place". Wells, W.

Histoire du roman policier. Hoveyda, F.

Histoire et technique du roman-policier. de Traz, G. A. E.

The historian as detective. Winks, R., (ed.).

A history of the comic strip. Musee des Arts Decoratifs, Paris.

Hitchcock's films. Wood, R.

"Hitchcock's 'Psycho'". Wood, R.

"Holiday homicide". Harwood, H. C.

"The Hollywood novel". See, C.

"Hollywoodunit". Mealand, R.

"Holmes; the Hamlet of crime fiction". Hill, R.

"Homage to Dashiell Hammett". Macdonald, R. [pseud.].

Homicide in American fiction, 1798-1860. Davis, D. B.

"Homicide in fiction". Boyd, S.

"Homicide West". Gerhardt, M. I.

"Les hommes, les hommes". Sullerot, E.

"Hoodlums". Siodmak, R.

"Hoodlums; the myth or reality?". Wilson, R.

"Hooverville West". Clarens, C.

"Horace McCoy, Captain Shaw, and the 'Black Mask'". Sturak, T.

"Horace McCoy's objective lyricism". Sturak, T.

The House of Beadle and Adams. Johannsen, A.

How to enjoy detective fiction. Thomas G.

"How to read a whodunit". Cuppy, W.

"How to tell Sam Spade from Philip Marlowe from Lew Archer".
Lingeman, R.

"How to write a detective story". Chesterton, G. K.

How to write detective novels. Morland, N.

How 007 got his name. Bond, M. W.

The hundred best crime stories. The Sunday Times (London).

"Hypothèse à propos de Maigret". Frank, N.

"I care who killed Roger Ackroyd". Leonard, J.

"I never called him Bill". Nanovic, J.

"I used to be a highbrow but look at me now". Wright, W.

Ian Fleming. Gant, R.

Ian Fleming. Zeiger, H.

Ian Fleming; a catalogue of a collection. Campbell, I.

"Der Ich-Erzähler im englisch-amerikanischen Detektiv- und
Kriminalroman". Ludwig, H.-W.

"If judges wrote detective stories". Waite, J.

"The illusion of the real". Barzun, J.

""I'm the eye"." Barnes, D. R.

"The imaginative world of John Buchan". Sykes, M.

"Impressionistic biography". Garden, Y. B. [pseud.?].

"In behalf of the puzzle novel". Boynton, H.

"In defense of the detective story". Reeve, A.

"In Rats' Alley". Ruhm, H.

"In re: Solar Pons". Starrett, V.

In search of Dr. Thorndyke. Donaldson, N.

In the Queen's parlor. Queen, E. [pseud.].

"In the tracks of Detective-Inspector 'Bony'". Trengove, A.

"Incitement against violence". French, P.

Index book for use with the plot genie. Hill, W.

The influence of Edgar Allan Poe in France. Cambiaire, C.-P.

Influences françaises dans l'oeuvre d'Edgar Poe. Messac, R.

An informal history of the pulp magazines. Goulart, R.

"An informal interview with Rex Stout". Bourne, M.

"The inheritance of the meek". Hamblen, A. A.

Innocence and arsenic. Borowitz, A.

"Introduction" (<u>The Continental Op.</u>). Marcus, S.

"Introduction" (<u>Crime and detection</u>). Wrong, E.

"Introduction" (<u>Crime on the lines</u>). Morgan, G.

"Introduction" (<u>Dee goong an</u>). Van Gulik, R.

"Introduction" (<u>The department of dead ends</u>). Bleiler, E.

"Introduction" (<u>The detective in fiction</u>). Seaborne, E.

"Introduction" (<u>Dimensions of detective fiction</u>).
Landrum, L. N., (et al).

"Introduction" (<u>Ellery Queen's Japanese golden dozen</u>).
Queen, E. [pseud.].

"Introduction" (<u>Famous plays of crime and detection</u>).
Chapman, J.

"Introduction" (<u>Father Brown</u>). Knox, R. A.

"Introduction" (<u>Fourteen great detective stories</u>). Haycraft, H.

"Introduction" (<u>The great American detective</u>). Kittredge, W.,
(jnt. auth.).

"Introduction" (<u>The great detective stories</u>). Wright, W.

"Introduction" (<u>Great short stories of detection, mystery and
horror</u>. First, second, and third series). Sayers, D.

"Introduction" (<u>The hard-boiled detective</u>). Ruhm, H., (ed.).

"Introduction" (<u>The hard-boiled omnibus</u>). Shaw, J.

"Introduction" (<u>The John Franklin Bardin omnibus</u>). Symons, J.

"Introduction" (<u>Kenneth Millar/Ross Macdonald</u>). Macdonald, R.
[pseud.].

"Introduction" (<u>Killer in the rain</u>). Durham, P. C.

"Introduction" (<u>Lady Audley's secret</u>). Donaldson, N.

"Introduction" (<u>Latin blood</u>). Yates, D. (comp.).

"Introduction" (<u>Lew Archer</u>). Macdonald, R. [pseud.].

"Introduction" (<u>The locked room reader</u>). Santesson, H.

"Introduction" (<u>Lord Peter</u>). Sandoe, J.

"Introduction" (<u>The Maltese falcon</u>). Hammett, D.

"Introduction" (<u>Memoirs of Solar Pons</u>). Queen, E. [pseud.].

"Introduction" (<u>Monseiur Lecoq</u>). Bleiler, E.

"Introduction" (<u>The moonstone</u>). Eliot, T.

"Introduction" (<u>The moonstone</u>). Sayers, D.

"Introduction" (<u>Mountain meadow</u>). Swiggett, H.

"Introduction" (<u>Murder for pleasure</u>). Day Lewis, C.

"Introduction" (<u>Nick Carter, detective</u>). Clurman, R.

"Introduction" (<u>Nightwebs</u>). Nevins, F.

"Introduction" (<u>Novels of mystery from the Victorian age</u>). Richardson, M.

"Introduction" (<u>101 years entertainment</u>). Queen, E. [pseud.].

"Introduction" (<u>The passenger from Scotland Yard</u>). Bleiler, E.

"Introduction" (<u>Philo Vance murder cases</u>). Wright, W.

"Introduction" (<u>Plots and counterplots</u>). Stern, M.

"Introduction" (<u>The private memoirs and confessions of a justified sinner</u>). Adams, R. M.

"Introduction" (<u>The private memoirs and confessions of a justified sinner</u>). Carey, J.

"Introduction" (<u>The reminiscences of Solar Pons</u>). Boucher, A. [pseud.].

"Introduction" (<u>The return of Solar Pons</u>). Smith, E.

"Introduction" (<u>The riddle of the sands</u>). Donaldson, N.

"Introduction" (<u>The riddle of the sands</u>). Household, G.

"Introduction" (<u>The second century of detective stories</u>). Bentley, E. C.

"Introduction" (<u>The simple art of murder</u>). Chandler, R.

"Introductio" (<u>The skeleton key</u>). Chesterton, G. K.

"Introduction" (<u>The smell of fear</u>). Chandler, R.

"Introduction" (<u>The Solange Stories</u>). Jesse, F. M. T.

"Introduction" (<u>The stoneware monkey</u>). Bleiler, E.

"Introduction" (<u>Tales of detection</u>). Sayers, D.

"Introduction" (<u>Tales of mystery and imagination</u>). Colum, P.

"Introduction" (<u>The thirty-nine steps</u>). Gilbert, M.

"Introduction" (<u>Three Victorian detective novels</u>). Bleiler, E.

"Introduction" (To catch a spy). Ambler, E.

"Introduction" (<u>Uncle Silas</u>). Shroyer, F.

"Introduction" (<u>Wonder Woman</u>). Steinem, G.

"Introduction" (<u>The world of Raymond Chandler</u>). Highsmith, P.

"Introduction" (<u>World's great spy stories</u>). Starrett, V., (ed.).

"Introduction and afterwords" (<u>Ellery Queen's challenge to the reader</u>). Queen, E. [pseud.].

<u>An introduction to American movies</u>. Earley, S.

"An introduction to the private eye novel". Scott, M.

"An introduction to the world of Magistrate Pao". Comber, L.

"Irony as theme". Spector, R.

"Is Poe's 'A tale of the Ragged Mountains' a hoax?". Thompson, G.

"Is television necessary?". Alexander, D.

"Ishmael Reed's neo-hoodoo detection". Carter, S. R.

<u>Israel Zangwill</u>. Adams, E. B.

<u>Israel Zangwill</u>. Ben Guigui, J.

<u>Israel Zangwill</u>. Leftwich, J.

<u>Israel Zangwill</u>. Wohlgelernter, M.

<u>Israfel</u>. Allen, W.

<u>It's elementary</u>. Janeczko, P.

"I've been reading thrillers". Stade, G.

"J. Edgar Hoover and the detective hero". Powers, R.

"James Bond". Eco, U.

"James Bond". Martin, B.

<u>James Bond</u>. Pearson, J.

The James Bond dossier. Amis, K.

James Bond in the cinema. Brosnan, J.

"James Bond unmasked". Richler, M.

James Hogg. Simpson, L.

"James Hogg's 'Confessions of a justified sinner'".
Chianese, R. L.

James M. Cain. Madden, D.

"James M. Cain and the movies of the thirties and forties".
Madden, D.

"James M. Cain and the pure novel". Madden, D.

"James M. Cain and the tough guy novelists of the 30's".
Madden, D.

"James M. Cain, 1922-1958". Hagemann, E. R., (jt. comp.).

"James M. Cain; twenty-minute egg of the hard-boiled school".
Madden, D.

"Jane Austen and detective stories". Jarrett, E.

"The Janus resolution". McSherry, F.

"John Appleby". Innes, M.

"John Buchan". Sandison, A.

John Buchan. Smith, J.

"John Buchan; a philosophy of high adventure". Cox, J.

"John Buchan; an untimely appreciation". Himmelfarb, G.

"John Buchan and Alfred Hitchcock". Camp, J.

John Buchan, 1875-1940. Hanna, A.

"John Creasey - fact or fiction". Creasey, J.

John D. MacDonald. Campbell, F.

"John D. MacDonald". Doulis, T.

"John Dickson Carr". Herzel, R.

"John Huston". Archer, E.

John Steed. Heald, T.

A list of the original appearances of Dashiell Hammett's magazine work. Mundell, E.

Die literarische Angst. Conrad, H.

Der literarische Mord. Wölcken, F.

"A literary crisis". Steel, K.

Die Literatur der Gewalttatigkeit und der Verfolgung. Shrapnel, N.

"Literatur unterm Tisch". Kaemmel, E.

"Literature high and low". Hartman, G. G.

Literature of mystery and detection. Arno Press.

The literature of roguery. Chandler, F. W.

"The literature of the subject". Briney, R. E.

The literature of the Victorian era. Walker, H.

"The literature on the detective story". Olle, J.

"Littérature 'populaire' et roman-policier". Hankiss, J.

"'Little Caesar' and its role in the gangster film genre". Kaminsky, S.

"The locked house; an essay on locked rooms". Yates, D.

"The locked room". Yates, D.

"The locked room lecture". Carr, J. D.

Locked room murders. Adey, R.

"Locked rooms and puzzles". Yates, D.

"'The long goodbye' from 'Chinatown'". Stewart, G.

"Long life: to some detectives". Stone, P.

The long weekend. Graves, R., (jt. auth.).

"Lost fortnight". Houseman, J.

Love and death. Legman, G.

Love and death in the American novel. Fiedler, L. A.

"The lure of the crime book". Wyndham, H.

Une machine à lire. Narcejac, T.

"'McWatters' Law'". Gilbert, E. G.

Magazín Labyrintu. Krkošková, M.

Magiciens et logiciens. Maurois, A.

"Maigret and Adler". Austin, R.

"Maigret and Co.". Dubourg, M.

"Maigret and women". Eisinger, E.

Os maiores detetives de todos os tempos. Albuquerque, P. de M.e.

Maker and craftsman. Dale, A.

"'The Maltese Falcon'". Crowther, B.

"A man and his books". Wallace, P.

The man behind Doc Savage. Weinberg, R. (ed.).

"The man behind Sherlock Holmes". Mackenzie, C.

"The man of letters (1908-12)". Homberger, E.

"Man under sentence of death". Oates, J.

The man who was Sherlock Holmes. Hardwick, J. M. D., (jt. auth.).

"Man with a toy gun". Pollock, W.

"Mark McPherson". Caspary, V.

"Marlowe, men, and women". Mason, M.

"Marlowe's victim". Symons, J.

"Martinis without olives". Godfry, L.

"Mary Rogers, John Anderson, and others". Wimsatt, W.

"A master of suspense". Pett, J.

Master of villainy. Van Ash, C.

Masters of mystery. Thomson, H.

"Matt Helm". Hamilton, D.

"Mayhem Parva and wicked Belgravia". Watson, C.

"The mean streets of Europe". Becker, J. P.

Med hälsningar. Queen, E. [pseud.].

Med venlig hilsen fra Ellery Queen. Queen, E. [pseud.].

"Media Marlowes". French, P.

"Meditations on the literature of spying". Barzun, J.

"Meet Sam Spade". Queen, E. [pseud.].

Melodrama; plots that thrilled. Disher, M. W.

Melville Davisson Post. Norton, C.

"Melville Davisson Post". Wood, W.

Mémoires. Vidocq, F.

Memories and adventures. Conan Doyle, Sir A.

Memory hold-the-door. Buchan, J.

The men behind boys' fiction. Lofts, W., (jt. auth.).

"Men, women, and thrillers". Gerould, K. F.

Meningar om mord. Broberg, J.

"Mental holidays". Quiz, Q. [pseud.].

"The message of Mayhem Parva". Watson, C.

Mesterdetektiver under Lup. Lauritzen, H.

"Die metaphysische Bedeutung des Detektivromans".
Rickmann, H.

La méthode intellectuelle d'Edgar Poe. Marion, D.

"Michael Butor's 'Passing time' and the detective hero".
O'Donnell, T.

"Michael Shayne". Halliday, B.

"Mickey Spillane and his bloody Hammer". La Farge, C.

"Mickey Spillane as a fifties phenomenon". Weibel, K.

"A midas gift to the theatre". Trewin, J.

The mind of Chesterton. Hollis, C.

The mind of Poe. Campbell, K.

The Minerva Press, 1790-1820. London. Bibliographical Society.

"A misrated author?". Ridley, M.

"Miss Marple". Brand, C.

"Mr. and Mrs. North". Lockridge, R.

Mr. Buchan, writer. Turner, A.

"Mr. Holmes, they were the footprints of a gigantic hound!".
Wilson, E.

"Mr. R. Austin Freeman". Adams, J.

"The mistress of complication". Symons, J.

"The mistress of simplicity". Crispin, E.

"Mistresses of malfeasance". Hoffman, N.Y.

Mistresses of mystery. Manley, S., jt. comp.

"The moment of violence". Gilbert, M.

"Mon ami Simenon". Moremans, V.

"Mon maître Simenon". Debray-Ritzen, P.

"The monitor image". Downer, A. S.

"Monsieur Hercule Poirot". La Cour, T.

Mord för ro skull. Broberg, J.

Mord i biblioteket. Elgström, J., (jt. auth.).

Mord i Biblioteket. La Cour, T.

Mord i minne. Broberg, J.

Mord mem moral - og uden. La Cour, T.

Mordbogen. La Cour, T., (jt. auth.).

"Du Mörder des Juden Aaron". Freund, W.

Mordets enkla konst. Lundin, B.

Mordisk familjebok. Broberg, J.

More rivals of Sherlock Holmes. Greene, Sir H., (ed.).

Mortal consequences. Symons, J.

"The most private eye". Slopen, B.

"Le mot du coffre". Mambrino, J.

"Movement as metaphor; 'The long goodbye'". Tarantino, M.

Multiplying villanies. Boucher, A. [pseud.].

Die Mumie im Glassarg. Pfeiffer, H.

No mundo do romance policial. Lins, A.

"Music and mystery". Weaver, W.

"Murder a minute". Whiteside, T.

"Murder and Karl Marx". McCarthy, M.

"Murder and the mean streets". Grella, G.

"Murder and morality". Hamilton, K.

"Murder and motives". Lucas, E.

"Murder and manners". Grella, G.

"Murder at large". Ball, J. D.

The murder book. SEE Mordbogen.

Murder by mail. Cook, M.

"Murder for pastime". Gerould, K. F.

Murder for pleasure. Haycraft, H.

Murder in Albemarle St. National Book League. London.

Murder in fact and fiction. Brookes, J. A. R.

"Murder in fiction". Lowndes, Mrs. B.

"Murder makes merry". Rice, C.

"Murder, Marx, and McCarthy". Seagle, W.

"Murder, mythology, and Mother Goose". Cabana, R.

Murder must appetize. Keating, H. R. F.

"The murder of Mary Cecilia Rogers". Crouse, R.

"Murder on Parnassus". Very, P.

Murder on the menu. Larmoth, J.

"Murder she says". Holquist, M.

Murder trilogy. Wilson, C.

"The murderers among us". Dyer, P. J.

"The murders in the Rue Morgue". Bonaparte, M., Princess.

"My favourite sleuths". Amis, K.

My life of absurdity. SEE The autobiography of Chester Himes.

"My murder story". Lucas, E.

"My servant Caleb". Ousby, I.

My story. Rinehart, M.

"My years with the Shadow". Gibson, W.

"Myshelovka". Ennok, E.

"The mysteries of 'Gaudy Night'". Ray, L.

"Mysteriet om en Hansom Cab". La Cour, T.

The mysterious world of Agatha Christie. Feinman, J.

Mystery. Haining, P.

Mystery and crime. Allinson, A. A. (jnt. auth.).

"The mystery as mind-stretcher". Evans, V.

"Mystery fans and the problem of potential murders".
Bergler, E.

"Mystery fiction in the nineteenth century". Smith, W.

Mystery fiction; theory and technique. Rodell, M.

"The mystery film". Connor, E.

[The Mystery Library]. California. University. University
at San Diego. University Extension.

"Mystery midwife". Taylor, I.

The mystery of Agatha Christie. Robyns, G.

"The mystery of Marie Rogêt". Benton, R. P.

"The mystery of mysteries". Hartman, G. H.

"The mystery of social reaction". Christopher, J. R.

"Mystery stories in Japan". Jinka, K.

"Mystery story". Boston, R.

"The mystery story". Ulanov, B.

"The mystery story in cultural perspective". Stein, A.

"The mystery story today and yesterday". Wallace, E.

"The mystery vs. the novel". Waugh, H.

The mystery writer's art. Nevins, F.

The mystery writer's handbook. Mystery Writers of America.

Mythologie du roman policier. Lacassin, F.

"Nachahmung der Vorsehung". Daiber, H.

"Name games". Nevins, F.

"Namen als Symbol". Gerber, R.

"Nancy Drew". Jones, J. P.

"Nancy Drew". Keene, C.

"Nancy Drew, ballbuster". Zacharias, L.

The Nancy Drew cookbook. Keene, C.

Nápady Čtenáře detektivek. Skvorecký, J.

"Negro stereotypes". Jones, J.

Nero Wolfe of West Thirty-fifth Street. Baring-Gould, W. S.

"Die neue Gattung". Škreb, Z.

"Neue Häuser in der Rue Morgue". Fischer, P.

"A new category of the mystery story". McSherry, F.

"New patents pending". Keating, H.

"The new wave in crime". Symons, J.

The Newgate novel. Hollingsworth, K.

"Ngaio Marsh". Shadbolt, M.

"Night moves". Gallagher, T.

"Night today". Kolker, R. P.

"Nightmare Alley". Shapiro, C.

Nihon suiri shōsetsu shi. Nakajima, K.

"Nine most devilish murders". Edmiston, S.

"The nine Philo Vances". Connor, E.

"'The nine tailors' and the complexity of innocence".
Basney, L.

XIX century fiction. Sadleir, M.

Ninkyō eiga no sekai. Kusumoto, K.

"Nirvana for two dollars". Whipple, L.

"Normative attitudes of spies in fiction". Rockwell, J.

"The not so literary digests". Turner, R.

"Not 'whodunit' but 'how'?". Barzun, J.

"A note on the inadequacy of Poe as a proofreader". Barzun, J.

"A note on 'The murder of Roger Ackroyd'". Barnes, D. R.

The notebooks of Raymond Chandler. Chandler, R.

"Notes on additions to a cornerstone library". SEE "From
Poe to Hammett".

"Notes on 'The big sleep' thirty years after". Monaco, J.

"Notes on the mystery". Chandler, R.

"Novel and narrative". Kermode, J. F.

The novel of violence in America, 1920-1950. Frohock, W. M.

"The novel turns tale". Barzun, J.

La novela criminal. Gubern, R., comp.

La novela de intrigua. Rodríguez Joulia Saint-Cyr, C.

La novela policíaca. Díaz, C. E.

Novelle und Kriminalschema. Schonhaar, R.

"The novels of Émile Gaboriau". Hardy, A. E. G.

The novels of G. K. Chesterton. Boyd, I.

The novels of Theodore Dreiser. Pizer, D.

"Nur ein Detektivroman". SEE "Only a detective story".

O och A. Tullberg, S.

The objective treatment of the hard-boiled hero in American
fiction. Durham, P. C.

"Of detective literature". Starrett, V., ed.

"Oh, England! full of sin". Casey, R. J.

"Old mystery books". Rosenbach, A.

Om norsk kriminallitteratur. Kvam, L. N.

"Omnes me impune lacessunt". Davies, R.

"The omnibus of crime". Sayers, D.

"On 'Caleb Williams'". Cruttwell, P.

"On Chesterton". Borges, J. L.

"On crime fiction". Williams, G.

On crime writing. Macdonald, R. [pseud.].

On detective fiction and other things. McCleary, G.

"On detective novels". Chesterton, G. K.

"On detective story writers". Chesterton, G. K.

"On holiday with the bodies". Priestley, J.

"On Raymond Chandler". Jameson, F.

"On the floor of the library". Strunsky, S.

"On the fourth floor of Paramount". Moffat, I.

"On the novels of Raymond Chandler". Parsons, L.

Onder de gordel. Visser, A.

"Only a detective story". Krutch, J. W.

Order of assassins. Wilson, C.

"The origin of Lord Peter Wimsey". Reynolds, B.

"The original of Hortense". Valentine, B.

"Origines du roman policier". Galtier-Boissiere, J.

Pages from an adventurous life. Preston-Muddock, J.

Pages from the Goncourt journal. Goncourt, E. L. A. de (jt.
auth.).

"The poetics of the private eye". Edenbaum, R.I.

Poetika kriminalističkog romana. Lasić, S.

"The poet's purloined letter". Roth, M.

"Le point Omega". Narcejac, T.

Points of view from Kipling to Graham Greene. Maurois, A.

"The police procedural". Waugh, H.

"Police report on the T.V. cop shows". Daley, R.

Policiers de roman et policiers de laboratoire. Locard, E.

"The political and social background of 'The secret agent'".
Watt, I.

"Poor Scotland Yard". Hammett, D.

The popular book. Hart, J.

Popular fiction 100 years ago. Dalziel, M.

The popular novel in England, 1770-1800. Tompkins, J.

"Pornography of moral indignation". Basney, L.

"Portrait of a tough guy". Nolan, W.F.

"A portrait of the artist as a criminal". Ziolkowski, T.

Positive images of aging. Bedell, J.

"The Postman and the Marathon". Wells, W.

"A postwar sympton". Swinnerton, F.

"Pourquoi le "nouveau roman" policier?" Charney, H.

A Praed Street dossier. Derleth, A.W.

"The precarious world of John D. Macdonald". Kelly, R.G.

"Preface" (Ashenden). Maugham, W.S.

"Preface" (Lord Peter devant le cadavre). Morand, P.

"Preface" (The face of violence). Bronowski, J.

"Preface" (The thirteen). Saintsbury, G.

"Preface" (Three of a kind). Cain, J.M.

"Preface" (<u>Three of hearts</u>). Cain, J.M.

"Preface" (<u>Zelty pes</u>). d'Astier de la Vigerie, E.

"A preface to 'the Galton Case'". Macdonald, R. (pseud.)

"Preface to William Faulkner's 'Sanctuary'". Malraux, A.

<u>A preliminary checklist of the detective novel and its</u>
<u>variants</u>. Shibuk, C. (comp.)

"The present conventions of the mystery story". MacDonnell, A.

"The present status of the mystery story". Sayers, D.

<u>The prince of storytellers</u>. Standish, R. (pseud.)

"Private eye in an evil time". Nevins, F.M.

<u>The private lives of private eyes</u>. Penzler, O.M.

<u>The problem of moral vision in Dashiell Hammett's detective</u>
<u>novels</u>. Thompson, G.

"Professionals in crime". Fishman, K.D.

"The professor and the detective". Nicolson, M.

"Progress of a crime writer". Symons, J.

"The private eye". Houston, P.

"The private eye". Sandoe, J.

"The private eye as illegal hero". Higgins, G.V.

"The private eye:from print to television". Charland, M.

<u>The private eye hero</u>. Crider, A.

"Private eyes and public critics". Cohen, R.

"Private eyes - from Sam Spade to J. J. Gittes". Miller, D.

"Psychology of detective stories". Bellak, L.

"The publication of Raymond Chandler's 'The long goodbye'".
Miller, R.

<u>The pulp jungle</u>. Gruber, F.

<u>The pulps</u>. Goodstone, T., comp.

<u>The puritan pleasures of the detective story</u>. Routley, E.

"Putting the shock into shockers". Williams, G.

The quality of hurt. SEE The autobiography of Chester Himes.

Quand j 'etais vieux. Simenon, G.

Queen's quorum. Queen, E. (pseud.)

("Quel dommage d l'avoir recontré si tard dans ma vie!")
Miller, H.

"Quelque chose de changé dans le roman policier". Boileau, P.

Quelques aspects du roman policier psychologique. Radine, S.

(Qui êtes-vous) Georges Simenon? Thoorens, L.

"Quiller". Hall, A.

Quotations from Charlie Chan. Chertok, H. (Jt. comp.)

"R. Austin Freeman" SEE In search of Dr. Thorndyke.

"Race Williams - private investigator". Crider, A.B.

"Raffles and Miss Blandish". Orwell, G.

Rascals at large. Prager, A.

"Raskolnikov's motives". Wasiolek, E.

"Ray and Cissy". Powell, D.

Raymond Chandler. Bruccoli, M.J.

Raymond Chandler. Finch, G.

"Raymond Chandler". Fleming, I.

"Raymond Chandler". Ruhm, H.

"Raymond Chandler and an American genre". Beeckman, E.M.

"Raymond Chandler and Hollywood". Desilets, M.

"Raymond Chandler and the traditions". Whitley, J.

"Raymond Chandler on crime and punishment". Sington, D.

Raymond Chandler on screen. Pendo, S.

Raymond Chandler speaking. Chandler, R.

"Raymond Chandler thirteen years after". Sissman, L.

"Raymond Chandler's last novel". Orel, H.

"Raymond Chandler's Los Angeles". Reck, T.

"Raymond Chandler's Philip Marlowe". Pendo, S.

"Raymond Chandler's private eye". Schickel, R.

"Reader's choice". Handlin, O.

"A readers' list of detective story 'cornerstones'".
SEE "From Poe to Hammett".

The real Le Queurx. Sladen, N.

"Recalled and awakened". Adams, D.K.

The recognition of Edgar Allan Poe. Carlson, E.W., (ed.)

Les récréants. Poupart, J.

"Redécouverte du roman d'aventure anglais". Bergier, J.

"The Red-headed League and 'The Rue Morgue'". Roberts, D.

Reflections on the Newgate calendar. Heppenstall, R.

"Reflections sur le roman-policier". Morand, P.

Remembering Mr Maugham. Kanin, G.

"Renaissance of wonder". Woods, K.

"Reply to "Cops" by P. French". Sparne, K.

"Reply to Edmund Wilson on detective stories". De Voto, B.

"Reply to J. P. Sisk, 'Crime and Criticism'". Cashman, G.

"Reply to N. Muhlen's 'Thinker and the tough guy'".
Boucher, A. (pseud.)

"Reply to: Waite, J.B." Denbie, R.

"Reply with rejoinder to: John Paterson". Boucher, A.
(pseud.)

"A resolution and a protest". Quiz, Q. (pseud.)

"Response to John Houseman". Asheim, L.

"Retrospective review". Kabatchnik, A.

"Return of the outlaw couple". Kinder, M.

"Reverens för Rinehart". Broberg, J.

Rex Stout: a biography. McAleer, J.

"Rex Stout and the detective story". Tuska, J.

The riddle of Erskine Childers. Boyle, A.

"The riddle of the sands". Cockburn, C.

The rivals of Sherlock Holmes. Greene, Sir H. (ed.)

"Robert Pinget et le roman policier". Zeltner, G.

Rock my socks off, baby. McCloy, S.

"The Rocky Steele novels of John B. West". Turner, D.

"Roderick Alleyn". Marsh, E.N.

"The role of detective stories in a child analysis".
Buxbaum, E.

"Un roman ininterrompu". Juin, H.

Le roman noir américain. Lacombe, A.

Le roman policier. Boileau, P.

Le roman policier. Caillois, R.

Le roman policier. Dupuy, J.

"Le roman policier et vérité". Chastaing, M.

"Roman policiers". Marcel, G.

"The romance of crime". Hardy, T.J.

"Les romans policiers de M. Georges Simenon".
Daniel-Rops.

"The roots of detection". Pritchett, V.

"Ross MacDonald". Carter, S.R.

"Ross Macdonald". Cook, B.

"Ross Macdonald". Leonard, J.

"Ross Macdonald". Speir, J.

"Ross Macdonald; at the edge". Grogg, S.

"Ross Macdonald in raw California". Carroll, J.

"Sex murder incorporated". Cowley, M.

"The Sexton Blake file". Cox, R.

"The Shadow". Grant, M.

"The shape of crimes to come". McSherry, F.

Sheridan Le Fanu. Browne, N.

Sherlock Holmes. Vigniel, D.

Sherlock Holmes & Co. Becker, J.P.

"Sherlock Holmes and Nero Wolfe". Rauber, D.

"Sherlock Holmes and the detective story". Ridley, M.

Sherlock Holmes is alive and well at the Metropolitan Toronto Library. Metropolitan Toronto Central Library.

"Sherlock Holmes on the screen". Connor, E.

Sherlock Holmes, Raffles, and their prototypes. SEE Sherlock Holmes, Raffles, und Ihre Vorbilder.

Sherlock Holmes, Raffles und Ihre Vorbilder. Depken, F.

Shitai o buji ni kesu made. Tsuzuki, M.

The shudder pulps. Jones, R.K.

Shukumei no bigaku. Gonda, M.

A sign for Cain. Wertham, F.

"Simenon". Collins, C.

Simenon. Fallois, B. de

Simenon. Lacassin, F. (comp.)

Simenon. Ritzen, Q. (pseud.)

"Simenon". Whiteley, J.

"Simenon and Chandler". Parsons, L.

"Simenon and Highsmith". Richardson, M.

"Simenon and Maigret". Grella, G.

"Simenon and Spillane". Rolo, C.

"Simenon et la fugue initiatique". Lacassin, F.

"Simenon et l'enfant de Choeur". Moré, M.

Simenon in court. Raymond, J.

"Simenon ou l'appétit de Maigret". Courtine, R.-J.

"Simenon's mosaic". Jacobs, J.

"Simenon's mosaic of small novels". Galligan, E.

"The simple art of murder". Chandler, R.

Sincerely, Tony/Faithfully, Vincent. Boucher, A. (pseud.) (jt. auth.)

"Sir Arthur Conan Doyle". Adcock, A. St J.

"Sir Arthur Conan Doyle". Hodder Williams, J.E.

Sir Arthur Conan Doyle. Nordon, P.

"The six Charlie Chans". Connor, E.

"Six mystery movies and their makers". Everson, W.K.

"Den skarpsinnige snobben". Lundin, B.

"The sleuth in sci-fi". Moskowitz, S.

Sleuths. MacGowan, K. (ed.)

Sleuths, Inc. Eames, H.

Snobbery with violence. Watson, C.

"A sober word on the detective story". Steeves, H.

"Social interaction in John O'Hara's 'The gangster'". Shawen, E.

"Solar Pons and Dr. Parker". De Waal, R.B.

"Some Chinese detective stories". Starrett, V.

Some less known detective stories. Indianapolis, Ind. Public Library.

Some mid-Victorian thrillers. Edwards, P.D.

"Some notes on violence". West, N.

Some rogues and vagabonds of Dickens. Dickens, C.

"Some silent sinners". Dyer, P.J.

"Some thoughts on fifties ganster films".   Whitehall, R.

"Some uncollected authors, XXXI: Dashiell Hammett".
Stoddard, R.

Somerset Maugham.   Cordell, R.

Sophocle et Archimède.   Achard, M.

"Sophocles and the rest of the boys in the pulps".
Van Meter, J.

"A source for ballistics in Poe".   Murphy, G.

South African detective stories in English and Afrikaans.
Friedland, S.

Soziologie als Wissanschaft : Der Detektivroman; Die
Angestellten.   SEE   Schriften.

Sparhundarna.   Lundin, B.

"Spies and ideologies".   Durgnat, R.

"Spielregein des Kriminalromans".   Heissenbüttel, H.

"The Spillane phenomenon".   Cawelti, J.

"Spillane's anti-establishmentarian heroes".   Banks, R.J.

"The sport of noble minds".   Sayers, D.

"Spring, three one hundred".   Pearson, E.

"The spy in fact and fiction".   Gilbert, M.F.

"The spy who came in for the gold".   Kanfer, S.

The spy's bedside book.   Greene, G. (jt. ed.)

"S. S. Van Dine at 20th Century Fox".   Smith, D.

"S. S. Van Dine filmography".   Thiede, K.

"S. S. Van Dine - Willard Huntington Wright".
Braithwaite, W.S.

"Starting with people".   Marsh, Dame N.

Stene for brød.   Jensen, V.

"Stolen privacy".   Denley, D.

The Strand Magazine 1891-1950.   Pound, R.

'The Strand Magazine', 1891-1950. Whitt, J.

"The strange case of Alfred Hitchcock". Durgnat, R.

"Strangers within, enemies without". Carlisle, C.R.

Studier i rødt. La Cour, T.

Studies in Agatha Christie's writings. Behre, F.

Studies in the Newgate novel. Lucas, A.

"Sua maestà Agatha Christie". Pensa, C.

"Success without the excess". Gow, G.

Such a strange lady. Hitchman, J.

Suiri bundan sengo shi. Yamamura, M.

The superhero women. Lee, S.

"Superintendent Pibble". Dickinson, P.

The supernatural in fiction. Penzoldt, P.

"The supersleuths of sci-fi". Moskowitz, S.

"Supreme moments in detective fiction". Stevenson, B.

"Sur la vieillesse et sur la mort". Kanters, R.

Suspense in the cinema. Gow, G.

"Suspense suspended". Barzun, J.

Svensk deckare - & thrillerbibliografi. Hedman, I.

Svensk mordbok. Elgstrom, J. (jt. auth.)

"The symbolic world of 'The secret agent'". Fleishman, A.

Tantei shosetu hyakka. Kuki, S.

"A taxonomy of American crime film themes". Grace, H.

The technique of the mystery story. Wells, C.

Television's private eye. Larka, R.

Les terribles. Peske, A. (jt. auth.)

Theodore Dreiser. Pizer, D. (jt. auth.)

"There's murder in the air". Crossen, K.

"These grapes need sugar". Stout, R.

"'The Thin Man'". Quennell, P.

Things I know. Le Queux, W.

"Thinker and the tough guy". Muhlen, N.

Thirteen classic detective stories. Liebman, A. (comp.)

"Thorndykiana". Freeman, R.A.

Those days. Bentley, E.C.

The thriller : the suspense film from 1946. Davis, B.

Thriller movies. Hammond, L.

Thrillers. Palmer, J.

"The thrillers of Chester Himes". Margolies, E.

"Thrillers; the deviant behind the consensus". Palmer, J.

"Through seas of blood". Mierow, C.

The time has come. Wheatley, D.

"The time of the assassins". Bogan, L.

"The time-space dimension in the Lew Archer detective
novels". Holtan, J. (jt. auth.)

"Today's hero". Houseman, J.

"Too many murders". O'Neill, D.

Tough guy writers of the Thirties. Madden, D. (ed.)

The tough guys. Parish, J.

"The tough Hemingway and his hard-boiled children".
Grebstein, S.N.

"A tout âge d'ailleurs". Mauriac, F.

Toward a definition of the American 'film noir'.
Karimi, A.M.

"Traffic in souls". Allen, R.C.

"The trail of scarlet". Rosenbach, A.

"The train in fiction and on the screen". Cookridge, E.

"Translator's preface" (Japanese tales of mystery and imagination). Harris, J.B.

"Trojan horse opera". Boucher, A. (pseud.)

The true Conan Doyle. Canon Doyle, A.M.

T.S. Stribling. Eckley, W.

"The twelve Bulldog Drummonds". Connor, E.

"Twentieth century interpretations of 'Bleak House'". Korg, J.

"Twenty rules for writing detective stories". Wright, W.

"Two authors in an attic : (John Dickson Carr)". Taylor, R.

"Tung mans liv". Mühlenbock, K.

"Uber die Popularität des Kriminalromans". Brecht, B.

Umění detektivky. Cizánek, J.

"The UNC detective collection". Carr, J.D.

"Under two flags". McSherry, F.

Underworld U.S.A. McArthur, C.

The unembarassed muse. Nye, R.

An unfinished woman. Hellman, L.

Das Unheimliche und die Detektivliteratur. Reinert, C.

Unpopular opinions. Sayers, D.

"Unreal policemen". Avis, K.

"The unromantic detective". Edgar, G.

Untersuchungen über die Romankunst von Wilkie Collins. Sehlbach, H.

"The uppity private eye as movie hero". Monahan, A.

"Van Dine and his public". Seldes, G.

"Variation und Innovation". Smuda, M.

"Das verbrecherische Pfarshaus" SEE "The guilty vicarage".

"A very English lady". Gilbert, M.F.

"The vicious circle". O'Riordan, C.

Wilkie, Collins : 'The Moonstone'. Bunnell, W.S.

William Faulkner. McHaney, T.

"William Faulkner and the art of the detective story". French, W.

"William Faulkner and the tradition of tough-guy fiction". Tallack, D.

William Harrison Ainsworth and his friends. Ellis, S.

"William Hope Hodgson". Christensen, P.

"William Powell". Jacobs, J.

William Somerset Maugham. Ward, R.

The Wimsey family. Scott-Giles, C.

"Windows, detectives, and justice in Durrenmatt's detective stories". Pfeiffer, J.

"The wings of Henry James". Thurber, J.

"With acknowledgements to Thomas De Quincy". Pearson, E.

With prejudice. Fairlie, G.

Without stopping. Bowles, P.F.

Der wohltemperierte Mord. Zmegac, V.

"Women in detective fiction". Slung, M.

Women in comics. Horn, M.

Wonder Woman. SEE Encyclopedia of comic book heroes.

"A word from Dr. Lyndon Parker". Parker, L.

Works of M. P. Shiel. Morse, A.

The world bibliography of Sherlock Holmes and Dr. Watson. De Waal, R.B.

"The world of Eric Ambler". Ambrosetti, R.

"The world of Erle Stanley Gardner". Morton, C.

"The world of Perry Mason". Robbins, F.

The world of Raymond Chandler. Gross, M. (ed.)

"The world of the detective story". Spiller, R.

The world of the thriller. Harper, R.

"The world we live in". Davis, P.

"Wozu Detektivgeschichten. SEE "Introduction" (Murder for pleasure).

"The writer as detective hero". Macdonald, R. (pseud.)

"The writer in America". Dolmetsch, C.

Writing detective and mystery fiction. Burack, A.S. (ed.)

Writing mysteries for young people. Nixon, J.

Writing thrillers for profit. Hogarth, B.

You only live once. Bryce, I.

"Young and innocent". Dyer, P.J.

De Zadig au Riffifi. Chassaing.

The zeal of the convert. Wilkinson, B.

"Zehn Regeln für einenguten Detektivroman". SEE "Introduction" (Best detective stories).

"007". Houston, P.

"007 and the myth of the hero". Carpenter, R.C.

"007 James Bond". Snelling, O.

"007 + 4". Johnson, I.

"Zur Typologie des Kriminalromans". Naumann, D.

SUBJECT INDEX

THE AFRICAN POISON MURDERS (Novel)

Barzun, J.M. A book of prefaces.

AINSWORTH, WILLIAM HARRISON (1805-1882)

Ellis, S.M. William Harrison Ainsworth and his friends.

Hollingsworth, K. The Newgate novel.

ALARUM AND EXCURSION (Novel)

Barzun, J.M. A book of prefaces.

ALCOTT, LOUISA MAY (1832-1888)

Stern, M.B. "Introductions" (Behind a mask and Plots and counterplots).

ALLAIN, MARCEL

Peske, A. Les terribles.

ALLARD, KENT (char.)

Grant, M. "The Shadow".

ALLEYN, RODERICK (char.)

Marsh, E.N. "Roderick Alleyn".

ALLINGHAM, MARGERY LOUISE (1904-1966)

Panek, L.L.   Watleau's shepherds.

See also DANCERS IN MOURNING (novel)

AMBLER, ERIC

Ambrosetti, R.   "The world of Eric Ambler".

Byrne, E.B. (jnt. comp.)   Attacks of taste.

Davis, P.   "The world we live in".

Eames, H.   Sleuths, Inc.

Hopkins, J.   "An interview with Eric Ambler".

James, C.   "Eric Ambler".

Lambert, G.   The dangerous edge.

AMERICAN CRIME FICTION

Becker, J.P.   Sherlock Homes & Co.

Buchloh, P.G. (jnt. auth.)   Der Detektivroman.

Gonda, M.   Shukumei no bigaku.

Nakauchi, M.   Amerika fubutsushi.

Narcejac, T.   La fin d'un bluff.

AND ON THE EIGTH DAY (novel)

Erisman, F. " 'Where we plan to go' ".

APPLEBY, JOHN (char.)

Innes, M.   "John Appleby".

ARCHER, Lew (char.)

Broberg, J.   "Lew Archer och hans värld".

Macdonald, R.   "Introduction" (Archer in Hollywood).

Macdonald, R.   "Introduction" (Lew Archer).

Macdonald, R.   "Lew Archer".

ARCHIMEDES (287?-212 B.C.)

Achard, M. Sophocle et Archimède.

ARGENTINIAN CRIME FICTION

Yates, D.A. The Argentine detective story.

ASIMOV, ISAAC.

Patrouch, J.F. "..a detailed discussion of Isaac Asimov's 'The caves of steel' and 'the naked sun'.."

AUBREY-FLETCHER, Sir HENRY LANCELOT, bart. (1887-1963)

Shibuk, C. "Henry Wade".

See also The DYING ALDERMAN (novel)

AUSTEN, JANE (1775-1817)

Jarrett, C. "Jane Austen and detective stories".

BAILEY, HENRY CHRISTOPHER (1878-1961)

See MR FORTUNE : EIGHT OF HIS ADVENTURES (short stories)

BALZAC, HONORE de (1799-1850)

Roux, F. Balzac.

Saintsbury, G.E.B. "Preface" (The thirteen).

BARDIN, JOHN FRANKLIN

Symms, J. "Introduction" (The John Franklin Bardin omnibus).

BATMAN (char.)

Encyclopedia of comic book heroes.

BEADLE AND ADAMS, PUBLISHERS

Johannsen, A. The House of Beadle and Adams.

The BENSON MURDER CASE (novel)

Hammett, D. "Poor Scotland Yard".

BENTLEY, EDMUND CLERIHEW (1875-1956)

Baker, I.L. E.C. Bentley.

Bentley, E.C. Those days.

Panek, L.L. Watteau's shepherds.

See also TRENT'S LAST CASE (novel)

BEYNON, JANE LEWIS (1915-   )

See The BIRTHDAY MURDER (novel).

BEYOND A REASONABLE DOUBT (novel)

Barzun, J.M. A book of prefaces.

BIBLIOGRAPHY - TEXTS

See TEXTS-BIBLIOGRAPHY.

The BIG BOW MYSTERY (novel)

Bleiler, E.F. "Introduction" (Three Victorian detective novels).

The BIG CLOCK (novel)

Barzun, J.M. A book of prefaces.

"The BIG SLEEP" (film)

Monaco, J. "Notes on 'The Big Sleep' ".

BIGGERS, EARL DER

See CHAN, CHARLIE (char.)

The BIRTHDAY MURDER (novel)

Barzun, J.M. A book of prefaces.

BLACK MASK MAGAZINE

Borneman, E. "'Black Mask'".

California University. University at Los Angeles. Library.
The boys in the Black Mask.

Durham, P.C. "The 'Black Mask' school".

Ruhm, H. "Introduction" (The hard-boiled detective).

Shaw, J.T. "Introduction" (The hard-boiled omnibus).

Sturak, T. "Horace McCoy, Captain Shaw, and the 'Black
Mask'".

BLAIR, ERIC

See ORWELL, GEORGE (pseud.)

BLAKE, NICHOLAS (pseud.)

See DAY LEWIS, CECIL.

BLAKE, SEXTON (char.)

Cox, R. "The Sexton Blake file".

A BLUNT INSTRUMENT (novel)

Barzun, J.M. A book of prefaces.

BLEAK HOUSE (novel)

Daniel, P. Bleak House.

Dyson, A.E. Dickens 'Bleak House'.

Korg, J. Twentieth century interpretations of 'Bleak House'.

Newsom, R. Dickens on the romantic side of familiar things.

Smith, G. Charles Dickens : 'Bleak House'.

Valentine, B.B. "The original of Hortense and the trial of
Marcia (sic) Manning for murder".

BLOOD ON THE BOSOM DIVINE (novel)

Barzun, J.M. A book of prefaces.

'The BLUE DAHLIA' (film)

Houseman, J. "Lost fortnight".

BOGART, HUMPHREY

Cooke, A. "Epitaph for a tough guy".

BONAPARTE, NAPOLEON (char.)

See UPFIELD, ARTHUR

BOND, JAMES (char.)

Amis, K. The James Bond dossier.

Carpenter, R.C. '007 and the myth of the Law".

Dear, A. "Intellectuals and 007".

Eco, U. "James Bond.

Glass, R. "The gunnery of James Bond".

Houston, P. "007".

Johnson, I. "007+4"

Lane, S. For Bond lovers only.

Martin, B. "James Bond".

Ormerod, D. "The Bond game".

Pearson, J.G. James Bond.

Richler, M. "James Bond unmasked".

Snelling, O.F. Double O Seven.

Tanner, W. The book of Bond.

Trahair, R.C.S. "A contribution to the psychoanalytic study of the modern hero".

See also FLEMING, IAN.

BOND, JAMES (char.) - FILMS

Brosnan, J. James Bond in the cinema.

The BOND IS POINTED (novel)

Barzun, J.M. A book of prefaces.

"BONNIE and CLYDE" (film)

Cawelti, J.G. Foursom 'Bonnie and Clyde'.

BOOK CLUB EDITIONS

Cook, M.L. Murder by mail.

BOUCHER, ANTHONY (pseud.)

Boucher, A. Sincerely, Tony/Faithfully, Vincent.

BOWLES, PAUL FREDERIC (1911-   ).

Bowles, P. F. Without Stopping.

Byrne, E.B. (int. comp.) Attacks of taste.

Stewart, L.D. "Paul Bowles".

The BOX OFFICE MURDERS (novel)

Barzun, J.M. A book of prefaces.

BOYS' FICTION

Lofts, W.O.G. The men behind boys' fiction.

Turner, E.S. Boys will be boys.

BRADDON, MARY ELIZABETH (1937-1915)

See LADY AUDLEY'S SECRET (novel)

BRADY, KING (char.)

Leithead, J.E. "The great detective team".

BRAMAH, ERNEST (pseud.)

White, W. "Bramah"

See also CARRADOS, MAX (char.)

See also MAX CARRADOS (short stories)

BRAZILIAN CRIME FICTION

Lemos Britto, J.G. de.   O crime e os criminosos na literatura brasileira.

BREDDER, Father JOSEPH (char.)

Holton, L.   "Father Bredder".

BRIGHTON ROCK (novel)

Price, A.   Brighton Rock.

BRITISH CRIME FICTION

Oswell, C.   "Grandeur et decadence du roman policier Anglais".

Ousby, I.   Bloodhounds of heaven.

Panek, L.L.   Watteau's shepherds.

BRODIE, Deacon

la Cour, T.   "Dr Jekyll og Mr. Brodie".

BROWN, Father JOHN PAUL (char.)

Knox, R.A.   "Introduction" (Father Brown).

Robson, W.W.   "G.K. Chesterton's 'Father Brown' stories".

BROWNING, ROBERT (1812-1889)

See 'The RING AND THE BOOK' (poem)

BUCHAN, JOHN, 1st Baron Tweedsmuir (1875-1940)

Buchan, J.   Memory-hold-the-door.

Cox, J.R.   "John Buchan"

Daniell, D.   The interpreter's house.

Greene, G. "The last Buchan".

Himmelfarb, G. "John Buchan".

John Buchan.

Lambert, G. The dangerous edge.

Ridley, M.R. "A misrated author?".

Sandison, A. "John Buchan".

Schubert, L. "Almost real reality".

Smith, J.B.A. John Buchan.

Swiggett, H. "Introduction" (Mountain meadow).

Sykes, M. "The imaginative world of John Buchan".

Turner, A.C. Mr. Buchan, writer.

Usborne, R. Clubland heroes.

BUCHAN, JOHN - BIBLIOGRAPHY

Hanna, A. John Buchan.

JOHN BUCHAN

See also HANNAY, RICHARD (char.)

See also 'The THIRTY-NINE STEPS' (film).

See also The THIRTY-NINE STEPS (novel).

BULLETT, GERALD (1893-1958)

See The JURY (novel).

BULWER-LYTTON

See LYTTON, E.G.E.L.B., 1st Baron.

BURIED FOR PLEASURE (novel)

Barzun, J.M. A book of prefaces.

BURTON, MILES (pseud.)

See STREET, CECIL JOHN CHARLES.

BUTOR, MICHAEL

See PASSING TIME (novel)

CAIN, JAMES MALLAHAN (1892-1958)

Byrne, E.B. Attacks of taste.

Farrell, J.T. "Cain's movietone realism".

Macdonald, R. "Cain X 3".

Madden, D.T. "James M. Cain".

Madden, D.T. James M. Cain.

Madden, D.T. "James M. Cain and the movies of the thirties
and forties".

Madden, D.T. "James M. Cain and the pure novel".

Madden, D.T. "James M. Cain and the tough guy novelists
of the 30's".

Oates, J.C. "Man under sentence of death".

Wilson, E.G. The boys in the back room".

Wolfe, T. "Introduction" (Cain X 3).

Hagemann, E.R. "James M. Cain, 1922-1958".

See also 'DOUBLE INDEMNITY' (film).

See also The POSTMAN ALWAYS RINGS TWICE (novel).

CALDWELL, ERSKINE PRESTON (1903-   )

Gossett, L.Y. "The climate of violence".

CALEB WILLIAMS (novel)

Gruttwell, P. "On 'Caleb Williams'".

McCracken, D. "Introduction" (Caleb Williams).

Rothstein, E.   "Allusion and analogy in the romance of 'Caleb Williams'".

CANADAY, JOHN EDWIN (1907-   )

See The CONGO VENUS (novel).

CANADIAN CRIME FICTION

Batten, J.   "Who will wear the sacred trench coat for Canada?".

Drew, B.   "The land of the Midnight Pulps".

Hirsh, M.   The great Canadian comic books.

CAPOTE, TRUMAN

Tschimmel, I.   Kriminalroman und Gesellschaftsdarstellung.

CARELLA, STEVE (char.)

McBain, E.   "The 87th Precinct".

CARNACKI, THOMAS (char.)

See HODGSON, WILLIAM HOPE.

CARR, JOHN DICKSON (1905-1978)

Herzel, R.   "John Dickson Carr".

Notes for the curious.

Panek, L.L.   Watteau's shepherds.

Taylor, R.L.   "Two authors in an attic".

CARRADOS, MAX (char.)

Bleiler, E.F.   "Introduction" (Best Max Carrados detective stories).

CARTER, NICK (char.)

Clurman, R.   "Introduction" (Nick Carter, detective).

Reck, T.S.   "Raymond Chandler's Los Angeles".

Ruhm, H.   "Raymond Chandler"

Russell, D.C.   "The Chandler books".

Schickel, R.   "Raymond Chandler".

Longton, D.   "Raymond Chandler on crime and punishment".

Lissman, L.E.   "Raymond Chandler thirteen years after".

Spender, N.   "His own long goodbye".

Symons, J.   "An aesthete discovers the pulps".

Symons, J.   "Marlowe's victim".

Wells, W.   "Grey Knight in the Great Wreng Place".

Whitley, J.   "Raymond Chandler and the traditions".

See also 'THE BIG SLEEP' (film).

See also The LADY IN THE LAKE (novel).

See also The LONG GOODBYE (novel).

CHANDLER, RAYMOND THORNTON (1888-1959) - BIBLIOGRAPHY

Bruccoli, M.J.   Raymond Chandler.

CHANDLER, RAYMOND THORNTON (1888-1959) - CRITICISM,
BIBLIOGRAPHY

McCloy, S.A.   Rock my socks off, baby.

CHARACTERS - DICTIONARY

Detectionary.

CHARACTERS IN NOVELS

Penzler, O.M.   The great detectives.

Penzler, O.M.   The private lives of private eyes.

CHARACTERS IN SERIES

See SERIES CHARACTERS

Cockburn, C.   "'The riddle of the sands'".

Donaldson, N.   "Introduction" (The riddle of the sands).

Wilkinson, B.   The zeal of the convert.

See also The RIDDLE OF THE SANDS (novel).

CHILDREN'S LITERATURE

Hasubek, P.   Die Detektivgeschichte für junge Leser.

CHILDREN'S LITERATURE - BIBLIOGRAPHY

Dikty, A.S.   The American boys' book series bibliography
1895-1935.

CHINESE CRIME FICTION

Comber, L.   "An introduction to the world of Magristrate Pao".

Hayden, G.A.   "Courtroom plays of the Yüan and early Ming
periods".

Hayden, G.A.   The Judge Pao plays of the Yüan Dynasty.

Lach, D.F.   "Introduction" (The Chinese Bell murders).

Starrett, V.   "Some Chinese detective stories".

Van Gulik, R.H.   "Introductions"   (Judge Dee series of novels).

CHRISTIE, Dame AGATHA MARY CLARISSA MILLER (1890-1976)

Behre, F.   Get, come, and go.

Behre, F.   Studies in Agatha Christie's writings.

Brand, C.   "Miss Marple".

Byrne, E.B.   Attacks of taste.

Christie, A.   Agatha Christie.

Christie, A.   An autobiography.

Crispin, E.   "The mistress of simplicity".

Cristea, V.   "Voluptatea teroarei".

East, A.R.   Agatha Christie quizbook.

See also The MURDER OF ROGER ACKROYD (novel).

See also POIROT, HERCOLE (char.)

The CIRCULAR STUDY (novel)

Barzun, J.M. A book of prefaces.

CLARK, ALFRED ALEXANDER GORDON (1900-1958)

See HARE, CYRIL (pseud.)

COE, TUCKER (pseud.)

Bakerman, J.S. "Patterns of quilt and isolation in five novels by 'Tucker Coe'".

COLE, GEORGE DOUGLAS HOWARD (1890-1959)

See The MURDER AT CROME HOUSE (novel).

COLE, MARGARET ISABEL (1893-   )

See The MURDER AT CROME HOUSE (novel).

COLLECTING

Carter, J. "Detective fiction".

Osborne, E.A. "Collecting detective fiction".

Penzler, O. "Detective fiction".

Quayle, E. The collector's book of detective fiction.

Quayle, E. "Detective fiction".

Rosenbach, A.S.W. "Old mystery books" and "The trail of scarlet".

Sheppard, R. Crime and detective fiction.

Stewart, S. "Adventure, detection and children's books".

COLLECTIONS

Carr, J.D. "The UNC detective collection".

COLLINS, WILLIAM WILKIE (1824-1889)

Andrews, R.V. Wilkie Collins.

Ashley, R. Wilkie Collins.

Davis, N.P. The life of Wilkie Collins.

Eliot, T.S. "Dickens and Collins".

Ellis, S.M. Wilkie Collins, Le Fame, and others.

Gregory, E.R. "Wilkie Collins and Dorothy L. Sayers".

Hyder, C.K. "Wilkie Collis and 'The woman in white'".

Lambert, G. The dangerous edge.

Marshall, W.H. Wilkie Collins.

Phillips, W.C. Dickens, Reade and Collins.

Robinson, K. Wilkie Collins.

Sadkin, M.T.H. "Wilkie Collins".

Sayers, D.L. Wilkie Collins.

Sehlbach, H. Untersuchungen über die Romankunst von Wilkie
Collins.

Swinburne, A.C. "Wilkie Collins".

See also The MOONSTONE (novel).

See also MY LADY'S MONEY (novel).

See also The WOMAN IN WHITE (novel).

COLLINS, WILKIE - BIBLIOGRAPHY

Parrish, M.L. Wilkie Collins and Charles Reade.

"COLUMBO" (TV series)

Marill, A.H. "Films on TV".

COMICS

Becker, S.D. Comic art in America.

Daniels, L. Comix.

Encyclopedia of comic book heroes.

Feiffer, J. The great comic book heroes.

Hirsh, M. The great Canadian comic books.

Horn, M. Woman in the comics.

Lee, S. The superhero woman.

Musee des Arts Decoratifs. Band dessinee.

Thompson, D. The comic-book book.

Waugh, C. The comics.

The world encyclopedia of comics.

CONAN DOYLE, Sir ARTHUR (1859-1930)

Adcock, A. St. J. "Sir Arthur Conan Doyle".

Brown, I.J.C. Conan Doyle.

Carr, J.D. The life of Sir Arthur Conan Doyle.

Conan Doyle, Sir A. Memories and adventures.

Conan Doyle, A.M. The true Conan Doyle.

Cromie, R. "Dr. Conan Doyle's place in Modern literature".

Eames, H. Sleuths, Inc.

Hardwick, J.M.D. The man who was Sherlock Holmes.

Higham, C. The adventures of Conan Doyle.

Hodder Williams, J.E. "Sir Arthur Conan Doyle".

Hollyer, C. "Arthur Conan Doyle".

Kittle, C.F. "Arthur Conan Doyle".

Lambert, G. The dangerous edge.

Lamond, J. Arthur Conan Doyle.

Mackenzie, C. "The man behind Sherlock Holmes".

Nordon, P. Sir Arthur Conan Doyle.

"The novels of Sir Arthur Conan Doyle".

Pearsall, R. Conan Doyle.

Pearson, H. Conan Doyle.

Sir Arthur Conan Doyle.

See also HOLMES, SHERLOCK.

See also The HOUND OF THE BASKERVILLES (novel).

See also The RED-HEADED LEAGUE (story).

CONAN DOYLE, Sir ARTHUR - BIBLIOGRAPHY

Locke, H. A bibliographical catalogue of the writings of Sir Arthur Conan Doyle.

CONAN DOYLE, Sir ARTHUR - COLLECTIONS

Metropolitan Toronto Central Library. A checklist of the Arthur Conan Doyle collection in the Metropolitan Toronto Central Library.

Metropolitan Toronto Central Library. Sherlock Holmes is alive and well at the Metropolitan Toronto Library.

The CONGO VENUS (novel)

Barzun, J.M. A book of prefaces.

CONRAD, JOSEPH (1857-1924)

Howe, I. "Joseph Conrad".

Pritchett, V.S. "An emigre".

See also The SECRET AGENT (novel).

The CONVERSATION" (film)

Denby, D. "Stolen privacy".

COOKBOOKS

Courtine, R.J. Le cahier de recettes de Madame Maigret.

Keene, C.   The Nancy Drew cookbook.

Larmoth, J.   Murder on the menu.

COOL, BERTHA

Robbins, F.E.   "The firm of Cool and Lam".

CORNWELL, DAVID

See LE CARRÉ, JOHN (pseud.)

COX, ANTHONY BERKELEY

Panek, L.L.   Watteau's shepherds.

CRANSTON, LAMONT (char.)

See ALLARD, KENT (char.)

CREASEY, JOHN

Creasey, J.   "John Creasey".

CRIME AND PUNISHMENT (novel)

Wasiolek, E.   Raskolnikov's motives.

CRIME FILMS

Alloway, L.   Violent America.

CRISPIN, EDMUND (pseud.)

See   BURIED FOR PLEASURE (novel).

CRITICISM-BIBLIOGRAPHY

Briney, R.G.   "The literature of the subject".

Hollyer, C.   The body in the library.

Skene Melvin, L.D.H. St C.   Crime, detective, espionage,
mystery, and thriller fiction and film.

CROFTS, FREEMAN WILLS (1879-1957)

Keddie, J. "Freeman Wills Crofts".

See also The BOX OFFICE MURDERS (novel).

The DAFFODIL AFFAIR (novel)

Barzun, J.M. A book of prefaces.

DANCERS IN MOURNING (novel)

Barzun, J.M. A book of prefaces.

DANISH CRIME FICTION

See SCANDINAVIAN CRIME FICTION

DA SILVA, JOSÉ (char.)

Fish, R.L. "Captain José Da Silva".

DAY LEWIS, CECIL (1904-1972)

Day Lewis, C. The buried day.

See also MINUTE FOR MURDER (novel).

DEATH IN HOLLYWOOD (novel)

Sturak, T. "A forword to 'Death in Hollywood'".

DEATH UNDER SAIL (novel)

Barzun, J.M. A book of prefaces.

DEE GOONG AN, Judge

Lach, D.F. "Introduction" (The Chinese Bell murders).

Van Gulik, R.H. "Introductions" (Judge Dee series of novels).

DE MAUPASSANT, GUY (1850-1898)

Fouyé, Y. Guy de Maupassant et les criminels.

DENT, LESTER

Weinberg, R.   The man behind Doc Savage.

The DEPARTMENT OF DEAD ENDS (short stories)

Bleiler, E.F.   "Introduction" (The department of dead ends).

The DETECTIVE (magazine)

Hutter, A.D.   "Who can be trusted?".

DETECTIVES (char's.)

MacGowan, K.   Sleuths.

Penzler, O.M.   The great detective.

Penzler, O.M.   The private lives of private eyes.

DICKENS, CHARLES (1812-1870)

Collins, P.A.W.   Dickens and crime.

Dickens, C.   Some rogues and vagabonds of Dickens.

Eliot, T.S.   "Dickens and Collins".

Hollingsworth, K.   The Newgate novel.

Monod, S.   Dickens romancier.

Phillips, W.C.   Dickens, Reade and Collins.

Poe, E.A.   "Charles Dickens".

Squires, P.C.   "Charles Dickens as criminologist".

See also BLEAK HOUSE.

DICKSON, CARTER (pseud.)

See CARR, JOHN DICKSON

DICKSON, HARRY

Lacassin, F.   "Alan Resnais and the quest for Harry Dickson".

DIME NOVELS

Bragin, C. Bibliography of dime novels.

Johannsen, A. The House of Beadle and Adams.

Pearson, E.L. Dime novels.

See also BRADY, KING (char.)

DINE, S.S. VAN

See WRIGHT, WILLARD HUNTINGTON

The DIVISION BELL MYSTERY (novel)

Barzun, J.M. A book of prefaces.

DR. JEKYLL AND MR. HYDE (story)

la Cour, T. "Dr. Jekyll og Mr. Brodie".

The DOCUMENTS IN THE CASE (novel)

Hart, H. "Accident, suicide, or murder?".

DONOVAN, DICK (pseud.)

See PRESTON-MUDDOCK, JOYCE EMMERSON (1843-1934).

DOSTOEVSKY, FEODOR MIKHAILOVICH (1821-1881)

See CRIME AND PUNISHMENT (novel)

'DOUBLE INDEMNITY' (film)

Allyn, J. "Double Indemnity".

DOYLE, Sir ARTHUR CONAN

See CONAN DOYLE, Sir ARTHUR

DRAMA

Chapman, J. "Introduction". (Famous plays of crime and detection).

Disher, M.W. Blood and thunder.

Disher, M.W. Melodrama.

Hayden, G.A. "Courtroom plays of the Yuam and early Ming periods".

Newton, H.C. Crime and the drama.

DREISER, THEODORE HERMAN ALBERT (1871-1945)

Pizer, D. The novels of Theodore Dreiser.

DREISER, THEODORE - BIBLIOGRAPHY

Pizer, D. (jnt.comp.) Theodore Dreiser.

DREW, NANCY (char.)

Jones, J.P. "Nancy Drew".

Jones, J.P. "Negro stereotypes in children's literature".

Keene, C. "Nancy Drew".

Keene, C. The Nancy Drew cookbook.

Mason, B.A. The girl sleuth.

Brager, A. Rascals at large.

Zacharias, L. "Nancy Drew, ballbuster".

DROSTE-HÜLSHOFFS, ANNETTE VON

Freund, W. "Der Mörder des Juden Aaron".

Rolleke, H. "Erzähltes Mysterium".

THE DROWNING POOL (novel)

Barzun, J.M. A book of prefaces.

DRUMMOND, HUGH (char.)

Connor, E. "The twelve Bulldog Drummonds".

DU MAURIER, DAPHNE (1907-   )

Du Maurier, D. Growing pains.

DUPIN, Chevalier AUGUSTE (char.)

Bandy, W.T. "Who was Monsieur Dupin".

Harrison, M. "Dupin; the reality behind the fictions".

DURAS, MARGUERITE

Eisinger, E.M. "Crime and detection in the novels of Marguerite Duras".

DÜRRENMATT, FRIEDRICH

Arnold, A. Friederich Dürrenmatt.

Ashbrook, B. "Dürrenmatt's detective stories".

Koropf, J. Friedrich Dürrenmatt.

Leah, G.N. "Dürrenmatt's detective stories".

Peppard, M.B. Friedrich Dürrenmatt.

Pfeiffer, J.R. "Windows, detectives, and justice in Dürrenmatt's detective stories".

Tschimmel, I. Kriminalroman und Gesellschaftsdarstellung.

The DYING ALDERMAN (novel)

Barzun, J.M. A book of prefaces.

EAST GERMANY

See GERMAN DEMOCRATIC REPUBLIC.

ENCYCLOPEDIAS

Reclams Kriminalromanführer.

Hagen, O.A. Who done it?

ENGLISH CRIME FICTION

Becker, J.P. Sherlock Holmes & Co.

Bergier, J. "Redécouverte du roman d'aventure anglais".

Buchloh, P.G. (jnt. auth.) Der detektivroman.

ESPIONAGE

See SPIES

ESSAYS

Der Detektiverzählung auf der Spin.

Dimensions of detective fiction.

Gilbert, M.F. Crime in good company.

Gonda, M. Shukumei no bigaku.

Haycraft, H. The art of the mystery story.

Ikushima, J. Hangyaku no kokoro o torimodose.

Kosakai, F. Kindai hanzai kenkyu.

Madden, D.T. Tough guy writers of the thirties.

The mystery story.

Nevins, F.M. The mystery writer's art.

Tsuzuki, M. Shitai o buji ni kesu made.

Vogt, J. Der Kriminalroman.

Zmegac, V. Der wohltemperierte Mord.

EUROPEAN CRIME FICTION

Becker, J.P. "The mean streets of Europe".

EUSTIS, HELEN WHITE (1916-   )

See The HORIZONTAL MAN (novel)

FAIR, A.A. (pseud.)

See GARDNER, ERLE STANLEY.

FAIRLIE, GERARD

Fairlie, G. With prejudice.

FAULKNER, WILLIAM HARRISON (1897-   )

Elsen, C. "Faulkner et le roman noire".

French, W. "William Faulkner and the art of the detective story".

Gidley, M. "Elements of the detective story in William Faulkner's fiction".

Gossett, L.Y. "The climate of violence".

McHaney, T.L. William Faulkner.

Malraux, A. "Preface to William Faulkner's 'Sanctuary'".

O'Brien, F.B. "Faulkner and Wright".

Tallack, D.C. "William Faulkner and the tradition of tough-guy fiction".

F.B.I.

Clarens, C. "Hooverville West".

FEARING, KENNETH (1902-1961)

See The BIG CLOCK (novel)

FEDERAL BUREAU OF INVESTIGATION

See F.B.I.

FELLOWS, FRED (char.)

Waugh, H. "Fred Fellows".

'FILM NOIR'

Borde, R. (jnt. auth.) Panorama du film noir américain.

Earley, S.C. An introduction to American movies.

Karimi, A.M. Toward a definition of the American 'film noir'.

Mirams, G. "Drop that gun!"

Monaco, J- "Notes on 'The Big Sleep'".

Monahan, A. "The uppity private eye as movie hero".

Nolan, J.E. "Graham Green's movies".

Paiva, S.C. de O ganster no cinema.

Parish, J.R. The great ganster pictures.

Parish, J.R. The great spy pictures.

Parish, J.R. The tough guys.

Pechter, W.S. "Anti-Western".

Peeples, S.A. "Films on 8 & 16".

Pendo, S. Raymond Chandler on screen.

Perry, G. The films of Alfred Hitchcock.

Pett, J. "A master of suspense".

Phillips, G.D. Graham Greene.

Pitts, M.R. Celluloid sleuths.

"Private eye".

Richie, D. "'High and low'".

Rosow, E. Born to lose.

Sacks, A. "An analysis of ganster movies of the early thirties".

Sayers, D.L. "Detective stories for the screen".

Shadoian, J. Dreams and dead ends.

Shearer, L. "Crime certainly pays on the screen".

Silver, A. "'Kiss me deadly'".

Siodmak, R. "Hoodlums".

Smith, D.R. "S.S. Van Dine at 20th Century-Fox".

Spoto, D. The act of Alfred Hitchcock.

Stewart, G. "'The long goodbye' from 'Chinatown'".

Bryce, I. You only live once.

Grant, R. Ian Fleming.

Pearson, J.G. The life of Ian Fleming.

Zeiger, H.A. Ian Fleming.

See also BOND, JAMES (char.)

FLEMING, IAN - BIBLIOGRAPHY

Campbell, I. Ian Fleming.

FORMULA STORIES

Cawelti, J.G. Adventure, mystery and romance.

FORRESTER, ANDREW

See The UNKNOWN WEAPON (novel).

FOUND DROWNED (novel)

Barzun, J.M. A book of prefaces.

FRASER, GEORGE MACDONALD

See FLASHMAN, HARRY (char.)

DAS FRAULEIN VON SCUDERI (novel)

Kanzog, K. "E.T.A. Hoffmans Erzählung 'Das Fraulein von
Scuderi' als Kriminalgeschichte".

Post, K.D. "Kriminalgeschichte als Heilsgeschichte".

Thalmann, M. "E.T.A. Hoffmans 'Fraulein von Scuderi".

FREEMAN, RICHARD AUSTIN (1862-1943)

Adams J. "Mr. R. Austin Freeman".

Bleiler, E. "Introduction" (The best Dr. Thorndyke
detective stories).

Donaldson, N. In search of Dr. Thorndyke.

See also The SINGING BONE (novel).

See also THORNDYKE, Dr. (char.)

FRENCH CRIME FICTION

Heppenstall, R.   French crime in the romantic age.

Tourteau, J.J.   D'Arsène Lupin à San-Antonio.

A FUNERAL IN EDEN (novel)

Barzun, J.M.   A book of prefaces.

FUTRELLE, JACQUES

Bleiler, E.   "Introduction" (Best "Thinking Machine" detective stories).

See also VAN DUSEN, S.F.X. (char.)

GABORIAU, ÉMILE (1835-1873)

Bleiler, E.   "Introduction" (Monsieur Lecoq).

Curry, N.E.L.   The life and works of Émile Gaboriau.

Hardy, A.E.G.   "Novels of Émile Gaboriau".

Sayers, D.L.   "Émile Gaboriau".

Williams, G.V.   "Gaboriau".

The GALTON CASE (novel)

Macdonald, R.   "A preface to 'The Galton Case'".

The GANGSTER (story)

Shawen, E.   "Social interaction in John O'Hara's 'The gangster'".

GANGSTER MOVIES

Baxter, J.   The gangster film.

Earley, S.C.   An introduction to American movies.

"Gang films".

Kaminsky, S.   "'Little Caesar' and its role in the ganster film genre".

Karpf, S.L.   The gangster film.

Lee, R.   Gangsters and hoodlums.

McArthur, C.   Underworld U.S.A.

Manchel, F.   Gangsters on the screen.

Paiva, S.C. de   O gangster no cinema.

Parish, J.R.   The great gangster pictures.

Rosow, E.   Born to lose.

Sacks, A.   "An analysis of gangster movies of the early thirties".

Shadoian, J.   Dreams and dead ends.

Warner, A.   "Gangster heroes".

Warshow, R.   "The gangster as tragic hero".

Whitehall, R.   "Crime, Inc."

Whitehall, R.   "Some thoughts on fifties gangster films".

Wilson, R.   "Hoodlums".

GARDNER, ERLE STANLEY (1889-1970)

Borrello, A.   "Evelyn Waugh and Erle Stanley Gardner".

Hughes, D.B.F.   Erle Stanley Gardner.

Johnston, A.   "The case of Erle Stanley Gardner".

Morton, C.W.   "The world of Erle Stanley Gardner".

Queen, E.   "Erle Stanley Gardner".

See also COOL, BERTHA (char.)

See also LAM, DONALD (char.)

See also MASON, PERRY (char.)

See also The CASE OF THE CROOKED CANDLE (novel).

GARDNER, ERLE STANLEY - BIBLIOGRAPHY

Mundell, E.H.   Erle Stanley Gardner.

GARVE, ANDREW (pseud.)

See NO TEARS FOR HILDA (novel).

GAUDY NIGHT (novel)

Ray, L.K.   "The mysteries of 'Gaudy Night'".

Sayers, D.L.   "Gaudy night".

GERMAN CRIME FICTION

Colbron, G.I.   "Detective story in Germany and Scandinavia".

Freund, W.   Die deutsche Kriminalnovelle von Schiller bis Hauptmann.

Greiner-Mai, H.   Die deutsche Kriminalerzählung von Schiller bis zur Gegenwart.

GERMAN DEMOCRATIC REPUBLIC

Dworak, A.   Der Kriminalroman der D.D.R.

GHOTE, GANESH V. (char.)

Keating, H.R.F.   "Inspector Ghote".

GIBSON, WILLIAM

Nanovic, J.L.   "I never called him Bill".

GILBERT, MICHAEL FRANCIS (1912-   )

See SMALLBONE DECEASED (novel).

The GLASS KEY (novel).

Pachovsky, G.   A brief appreciation of 'The glass key'.

GODWIN, WILLIAM (1756-1836)

Adams, D.K. "Recalled and awakened".

Barber, G.A. "Justice to Caleb Williams".

McCracken, D. "Introduction" (Caleb Williams).

Ousby, I. "My servant Caleb".

Pollin, B.R. "Poe and Godwin".

See also CALEB WILLIAMS (novel).

GODWIN, WILLIAM - CRITICISM - BIBLIOGRAPHY

Pollin, B.R. Godwin criticism.

The GOLD BUG (story)

Blanch, R.J. "The background of Poe's 'Gold Bug'".

GOTHIC MYSTERIES

Whitney, P.A. "Gothic mysteries".

GOTHIC NOVELS - BIBLIOGRAPHY

Summers, A.J-M.A.M. A Gothic bibliography.

GRAFTON, CORNELIUS WARREN (1909-   )

See BEYOND A REASONABLE DOUBT (novel).

GRANT, MAXWELL (pseud.)

See GIBSON, WILLIAM

GRAY, CURME

See MURDER IN MILLENIUM VI (novel).

GREAT BRITAIN

Great Britain. British Council. British crime fiction.

Panek, L.L. Watteau's shepherds.

GREAT BRITAIN - 17TH CENTURY

Peterson, S. The counterfeit lady unveiled.

GREAT BRITAIN - 19TH CENTURY

See NINETEENTH-CENTURY (GREAT BRITAIN).

The GREAT GATSBY (novel)

Stewart, L.D. "The dust jackets of 'The great Gatsby' and 'The long goodbye'".

Whitley, J.S. F. Scott Fitzgerald:'The great Gatsby'.

GREEN, ANNA KATHARINE (1846-1935)

See The CIRCULAR STUDY (novel)

GREENE, GRAHAM (1904-   )

Allott, K. The art of Graham Greene.

Atkins, J.A. Graham Greene.

Lambert, G. The dangerous edge.

Lodge, D. Graham Greene.

McCann, J. "Graham Greene".

Mesnet, M.B. Graham Greene and the heart of the matter.

Nolan, J.E. "Graham Greene's movies".

Phillips, G.D. Graham Greene.

Pryce-Jones, D. Graham Greene.

Stewart, D.G. "Graham Greene".

Wolfe, P. Graham Greene.

Wyndham, F. Graham Greene.

See also BRIGHTON ROCK (novel)

GREENE, GRAHAM - CRITICISM - BIBLIOGRAPHY

Vann, J.D. Graham Greene.

GRESHAM, WILLIAM LINDSAY

See NIGHTMARE ALLEY (novel)

GULIK, ROBERT H. van

See VAN GULIK, ROBERT H.

HAD I BUT KNOWN

See HIBK

HAGEN, ORDEAN

Barzun, J.M. "The book, the bibliographer, and the absence of mind".

HALLAS, RICHARD (pseud.)

See KNIGHT, ERIC

HAMMETT, SAMUEL DASHIELL (1894-1961)

Adams, D.K. "The first thin man".

Blair, W. "Dashiell Hammett".

Bazelen, D.T. "Dashiell Hammett's 'Private Eye'".

City of San Francisco Magazine.

Crider, A.B. The private eye hero.

Eames, H. Sleuths, Inc.

Edenbaum, R.I. "The poetics of the private eye".

Godshalk, W. "...a critical biography of Hammett...".

Gores, J.N. Hammett.

Gores, J.N. "Hammett the writer".

Hellman, L. (autobiography).

Hellman, L. "Dashiell Hammett".

Kenney, W.P. The Dashiell Hammett tradition...

Macdonald, R. "Homage to Dashiell Hammett".

McLaren, J.R.   "Chandler and Hammett".

Marcus, S.   "Dashiell Hammett and the Continental op".

Moss, L.   "Hammett's heroic operative".

Nolan, W.F.   Dashiell Hammett.

Parker, R.B.   The violent hero.

Phelps, D.   "Dashiell Hammett's microcosmos".

Popescu, C.   "Asta simplā a romanuliu polițrist".

Queen, E.   "Letter to the reader".

Sanderson, E.   "Ex-detective Hammett".

Symons, J.   "Dashiell Hammett".

Thompson, G.J.   The problem of moral vision in Dashiell
Hammett's detective novels.

White, W.   "About Dashiell".

Wolfe, P.   Beams falling.

Wolfe, P.   "Sam Spade, lover".

See also SPADE, SAM (char.)

See also The GLASS KEY (novel).

See also The MALTESE FALCON (novel).

See also The THIN MAN (novel).

HAMMETT, DASHIELL - BIBLIOGRAPHY

Mundell, E.H.   A list of the original appearances of
Dashiell Hammett's magazine work.

Stoddard, R.E.   "Some uncollected authors".

HAMMETT, DASHIELL - CRITICISM - BIBLIOGRAPHY

McCloy, S.A.   Rock my socks off, baby.

HANNAY, RICHARD (char.)

Voorhees, R.J.   "Flashman and Richard Hannay".

HARBAGE, ALFRED BENNETT (1901-   )

See BLOOD ON THE BOSOM DIVINE (novel).

HARD-BOILED

Durham, P. "The 'Black Mask' school".

Durham, P.C. The objective treatment of the hard-boiled hero in American fiction.

Goulart, R. The hardboiled dicks.

Grebstein, S.N. "The tough Hemingway and his hard-boiled children".

Grella, G. "Murder and the mean streets".

Madden, D.T. Tough-guy writers of the thirties.

Ruhm, H. "Introduction" (The hard-boiled detective).

Shaw, J.T. "Introduction" (The hard-boiled omnibus).

Xenophile (special issue).

See also BLACK MASK MAGAZINE.

HARD-BOILED - BIBLIOGRAPHY

Sandoe, J. The hard-boiled dick.

HARDY BOYS (char's.)

McFarlane, L. Ghost of the Hardy Boys.

HARE, CYRIL (pseud.)

Gilbert, M. F. "Introduction" (Best detective stories of Cyril Hare.

Shibuk, C. "Cyril Hare".

See WHEN THE WIND BLOWS (novel).

HEAD, MATTHEWS (pseud.)

See CANADAY, JOHN EDWIN

HELLMAN, LILLIAN (1905-   )

Hellman, L. (autobiography).

HELM, MATT (char.)

Hamilton, D. "Matt Helm".

HEMINGWAY, ERNEST MILLER (1898-1961)

Grebstein, S.N. "The tough Hemingway and his hard-boiled children".

HERO

Burton, C.T. The hero as detective.

Carpenter, R.C. "007 and the myth of the hero".

Hill, L. "The Hero in criminal literature".

Howarth, P. Play up and play the game.

Murdoch, D. "The case of the vanishing hero".

Praz, M. The hero in eclipse in Victorian fiction.

HEYER, GEORGETTE (1902-1974)

See A BLUNT INSTRUMENT (novel).

HIBK

Nash, O. "Don't guess, let me tell you".

'HIGH AND LOW' (film)

Richie, D. "'High and low'".

HIGHSMITH, PATRICIA

Richardson, M. "Simenon and Highsmith".

HILTON, JAMES (1900-1954)

See WAS IT MURDER (novel).

HIMES, CHESTER B. (1909-   )

Cullaz, M.   "Chester Himes".

Himes, C.   The autobiography of Chester Himes.

Lundquist, J.   Chester Himes.

Margolies, E.   "The thrillers of Chester Himes".

Milliken, S.F.   Chester Himes.

Nelson, R.   "Domestic Harlem".

Reed, I.   ("Essay on Chester Himes").

HITCHCOCK, ALFRED

Bogdanovich, P.   The cinema of Alfred Hitchcock.

Durgnat, R.   "The strange case of Alfred Hitchcock".

Lambert, G.   The dangerous edge.

Perry, G.   The films of Alfred Hitchcock.

Spoto, D.   The art of Alfred Hitchcock.

Truffaut, F.   Le cinéma selon Hitchcock.

Wood, R.   Hitchcock's films.

See also 'NORTH BY NORTHWEST' (film).

See also 'The THIRTY-NINE STEPS' (film).

HODGSON, WILLIAM HOPE

Christensen, P.   "William Hope Hodgson".

HOFFMANN, ERNST THEODOR AMADEUS (1776-1822)

Kanzog, K.   "E.T.A. Hoffmanns Erzählung 'Das Fraulein von
Scuderi' als Kriminalgeschichte".

See also 'Das FRAULEIN VON SCUDERI' (story).

HOGG, JAMES (1770-1835)

Adams, R.M.   "Introduction" (The private memoirs and
confessions of a justified sinner).

Carey, J. "Introduction" (The private memoirs...).

Chianese, R.L. "James Hogg's 'Confessions of a justified sinner'".

Gide, A. "Afterword" (The private memoirs...).

Simpson, L.A.M. James Hogg.

HOLMES, SHERLOCK

Connor, E. "Sherlock Holmes on the screen".

Depken, F. Sherlock Holmes, Raffles, and Ihre Vorbilder.

Druxman, M.B. Basil Rathbone.

Hill, R. "Holmes".

Queen, E. "Who shall ever forget".

Rauber, D.F. "Sherlock Holmes and Nero Wolfe".

Ridley, M.R. "Sherlock Holmes and the detective story".

"The ultimate source of Sherlock Holmes".

Vigniel, D. Sherlock Holmes.

HOLMES, SHERLOCK - BIBLIOGRAPHY

De Waal, R.B. The world bibliography of Sherlock Holmes and Dr. Watson.

HOOVER, J. EDGAR

Dowers, R.G. "J. Edgar Hoover and the detective hero".

The HORIZONTAL MAN (novel)

Barzun, J.M. A book of prefaces.

The HOUND OF THE BASKERVILLES (novel)

Barzun, J.M. A book of prefaces.

HUGO, VICTOR MARIE (1802-1885)

Savey-Casard, P. Le crime et la peine dans l'oeuvre de Victor Hugo.

HUSTON, JOHN

Archer, E. "John Huston".

HUXLEY, ELSPETH JOSCELINE GRANT (1907-   )

See The AFRICAN POISON MURDERS (novel).

IN ACCORDANCE WITH THE EVIDENCE (novel)

Barzun, J.M. A book of prefaces.

INNES, MICHAEL (pseud.)

See The DAFFODIL AFFAIR (novel).

The INNOCENCE OF FATHER BROWN (short stories)

Barzun, J.M. A book of prefaces.

JAMES, HENRY (1843-1916)

Hamblen, A.A. "The inheritance of the meek".

McGill, V.J. "Henry James, master detective".

Thurber, J. "The wings of Henry James".

JAPANESE CRIME FICTION

Gonda, M. Shukumei no bigaku.

Harris, J.B. "Translator's preface" (Japanese tales of mystery & imagination).

Jinka, K. "Mystery stories in Japan".

Nakajima, K. Nihon suiri shōsetsu shi.

Queen, E. "Introduction" (Ellery Queen's Japanese golden dozen).

Yamamura, M. Suiri bundan sengo shi.

DIE JUDENBUCHE (novel)

Freund, W. "Der Mörder des Juden Aaron".

The JURY (novel)

Barzun, J.M. A book of prefaces.

JUVENILES

Nixon, J. Writing mysteries for young people.

"The KENNEL MURDER CASE' (film)

Everson, W.K. "'The Kennel Murder Case'".

KIM (novel)

Hardacre, K. Rudyard Kipling; 'Kim'.

KINDON, THOMAS

See MURDER IN THE MOOR (novel)

KIPLING, RUDYARD (1865-1936)

See KIM (novel).

'KISS ME DEADLY' (film)

Silver, A. "'Kiss me deadly'".

KNIGHT, ERIC

See YOU PLAY THE BLACK AND THE RED COMES UP (novel).

KNOX, RONALD

Waugh, E. The life of the Right Reverend Ronald Knox.

KOJAK, Sergeant (char.)

Sage, L. "Kojak and co.".

KUNNITZ, HARRY (1908-1968)

See The SHADOWY THIRD (novel).

KUROSAWA, AKIRA

See 'HIGH AND LOW' (film).

KYD, THOMAS (pseud.)

See HARBAGE, ALFRED BENNETT

LADY AUDLEY'S SECRET (novel)

Donaldson, N.   "Introduction" (Lady Audley's secret).

The LADY IN THE LAKE (novel)

Barzun, J.M.   A book of prefaces.

LAM, DONALD (char.)

Robbins, F.E.   "The firm of Cool and Lam".

LANG, FRITZ

Bogdanovich, P.   Fritz Lang in America.

Eisner, L.   Fritz Lang.

LAURA (novel)

Caspary, V.   "Mark McPherson".

LEBLANC, MAURICE

Peske, A.   Les terribles.

LE CARRÉ, JOHN (pseud.)

Kanfer, S.   "The spy who came in for the gold".

LE FANU, JOSEPH SHERIDAN (1814-1873)

Browne, N.   Sheridan Le Fanu.

Diskin, P. "Poe, Le Fanu, and the sealed room mystery".

Ellis, S.M. Wilkie Collins, Le Fanu and others.

Shroyer, F. "Introduction" (Uncle Silas).

LEGGETT, WILLIAM

Seelye, J. "Buckskin and ballistics".

LE QUEUX, WILLIAM (1864-1927)

Le Queux, W. Things I know.

Sladen, N. St B. The real Le Queux.

LEROUX, GASTON (1868-1927)

Peske, A. Les terribles.

L'ÉTRANGER (novel)

Madden, D.T. "Cain's 'The postman always rings twice' and
Camus' 'L'Étranger'".

LEWIS, CECIL DAY

See DAY LEWIS, CECIL

LEWIS, LANGE (pseud.)

See BEYNON, JANE LEWIS

'LITTLE CAESAR' (film)

Kaminsky, S. "'Little Caesar' and its role in the ganster
filme genre".

LOCKED ROOM

Adey, R. "A brief history of the early years of the locked
room".

Adey, R.C.S. Locked room murders.

Boucher, A. "...critical discussion of locked room theory..."

Carr, J.D.   "The locked room lecture".

Diskin, P.   "Poe, Le Fanu, and the sealed room mystery".

Rawson, C.   "...critical discussion of locked room theory...".

Santesson, H.S.   "Introduction" (The locked room reader).

Yates, D.A.   "The locked room".

Yates, D.A.   "Locked rooms and puzzles".

LONG, GABRIELLE MARGARET VERE CAMPBELL (1886-1952)

Lewis, S.   "Foreword" (The golden violet).

The LONG GOODBYE (novel)

Miller, R.H.   "The publication of Raymond Chandler's 'The long goodbye'".

Stewart, L.D.   "The dust jackets of 'The great Gatsby' and 'The long goodbye'".

'The LONG GOODBYE' (film)

Tarantino, M.   "Movement as metaphor".

LOS ANGELES

Reck, T.S.   "Raymond Chandler's Los Angeles".

LUPIN, ARSÈNE (char.)

Catogan, V.   Le secret des rois de France.

LYTTON, EDWARD GEORGE EARLE LYTTON BULWER-, 1st Baron (1803-1873)

Hollingsworth, K.   The Newgate novel.

MACLAIN, DUNCAN (char.)

Kendrick, B.H.   "Duncan Maclain".

MCCOY, HORACE (1897-1955)

Sturak, J.T.   "Horace McCoy, Captain Shaw, and the 'Black Mask".

Sturak, J.T.   "Horace McCoy's objective lyricism".

Sturak, J.T.   The life and writings of Horace McCoy.

See also THEY SHOOT HORSES, DON'T THEY? (novel).

MACDONALD, JOHN DANN

Abrahams, E.C.   Visions and values in the action detective novel.

Campbell, F.D.   John P. Macdonald and the colorful world of Travis McGee.

Doulis, T.   "John D. Macdonald".

Hills, L.R.   "Awesome beige typewriter".

Kelly, R.G.   "The precarious world of John D. Macdonald".

MACDONALD, (JOHN) ROSS (pseud.)

Abrahams, E.C.   Visions and values in the action detective novel.

Barnes, D.R.   "'In the eye'".

Broberg, J.   "Lew Archer och hans varld".

Carroll, J.   "Ross Macdonald in raw California".

Carter, S.R.   "Ross Macdonald".

Cook, B.   "Ross Macdonald".

Crider, A.B.   The private eye hero.

Grogg, S.L.   "Ross Macdonald".

Hazard, J.   "... Ph. D. dissertation...".

Holtan, J.   "The time-space dimension in the Lew Archer detective novels".

Leonard, J.   "Ross Macdonald".

Macdonald, R.   "Introduction" (Kenneth Millar/Ross Macdonald).

Pry, E.   "Lew Archer's 'Moral landscape'".

Ross Macdonald; in the first person.

Parker, R.B.   The violent hero.

Sipper, R.B.   "An interview with Ross Macdonald".

Slopen, B.   "The most private eye".

Speir, J.   Ross Macdonald.

Tutunjian, J.   "A conversation with Ross Macdonald".

Wolfe, P.   Dreamers who live their dreams.

See also ARCHER, LEW (char.)

See also The DROWNING POOL (novel).

See also The GALTON CASE (novel).

MACDONALD, ROSS (pseud.) - BIBLIOGRAPHY

Bruccoli, M.J.   Kenneth Millar.

MCFARLANE, LESLIE (1902-   )

McFarlane, L.   Ghost of the Hardy Boys.

Palmer, D.   "A last talk with Leslie McFarlane".

MCGERR, PATRICIA (1917-   )

See PICK YOUR VICTIM (novel).

MCGUIRE, DOMINIC PAUL (1903-   )

See A FUNERAL IN EDEN (novel).

MACLEAN, ALISTAIR

Lee, R.A.   Alistair MacLean.

MCNEILE, HERMAN CYRIL (1888-1937)

See "SAPPER" (pseud.)

McPHERSON, MARK (char.)

Caspary, V. "Mark McPherson".

The MAFIA

Carlisle, C.R. "Strangers within".

MAIGRET, JULES (char.)

Henry, G. Commissaire Maigret.

la Cour, T. "Jules Maigret's privat liv".

MALLOWAN, AGATHA

See CHRISTIE, Dame AGATHA MARY CLARISSA MILLER

The MALTESE FALCON (film)

Crowther, B. "'The Maltese Falcon'".

Eyles, A. "Great films of the century".

Nolan, W.F. "Bogie and the Black Bird".

The MALTESE FALCON (novel)

Malin, I. "Focus on 'The Maltese Falcon'".

Hammett, D. "Introduction" (The Maltese Falcon).

MANHUNT MAGAZINE (circa 1952-1962)

Turner, R. "The not so literary digests".

MARIE ROGÊT

See ROGÊT, MARIE

MARSH, Dame (EDITH) NGAIO (1899-   )

Marsh, Dame N. Black beech and honeydew.

Panek, L.L. Watteau's shepherds.

Shadbolt, M. "Ngaio Marsh".

See also A WREATH FOR RIVERA (novel).

MASON, ALFRED EDWARD WOODLEY (1865-1948)

Green, R.L. A.E.W. Mason.

MASON, PERRY (char.)

Kane, P. "Perry Mason".

Robbins, F.E. "The world of Perry Mason".

MAUGHAM, WILLIAM SOMERSET (1874-1965)

Cordell, R. Somerset Maugham.

Kanin, G. Remembering Mc. Maugham.

Ward, R.H. William Somerset Maugham.

Whitehead, J. "'Whodunit' and Somerset Maugham".

MAUPASSANT, GUY DE

See DE MAUPASSANT, GUY

MAX CARRADOS (short stories)

Barzun, J.M. A book of prefaces.

MEASURE FOR MURDER (novel)

Barzun, J.M. A book of prefaces.

MENDOZA, LUIS (char.)

Shannon, D. "Lieutenant Luis Mendoza".

MERCER, CECIL WILLIAM (1885-1960)

See YATES, DORNFORD (pseud.)

MEXICAN CRIME FICTION

Ortiz Vidales, S.   Los bandidos en la literatura mexicano.

MILLAR, KENNETH (1915-   )

See MACDONALD, ROSS (pseud.)

MILLAR, MARGARET

Slopen, B.   "The most private eye".

MILNE, ALAN ALEXANDER (1882-1956)

Panek, L.L.   Watteau's shepherds.

Swann, T.B.   A.A. Milne.

See also The RED HOUSE MYSTERY (novel).

The MINERVA PRESS

London.   Bibliographical Society.   The Minerva Press.

MINUTE FOR MURDER (novel)

Barzun, J.M.   A book of prefaces.

MR. FORTUNE: EIGHT OF HIS ADVENTURES (short stories)

Barzun, J.M.   A book of prefaces.

MONSIEUR LECOQ (novel)

Bleiler, E.   "Introduction" (Monsieur Lecoq).

MONTGOMERY, ROBERT BRUCE (1921-   )

See CRISPIN, EDMUND (pseud.)

The MOONSTONE (novel)

Bunnell, W.S. Wilkie Collins.

Eliot, T.S. "Introduction" (The Moonstone).

Reed, J.R. "English imperialism and the unacknowledged crime of 'The Moonstone'".

Sayers, D.L. "Introduction" (The Moonstone).

MORRAH, DERMOT MICHAEL MACGREGOR (1896-   )

See The MUMMY CASE (novel).

'The MOUSETRAP'

Ennok, E. "'Myshelovka'".

The MUMMY CASE (novel)

Barzun, J.M. A book of prefaces.

MURDER

Wilson, C. Murder trilogy.

The MURDER AT CROME HOUSE (novel)

Barzun, J.M. A book of prefaces.

MURDER IN MILLENNIUM VI (novel)

Knight, D.F. ("...a careful analysis of Curme Gray's 'Murder in Millenium VI'...").

MURDER IN THE MOOR (novel)

Barzun, J.M. A book of prefaces.

The MURDER OF ROGER ACKROYD (novel)

Barnes, D.R. "A note on 'The murder of Roger Ackroyd'".

Barzun, J.M. A book of prefaces.

The MURDERS IN THE RUE MORGUE (story)

Bonaparte, Princess M. "The murders in the Rue Morgue".

Hawkins, J. "Poe's 'The murders in the Rue Morgue'".

Roberts, D.M. "'The red-headed League' and 'The Rue Morgue'".

MY LADY'S MONEY (novel)

Bleiler, E.F. "Introduction" (Three Victorian detective novels).

The MYSTERY OF A HANSOM CAB (novel)

la Cour, T. "Mysteriet om en Hansom Cab".

The NAKED SUN (novel)

See ASIMOV, ISAAC

NEWGATE CALENDAR

Heppenstall, R. Reflections on the Newgate Calendar.

NEWGATE NOVEL

Hollingsworth, K. The Newgate novel.

Lucas, A. Studies in the Newgate novel of early Victorian England.

NIGHTMARE ALLEY (novel)

Shapiro, C. "'Nightmare Alley'".

The NINE TAILORS (novel)

Basney, L. "'The nine tailors' and the complexity of innocence".

NINETEENTH-CENTURY

Smith, W.J. "Mystery fiction in the nineteenth century".

NINETEENTH-CENTURY - FICTION - BIBLIOGRAPHY

Sadleir, M.T.H. XIX century fiction.

NINETEENTH-CENTURY (GREAT BRITAIN)

Altick, R.D. Victorian studies in scarlet.

Edwards, P.D. Some mid-Victorian thrillers.

Knoepflmacher, U.C. "The counterworld of Victorian fiction and 'The woman in white'".

Richardson, M. "Introduction" (Novels of mystery from the Victorian age).

NO TEARS FOR HILDA (novel)

Barzun, J.M. A book of prefaces.

NORTH, JERRY (char.)

Lockridge, R. "Mr. and Mrs. North".

NORTH, PAMELA (char.)

Lockridge, R. "Mr. and Mrs. North".

'NORTH BY NORTHWEST' (film)

Camp, J. "John Buchan and Alfred Hitchcock".

NORWEGIAN CRIME FICTION

Kram, L.N. Om norsk kriminallitteratur.

See also SCANDINAVIAN...

O'HARA, JOHN HENRY (1905-   )

Wilson, E.G. "The boys in the back room".

See also 'The GANGSTER' (story).

ONIONS, GEORGE OLIVER (1873-1961)

See IN ACCORDANCE WITH THE EVIDENCE (novel).

OPPENHEIM, EDWARD PHILLIPS (1866-1946)

Standish, R. The prince of storytellers.

ORCZY, EMMUSKA, Baroness (1865-1947)

Orczy, E. Links in the chain of life.

The ORIENT EXPRESS

Cookridge, E.H. "The train in fiction and on the screen".

ORWELL, GEORGE (pseud.)

Parrinder, P. "George Orwell and the detective story".

PAGE, MARCO (pseud.)

See KUNNITZ, HARRY

PAO Judge (char.)

Comber, L. "An introduction to the world of Magistrate Pao".

Hayden, G.A. The Judge Pao plays of the Fuau Dynasty.

PAPERBACKS

Breen, J.L. The girl in the pictorial wrapper.

PAPERBACKS - REVIEWS

See REVIEWS - PAPERBACKS

PARIS

Simenon, G.J.C. Le Paris de Simenon.

The PASSENGER FROM SCOTLAND YARD (novel)

Bleiler, E.F. "Introduction" (The passenger from Scotland Yard).

PASSING TIME (novel)

O'Donnell, T.D.   "Michael Burton's 'Passing time' and the detective hero".

The PASTOR OF VELBY (novel)

Larsen, A.P.   Sagen mod praesten i Vejlby.

PENNY DREADFULS

The penny dreadful.

PERDUE, VIRGINIA (1899-1945)

See ALARUM AND EXCURSION (novel).

PETRELLA, PATRICK (char.)

Gilbert, M.   "Patrick Petrella".

PHILLPOTTS, EDEN (1862-1960)

Girvan, W.   Eden Phillpotts.

Philpotts, E.   From the angle of 88.

Rowland, J.   "Phillpott's detective fiction".

See also FOUND DROWNED (novel).

PIBBLE, JAMES (char.)

Dickinson, P.   "Superintendent Pibble".

PICK YOUR VICTIM (novel)

Barzun, J.M.   A book of prefaces.

PINGET, ROBERT

Zeltner, G.   "Robert Pinget et le roman policer".

POE, EDGAR ALLAN (1809-1849)

Alexander, J. Affidavits of genius.

Allen, W.H. Israfel.

Asselineau, R. Edgar Allan Poe.

Barzun, J.M. "A note on the inadequacy of Poe as a proofreader and of his editors as French scholars".

Benton, R.P. "The mystery of Marie Roget".

Bittner, W.R. Poe.

Blanch, R.J. "The background of Poe's 'Gold Bug'".

Bonaparte, M., Princess   Edgar Poe.

Bonaparte, M., Princess   "The murders in the Rue Morgue".

Braddy, H. Glorious incense.

Buranelli, V. Edgar Allan Poe.

Cambiaire, C.P. The influence of Edgar Allan Poe in France.

Campbell, K. The mind of Poe.

Carlson, E.W. (ed.) The recognition of Edgar Allan Poe.

Christopher, J.R. "Poe and the detective story".

Coleem, P. "Introduction" (Tales of mystery and imagination).

Crouse, R. "The murder of Mary Cecilia Rogers".

Davidson, E.H. Poe.

Diskin, P. "Poe, Le Fanu, and the sealed room mystery".

Dorset, G. An aristocrat of intellect.

Falk, D.V. "Poe and the powers of animal magnetism".

Fisher, B.F. "Poe in the seventies".

Goncourt, E.L.A. de   Pages from the Goncourt Journal.

Hoffman, D. Poe Poe Poe Poe Poe Poe Poe.

Just, K.G. "Edgar Allan Poe und die Folgen".

Kennedy, J.G. "Limits of reason".

Lemonnier, L. Edgar Poe et les conteurs français.

See also 'A TALE OF THE RAGGED MOUNTAINS' (story).

See also DUPIN, CHEVALIER AUGUSTE (char.)

See also ROGERS, MARY

See also 'The MURDERS IN THE RUE MORGUE' (story).

See also 'The TELL-TALE HEART' (story).

POE - BIBLIOGRAPHY

Hyneman, E.F.   Edgar Allan Poe.

POE - CRITICISM - BIBLIOGRAPHY

Dameron, J.L.   Edgar Allan Poe.

POETRY

"A poetic investigation of detectives, mystery and murder".

POIROT, HERCULE (char.)

Keating, H.R.F.   "Hercule Poirot".

la Cour, T.   "Monsieur Hercule Poirot".

POLISH CRIME FICTION

Zegel, S.   "A l'est du nouveau dans le roman policier".

PONS, SOLAR (char.)

Boucher, A. (pseud.) "Introduction" (The reminiscences of Solar Pons).

Derleth, A.W.   A Praed Street dossier.

Parker, L.   "A word from Dr. Lyndon Parker".

Pattrick, R.   "A chronology of Solar Pons".

Queen, E.   "Introduction" (The memoirs of Solar Pons).

Smith, E.W.   "Introduction" (The return of Solar Pons).

Starrett, V.   "In re: Solar Pons".

PONS, SOLAR (char.) - BIBLIOGRAPHY

De Waal, R.B. "Solar Pons and Dr. Parker".

POST, MELVILLE DAVISSON (1871-1930)

Norton, C.A. <u>Melville Davisson Post</u>.

Overton, G.M. "The act of Melville Davisson Post".

Wood, W. "Melville Davisson Post".

The <u>POSTMAN ALWAYS RINGS TWICE</u> (novel)

Madden, D.T. "Cain's 'The postman always rings twice' and Camus' 'L'Étranger'".

Wells, W. "The Postman and the Marathon".

POWELL, WILLIAM

Jacobs, J. "William Powell".

PRESTON-MUDDOCK, JOYCE EMMERSON (1843-1934)

Preston-Muddock, J.E. <u>Pages from an adventurous life</u>.

PSEUDONYMS

Gibbin, L.S. <u>Who's whodunit</u>.

Nevins, F.M. "Name games".

PSYCHOANALYSIS

See PSYCHOLOGY

PSYCHOLOGY

Bellak, L. "Psychology of detective stories".

Bergler, E. "Mystery fans and the problem of potential murders".

Buxbaum, E. "The role of detective stories in a child analysis".

Pederson-Krag, G. "Detective stories and the primal scene".

Rycroft, C. "A detective story".

PULPS

Beaumont, C. "The bloody pulps".

The fantastic pulps.

Goodstone, T. The pulps.

Goulart, R. Cheap thrills.

Goulart, R. The hardboiled dicks.

Gruber, F. The pulp jungle.

Jones, R.K. The shudder pulps.

Weinberg, R. The hero pulp index.

See also The SHADOW MAGAZINE.

QUEEN, ELLERY (pseud.)

Boucher, A. (pseud.) Ellery Queen.

Christopher, J.R. "The mystery of social reaction".

Connor, E. "The four Ellery Queens".

Dannay, F. The golden summer.

Nevins, F.M. Royal bloodline.

Nevins, F.M. "The Drury Lane quartet".

A silver anniversary tribute to Ellery Queen...

Texas University. Humanities Research Center. An exhibition
on the occasion of the opening of the Ellery Queen collection.

See also AND ON THE EIGHTH DAY (novel).

QUILLER (char.)

Hall, A. "Quiller".

RADIO

Crossen, K. "There's murder in the air".

Fett, M.   "Crime on the radio".

Harmon, J.   The great radio heroes.

RAFFLES (char.)

Depken, F.   Sherlock Holmes, Raffles, and Ihre Vorbilder.

RAMPO, EDOGAWA (pseud.)

Harris, J.B.   "Translator's preface".

RATHBONE, BASIL

Druxman, M.B.   Basil Rathbone.

READE, CHARLES (1814-1884)

Phillips, W.C.   Dickens, Reade, and Collins.

READE, CHARLES - BIBLIOGRAPHY

Parrish, M.L.   Wilkie Collins and Charles Reade.

'The RED-HEADED LEAGUE' (story)

Roberts, D.M.   "'The red-headed League' and 'The Rue Morgue'".

The RED HOUSE MYSTERY (novel)

Barzun, J.M.   A book of prefaces.

REED, ISHMAEL

Carter, S.R.   "Ishmael Reed's neo-hoodoo detection".

RELIGIOUS DETECTIVES

Boucher, A. (pseud.)   "Introduction" (Ten adventures of Father Brown).

RESNAIS, ALAN

Lacassin, F.   "Alan Resnais and the quest for Harry Dickson".

RETIRED DETECTIVES

Bedell, J.F. Positive images of aging and active retirement in detective fiction.

REVIEWS-PAPERBACKS

Breen, J.L. The girl in the pictorial wrapper.

RHODE, JOHNE (pseud.)

See STREET, CECIL JOHN CHARLES

The RIDDLE OF THE SANDS (novel)

Cockburn, C. "'The riddle of the sands'".

Donaldson, N. "Introduction" (The riddle of the sands).

Household, G. "Introduction" (The riddle of the sands).

'THE RING AND THE BOOK' (poem)

Altick, R.D. Browning's Roman murder story.

Cortona Codex. Curious annals.

Treves, Sir. F. The country of 'The Ring and the Book'.

RINEHART, MARY ROBERTS (1876-1958)

Broberg, J. "Reverens for Rinehart".

Rinehart, M.R. My story.

ROGERS, MARY CECILIA

Crouse, R. "The murder of Mary Cecilia Rogers".

Wimsatt, W.K. "Poe and the mystery of Mary Rogers".

Wimsatt, W.K. "Mary Rogers, John Anderson, and others".

See also ROGÊT, MARIE

ROGÊT, MARIE (char.)

Benton, R.P. "The mystery of Marie Rogêt".

Crouse, R. "The murder of Mary Cecilia Rogers".

Walsh, J.E. Poe the detective.

ROHLFS, Mrs CHARLES

See GREEN, ANNA KATHARINE

ROHMER, SAX (1886-1959)

Briney, R.E. "Sax Rohmer".

Frayling, C. "Sax Rohmer and the devil doctor".

Van Ash, C. Master of villainy.

ROMAN À CLEF

Sandoe, J. "Criminal clef".

ROUGIER, Mrs. G.R.

See HEYER, GEORGETTE

RUSSIAN CRIME FICTION

Zegel, S. "A l'est du nouveau dans le roman policier".

SADLER, MARK

Nevins, F.M. "Private eye in an evil time".

'SAPPER' (pseud.)

Usborne, R. Clubland heroes.

See also DRUMMOND, HUGH (char.)

SAYERS, DOROTHY LEIGH (1893-1957)

As her whimsey took her.

Dale, A.S. Maker and craftsman.

Gregory, E.R. "Wilkie Collins and Dorothy L. Sayers".

Hannay, M.P. "Harriet's influence on the characterization of Lord Peter Wimsey".

Harrison, B.G. "Dorothy L. Sayers and the tidy art of detective fiction".

Heilbrun, C.G. "Sayers, Lord Peter, and God".

Hitchman, J. Such a strange lady.

Hone, R.E. Dorothy L. Sayers.

James, P.D. "Dorothy L. Sayers".

Leavis, Q.D. "The case of Miss Dorothy Sayers".

Morand, P. "Preface" (Lord Peter devant le cadavre).

Panek, L.L. Wattheau's shepherds.

Reaves, R.B. "Crime and punishment in the detective fiction of Dorothy L. Sayers".

Rickmann, H.P. "From detection to theology".

Sandoe, J. "Introduction" (Lord Peter).

Stock, R.D. (jnt. auth.) "The agents of evil and justice in the novels of Dorothy L. Sayers".

See also GAUDY NIGHT (novel).

See also STRONG POISON (novel).

See also The DOCUMENTS IN THE CASE (novel).

See also The NINE TAILORS (novel).

See also WIMSEY, Lord PETER (char.)

SAYERS, DOROTHY LEIGH - BIBLIORAPHY

Harman, R.B. An annotated guide to the works of Dorothy L. Sayers.

SCANDINAVIAN CRIME FICTION

la Cour, T. The Scandinavian crime-detection story.

Colbron, G.I. "Detective story in Germany and Scandinavia".

SCHILLER, JOHANN CHRISTOPH FRIEDRICH von (1759-1805)

Haslinger, A. "Friedrick Schiller und die Kriminalliteratur".

SCHMIDT, Inspector (char.)

Bagby, G. "Inspector Schmidt".

SCIENCE FICTION

Briney, R.E. "Death rays, demons, and worms unknown to science".

McSherry, F.D. "Under two flags".

Moskowitz, S. "The sleuth in sci-fi.".

See also ASIMOV, ISAAC.

See also MURDER IN MILLENIUM VI (novel).

SCOTLAND YARD

Wood, J.P. "Scotland Yard in fiction".

The SECRET AGENT (novel)

Fleishman, A. "The symbolic world of 'The secret agent'".

Gose, E.B. "'Cruel devourer of the world's light'".

Guérard, A.J. "Aversion of anarchy".

Gurko, L. "'The secret agent'".

Hagan, J. "The design of Conrad's 'The secret agent'".

Leavis, F.R. "'The secret agent'".

Mann, T. "Joseph Conrad's 'The secret agent'".

Miller, J.H. "'The secret agent'".

Race, H. Joseph Conrad: 'The secret agent'".

Sherry, N. "The Greenarch bomb outrage and 'The secret agent'".

Spector, R.D. "Irony as theme".

Walpole, Sir H.S. "'The secret agent'".

Watt, I.P. Conrad: 'The secret agent'.

Watt, I.P. "The political and social background of 'The secret agent'".

The SECRET OF HIGH ELDERSHAM (novel)

Barzun, J.M. A book of prefaces.

SECRET SERVICE

See SPIES

SENSATIONAL NOVEL

Edwards, P.D. Some mid-Victorian thrillers.

SERIALS

Lahue, K.C. Bound and gagged.

SERIES CHARACTERS

Hubin, A.J. "Patterns in mystery fiction".

SEX

Bullough, V.L. "Deviant sex and the detective story".

Grotjahn, M. "Sex and the mystery story".

The SHADOW (char.)

Gibson, W.B. "My years with The Shadow".

Grant, M. "The Shadow".

The SHADOW MAGAZINE

Murray, W. The 'Duende' history of 'The Shadow Magazine".

The SHADOWY THIRD (novel)

Barzun, J.M. A book of prefaces.

SHAKESPEARE, WILLIAM (1564-1616)

Goll, A. Criminal types in Shakespeare.

SHAW, JOSEPH THOMPSON (1874-   )

Sturak, T. "Horace McCoy, Captain Shaw and the 'Black Mask'".

SHAW, PAUL (char.)

Nevins, F.M. "Private eye in an evil time".

SHAYNE, MICHAEL (char.)

Halliday, B. "Michael Shayne".

SHEARING, JOSEPH (pseud.)

See LONG, GABRIELLE MARGARET VERE CAMPBELL

SHIEL, MATTHEW PHIPPS (1865-1947)

Morse, A.R. Works of M.P. Shiel.

Shiel, M.P. "About myself".

Shiel, M.P. Science, life and literature.

SHILLING SHOCKERS

See PENNY DREADFULS

SHORT STORIES

Ellin, S. "The crime short story".

Queen, E. Queen's quorum.

Strong, L.A.G. "The crime short story".

SHORT STORIES - BIBLIOGRAPHY

Mundell, E.H. A checklist of detective short stories.

Mundell, E.H. The detective short story.

Queen, E. The detective short story.

Whiteley, J.S. "Simenon".

See also MAIGRET, JULES (char.)

SIMENON - BIBLIOGRAPHY

Menguy, C. Bibliographie des éditions originales de
Georges Simenon...

Young, T. Georges Simenon.

The SINGING BONE (novel)

Barzun, J.M. A book of prefaces.

SLANG

See THIEVES' CANT

SMALLBONE DECEASED (novel)

Barzun, J.M. A book of prefaces.

SMITH, ERNEST BRAMAH (1869?-1942)

See BRAMAH, ERNEST (pseud.)

SNOW, Sir CHARLES PERCY (1905-   )

See DEATH UNDER SAIL (novel)

SOPHOCLES (495-406 B.C.)

Achard, M. Sophocle et Archimède.

SOVIET CRIME FICTION

See RUSSIAN CRIME FICTION

SOUTH AFRICAN CRIME FICTION

Miller, A. Afrikaanse speurverhole uitgegee tot die ende
van 1950.

SOUTH AFRICAN CRIME FICTION - BIBLIOGRAPHY

Friedland, S. South African detective stories in English and Afrikaans from 1951-1971.

SOUTH AMERICAN CRIME FICTION

Yates, D.A. "Introduction" (Latin Blood).

SPADE, SAM (char.)

Queen, E. "Meet Sam Spade".

Wolfe, P. "Sam Spade, lover".

SPIES

Ambler, E. "Introduction" (To catch a spy)".

Barzun, J.M. "Meditations on the literature of spying".

Becker, J.P. Der englische Spionageroman.

Donaldson, N. "Introduction" (The riddle of the sands).

Durgnat, R. "Spies and ideologies".

Gilbert, M.F. "The spy in fact and fiction".

Greene, G. The spy's bedside book.

Hall, A. "Quiller".

McCormick, D. Who's who in spy fiction.

Maugham, W.S. "Preface" (Ashenden).

Merry, B. Anatomy of the spy thriller.

Pavish, J.R. The great spy pictures.

Penzler, O.M. The private lives of private eyes.

Rockwell, J. "Normative attitudes of spies in fiction".

Skene Melvin, L.D.H. St C. "The secret eye".

Smith, M.J. Cloak-and-dagger bibliography.

Starrett, V. "Introduction" (World's great spy stories).

Welcome, J. "Introduction" (Best secret service stories 2).

SPILLANE, MICHEY

Banks, R.J.   "Anti-professionalism in the works of Mickey Spillane".

Banks, R.J.   "Spillane's anti-establishmentarian heroes".

La Fargo, C.   "Mickey Spillane and his bloody Hammer".

Rolo, C.J.   "Simenon and Spillane".

Weibel, K.   "Mickey Spillane as a fifties phenomenon".

See also 'KISS ME DEADLY' (film)

S.S. VAN DINE

See WRIGHT, WILLARD HUNTINGTON

STARRETT, VINCENT

Boucher, A.   Sincerely, Tony/Faithfully, Vincent.

Murphy, M.   Vincent Starrett.

STEED, JOHN (char.)

Heald, T.   John Steed.

STEELE, ROCKY (char.)

Turner, D.T.   "The Rocky Steele novels of John B. West".

STEIN, GERTRUDE (1874-1946)

Stewart, L.D.   "Gertrude Stein and the vital dead".

STEWART, JOHN INNES MACKINTOSH (1906-   )

See INNES, MICHAEL (pseud.)

STOUT, REX TODHUNTER (1886-1975)

Barzun, J.M.   A birthday tribute to Rex Stout.

Bourne, M.   "An informal interview with Rex Stout".

Carnillon, J.   The androgynous orchid.

Corsage

De Voto, B.   "Alias Nero Wolfe".

Gerhardt, M.I.   "Homicide West".

McAleer, J.   Rex Stout.

Tuska, J.   "Rex Stout and the detective story".

See also WOLFE, NERO (char.)

See also TOO MANY COOKS (novel).

'The STRAND MAGAZINE'

Pound, R.   The Strand Magazine.

Whitt, J.F.   'The Strand Magazine'.

STREET & SMITH, publishers

Reynolds, Q.J.   The fiction factory.

STREET, CECIL JOHN CHARLES (1884-1964)

See The SECRET OF HIGH ELDERSHAM (novel).

STRIBLING, THOMAS SIGISMUND (1881-1965)

Eckley, W.   T. S. Stribling.

STRONG POISON (novel)

Barzun, J.M.   A book of prefaces.

SUSPECTS ALL (novel)

See The SHADOWY THIRD.

SWEDISH CRIME FICTION

Elgström, J.   Svensk mordbok.

Ord om mord.

See also SCANDINAVIAN CRIME FICTION.

SWEDISH CRIME FICTION - BIBLIOGRAPHY

Hedman, I. <u>Svensk deckare - & thrillerbibliografi</u>.

Tullberg, S. <u>O och A</u>.

!A TALE OF THE RAGGED MOUNTAINS' (story)

Thompson, F.R. "Is Poe's 'A tale of the Ragged Mountains' a hoax?".

TARO, HIRAI (1894-   )

See RAMPO, EDOGAWA (pseud.)

TECHNIQUE

Burack, A.S. (ed.) <u>Writing detective and mystery fiction</u>.

Champigny, R. <u>What will have happened</u>.

Chesterton, G.K. "How to write a detective story".

Corbett, J. "Art of writing thrillers".

Highsmith, P. <u>Plotting and writing suspense fiction</u>.

Hill, W.A. <u>Index book for use with the plot genie</u>.

Hogarth, B. <u>Writing thrillers for profit</u>.

Morland, N. <u>How to write detective novels</u>.

<u>Murder manual</u>.

Mystery Writers of America. <u>The mystery writer's handbook</u>.

Nixon, J.L. <u>Writing mysteries for young people</u>.

Rodell, M.F. <u>Mystery fiction</u>.

Wells, C. <u>The technique of the mystery story</u>.

White, T.W. "The detective story".

Wright, W.H. "Twenty rules for writing detective stories".

<u>Writing suspense and mystery fiction</u>.

TELEVISION

Alexander, D. "Is television necessary".

Daley, R. "Police report on the TV cop shows".

Larka, R. Television's private eye.

'The TELL-TALE HEART' (story)

Robinson, E.A. "Poe's 'The tell-tale heart'".

TEXTS - BIBLIOGRAPHY

Arno Press. Literature of mystery and detection.

Barnes, M.P. Best detective fiction.

Barzun, J.M. (jnt. comp.) A catalogue of crime.

Block, A. The English novel, 1740-1850.

Bragin, C. Bibliography of dime novels.

Chandler, F.W. The literature of roguery.

Detective fiction (catalogue).

Detective fiction; a century of crime.

Detective fiction; mysteries and crime.

Gardner, F.M. Sequels.

Glover, D. Victorian detective fiction.

Haycraft, H. "From Poe to Hammett".

Hedman, I. Svensk deckare - & thrillerbibliografi.

Herman, L. Corpus delecti of mystery fiction.

Hubin, A.J. The bibliography of crime fiction.

Indianapolis, Ind. Public Library. Some less known detective stories.

Indiana. University. Lilly Library. The first hundred years of detective fiction.

Maggs Bros. A gallery of rogues.

National Book League. Murder in Albemarle Street.

National Book League. Paging crime.

Scribner, publishers. Detective fiction.

Shibuk, C. A preliminary checklist of the detective novel and its variants.

Stevenson, W.B. Detective fiction.

Sunday Times. The hundred best crime stories.

Wright, L.H. American fiction.

THACKERAY, WILLIAM MAKEPEACE (1811-1863)

Hollingsworth, K. The Newgate novel.

THEATRE

Pond, J.B. Eccentricities of genius.

Vickers, R. "Crime on the stage".

See also DRAMA

THEY SHOOT HORSES, DON'T THEY? (novel)

Wells, W. "The Postman and the Marathon".

THIEVES' CANT

Goldin, H.E. A dictionary of American underworld lingo.

The THIN MAN (film)

Crowther, B. "...film history of 'The Thin Man'...".

The THIN MAN (novel)

Quennell, P. "'The Thin man'".

'The THIRTY-NINE STEPS' (film)

Camp, J. "John Buchan and Alfred Hitchcock".

The UNKNOWN WEAPON (novel)

Bleiler, E.F.   "Introduction" (Three Victorian detective novels).

UPFIELD, ARTHUR (1888-1964)

Hawke, J.   Follow my dust.

Sarjeant, W.A.S.   "The great Australian detective".

Trengove, A.   "In the tracks of Detective-Inspector "Bony".

See also The BONE IS POINTED (novel).

VAN DER VALK, PEET (char.)

Freeling, N.   "Inspector Van der Valk".

VAN DINE, S.S.

See WRIGHT, WILLARD HUNTINGTON

VAN DUSEN, S.F.X. (char.)

Bleiler, E.F.   "Introduction" (Best "Thinking Machine" detective stories).

VAN GULIK, ROBERT HANS (1910-1967)

Lach, D.F.   "Introduction" (The Chinese Bell murders).

"Necrology of R. H. Van Gulik".

VAN GULIK. ROBERT HANS - BIBLIOGRAPHY

Bibliography of Dr. R. H. van Gulik.

VANCE, PHILO (char.)

Connor, E.   "The nine Philo Vances".

Field, L.M.   "Philo Vance & Co.".

Maltin, L.   "Philo Vance at the movies".

VICKERS, ROY

See The DEPARTMENT OF DEAD ENDS (short stories)

VICTORIAN ERA

See NINETEENTH-CENTURY (GREAT BRITAIN)

VIDOCQ, FRANCOIS EUGENE (1775-1857)

Vidocq, F.E. Mémoires.

VILLAINS

Cameron, I.A. (jnt. auth.)

The heavies.

Everson, W.K. The bad guys.

Pate, J. The great villains.

WADE, HENRY (pseud.)

See AUBREY-FLETCHER, Sir HENRY LANCELOT

WALLACE, RICHARD HORATIO EDGAR (1875-1932)

Lane, M. Edgar Wallace.

Wallace, V.K. Edgar Wallace.

Wallace, P. "A man and his books".

WALLACE, EDGAR - BIBLIOGRAPHY

Lofts, W.O.G. The British bibliography of Edgar Wallace.

WARD, ARTHUR SARSFIELD

See ROHMER, SAX

WAS IT MURDER (novel)

Barzun, J.M. A book of prefaces.

WAUGH, EVELYN

Borrello, A. "Evelyn Waugh and Erle Stanley Gardner".

WEBSTER, HENRY KITCHELL (1875-1932)

See WHO IS THE NEXT (novel).

WEST, JOHN B.

See STEELE, ROCKY (char.)

WESTMACOTT, MARY (pseud.)

See CHRISTIE, Dame AGATHA MARY CLARISSA MILLER

WHEATLEY, DENNIS

Hedman, I. Fyra decennier med Dennis Wheatley.

Wheatley, D. The time has come.

WHEN THE WIND BLOWS (novel)

Barzun, J.M. A book of prefaces.

WHO DONE IT (encyclopaedia)

Barzun, J.M. "The book, the bibliographer, and the absence of mind".

WHO IS THE NEXT (novel)

Barzun, J.M. A book of prefaces.

WILKINSON, ELLEN C. (? - 1947)

See The DIVISION BELL MYSTERY (novel).

WILLIAMS, CALEB (char.)

Stone, E. "Caleb Williams and Martin Faber".

WILLIAMS, RACE (char.)

Crider, A.B. "Race Williams".

WIMSEY, Lord Peter (char.)

Hannay, M.P. "Harriet's influence on the characterization of Lord Peter Wimsey".

Reynolds, B. "The origin of Lord Peter Wimsey".

Scott-Giles, C.W. The Wimsey family.

WINTERTON, PAUL (1908-   )

See GARVE, ANDREW (pseud.)

WITTING, CLIFFORD (1907-   )

See MEASURE FOR MURDER (novel)

WOLFE, NERO (char.)

Baring-Gould, W.S. Nero Wolfe of West Thirty-fifth Street.

Goodwin, A. "Why Nero Wolfe likes orchids".

Muhlenbock, K. "Tung mans liv".

Rauber, D.F. "Sherlock Holmes and Nero Wolfe".

WOLFE, THOMAS

Gossett, L.Y. "The climate of violence".

The WOMAN IN WHITE (novel)

Knoepflmacher, U.C. "The counterworld of Victorian fiction and 'The woman in white'".

WOMEN

Cameron, I.A. (jnt. auth.) Broads.

Chester, P. "The amazon legacy".

Hoffman, N.Y. "Mistresses of malpleasure".

Horn, M. Women in the comics.

APPENDIX: MATERIALS IN OTHER LANGUAGES

AFRIKAANS

Miller, A. Afrikaanse speurverhale uitgegee tot die einde van 1950.

Nienaber, P.J. Bronnegids by die studie van die Afrikaanse taal en letterkunde.

CZECHOSLOVAKIAN

Cigánek, J. Umění detektivky.

Krkošková, M. Magazín Labyrintu.

Skvorecký, J. Nápady čtenáře detektivek.

DANISH

Dansk og udenlandsk kriminallitteratur.

Hansen, R. Kriminal romaner.

Jensen, V. Stene for brød.

la Cour, T. "Damer pä den litteraere forbryderbane".

la Cour, T. "Dr. Jekyll og Mr Brodie".

la Cour, T. Den grønne o i fantasiens...

la Cour, T. "Jules Maigret's privat liv".

la Cour, T. Kaleidoskop.

la Cour, T. "Monsieur Hercule Poirot".

la Cour, T. "Mord i Biblioteket".

la Cour, T. Mord mem moral.

la Cour, T. Mordbogen.

la Cour, T. "Mysteriet om en Hansom Cab".

la Cour, T. "Skandinaviske Kriminalfortaellinger".

la Cour, T. Studier i rødt.

Larsen, A.P. Sagen mod praesten i Vejlby.

Lauritzen, H. Mesterdetektiver under Lup.

Mord Som Hobby.

Pouplier, E. Ti kriminelle minutter.

Queen, E. Med venlig hilsen fra Ellery Queen.

ESTONIAN
Ennok, E. "'Myshelovka'".

FRENCH

Achard, M. Sophocle et Archimède.

Alter, J. "L'Enquête policière dans le nouveau roman".

d'Astier de la Vigerie, E. "Preface" (Zelty pes;...)

Bergier, J. "Redécouverte du roman d'aventure anglais".

Boileau, P. Quelque chose de changé dans le roman policier".

Borde, R. (jnt. auth.) Panorama du film noir américain.

Boverie, D. "Georges Simenon".

Caillois, R. Le roman policier.

Campinchi, C. "Le crime et le mystère d'Edgar Poe à Geo. London".

Catogan, V. Le secret des rois de France.

Cauliez, A.J. Le film criminel.

Chassaing. De Zadig au Riffifi.

Chastaing, M. "Le roman policier et vérité".

Courtine, R.J. Le cahier de recettes de Madame Maigret.

Courtine, R.J. "Simenon ou l'appétit de Maigret".

Daniel-Rops. "Les romans policiers de M. Georges Simenon".

de Traz, G.A.E. Histoire et technique du roman-policier.

Debray-Ritzen, P. "Mon maître Simenon".

Deniker, Prof. "Georges Simenon".

Dubourg, M. "Géographie de Simenon".

Duperray, J. "Au nom du Père".

Dupuy, J. Le roman policier.

Eco, U. "James Bond".

Elsen, C. "Faulkner et le roman noire".

Fallois, B. de Simenon.

Fouyé, Y. Guy de Maupassant et les criminels.

Frank, N. "Hypothèse à propos de Maigret".

Freustié, J. "Une petite tente au milieu du jardin".

Galtier-Boissiere, J. "Origines du roman policier".

Hankiss, J. "Littérature 'populaire' et roman-policier".

Henry, G. Commissaire Maigret.

Hoveyda, F. Histoire du roman policier.

Hoveyda, F. Petite histoire du roman policier.

Janvier, L. Une parole exigeante.

Juin, H. "Un roman ininterrompu".

Kanters, R. "Sur la vieillesse et sur la mort".

Lacassin, F. (jnt. comp.) Simenon.

Lacassin, F. "Simenon et la fugue initiatique".

Lacombe, A. Le roman noir américain.

Lemennier, L. Edgar Poe et les conteurs français.

Locard, E. La criminalistique.

Locard, E. Policiers de roman et de laboratoire.

Locard, E. Policiers de roman et policiers de laboratoire.

Magny, C.E. L'âge du roman américain.

Mambrino, J. "Le mot du coffre".

Marcel, G. "Roman policiers".

Marion, D. La méthode intellectuelle d'Edgar Poe.

Maurois, A. Magiciens et logiciens.

Manguy, C. Bibliographie des éditions originales de George Simenon.

Messac, R. Le 'detective novel' et l'influence de la pensée scientifique.

Messac, R. Influences françaises dans l'oeuvre d'Edgar Poe.

Messac, R. "Georges Simenon".

Miller, H. ("Quel dommage...").

Monod, S. Dickens romancier.

Morand, P. "Preface" (Lord Peter devant le cadavre).

Morand, P. "Reflexions sur le roman policier".

More, M. "Simenon et l'enfant de choeur".

Moremans, V. "Mon ami Simenon".

Musée de Arts Decoratifs. Band dessinée.

Narcejac, T. Le cas Simenon.

Narcejac, T. Esthétique du roman policier.

Narcejac, T. La fin d'un bluff.

Narcejac, T. Une machine à lire.

Narcejac, T. "Le point Omega".

Norden, P. Sir Arthur Conan Doyle.

Orwell, G. "Grandeur et décadence du roman policier Anglais".

Parinaud, A. Connaissance de Georges Simenon.

Paulhan, J. "Les anneaux de Bicetre".

Poupart, J.M. Les récréants.

"Quelques aspects d'une mythologie moderne".

Radine, S. Quelques aspects du roman policier psychologique.

Richter, A. Georges Simenon et l'homme desintegre.

Ritzen, Q. Simenon.

Roux, F. Balzac.

Savey-Casard, P. Le crime et la peine dans l'oeuvre de Victor Hugo.

Schraiber, E. "Georges Simenon et le littérature russe".

Sigaux, G. "Lire Simenon".

Simenon, G.J.C. Le Paris de Simenon.

Simenon, G.J.C. Pedigree.

Simenon, G.J.C. Quand j'etais vieux.

Stephane, R. Le dossier Simenon.

Sullerot, E. "Les hommes, les hommes...".

Thoorens, L. (Qui êtes-vous).

Truffaut, F. Le cinéma selon Hitchcock.

Vidocq, F.E. Mémoires.

Vigniel,D. Sherlock Holmes.

Zegel, S. "A l'est du nouveau dans le roman policier".

GERMAN

Alewyn, R. "Anatomie des detektivromans".

Alewyn, R. "Die Anfänge des Detektivromans".

Becker, J.-P. Der englische Spionageroman.

Becker, J.-P. Sherlock Holmes & Co.

Bien, G. "Abenteur und verborgene Wahrheit".

Bien, G. "Detektivroman un Unterricht".

Bloch, E. "Philosophische Ansicht des Detektivromans".

Brecht, B. "Über die Popularitat des Kriminalromans".

Buchloh, P.G. (jnt. auth.) Der Detektivroman.

Conrad, H. Die literarische Angst.

Dahncke, W. Kriminalroman und Wirklichkeit.

Daiber, H. "Nachahmung der Vorsehung".

Depken, F. Sherlock Holmes, Raffles, und Ihre Vorbilder.

Der Detektiverzählung auf der Spur.

Dworak, A. Der Kriminalroman der D.D.R.

Egloff, G. Detektivroman und englisches Bürgertum.

Epstein, H. Der Detektivroman der Unterschicht.

Fischer, P. "Neue Häuser in der Rue Morgue".

Frenzel, E. "Kriminalgeschichte".

Freund, W. Die deutsche Kriminalnovelle von Schiller bis Hauptmann.

Freund, W. "Der Mörder des Juden Aaron".

Gerber, R. "Namen als Symbol".

Gerteis, W. Detektive.

Greiner-Mai, H. Die deutsche Kriminalerzählung von Schiller bis zur Gegenwart.

Haslinger, A. "Friederich Schiller und die Kriminalliteratur".

Hasubek, P. Die Detektivgeschichte für junge Leser.

Heissenbuttel, H. "Spielregein des Kriminalromans".

Just, K.G. "Edgar Allan Poe und die Folgen".

Kaemmel, E. "Literatur untern Tisch".

Kanzog, K. "E.T.A. Hoffmans Erzählung 'Das Fraulein von Scuderi als Kriminalgeschichte".

Katholische Akademie Stuttgart-Hohenheim. Für und wider den Krimi.

Knobel, B. Krimifibel.

Knopf, J. Friederich Dürrenmatt.

Kracauer, S. Schriften.

Langenbrucher, E. "Geistes' Blitze aus Kriminal-Romanen".

Lennig, W. Edgar Allan Poe in Selbstzeugnissen und Bilddokumenten.

Lichtenstein, A. Der Kriminalroman.

Ludwig, H-W. Der Ich-Erzähler im englisch-amerikanischen Detektiv- und Kriminalroman.

Mager, H. Krimi und crimen.

Marsch, E. Die Kriminalerzählung.

Naumann, D. "Der Kriminalroman".

Naumann, D. "Kriminalroman und Dichtung".

Naumann, D. "Zur Typologie des Kriminalromans".

Pfeiffer, H. Die Mumie un Glassarg.

Post, K.D. "Kriminalgeschichte als Heilsgeschichte".

Reclams Kriminalromanführer.

Reinert, C. Detektivliteratur bei Sophokles, Schiller and Kleist.

Reinert, C. Das Unheimliche und die Detektivliteratur.

Rickmann, H.P. "Die metaphysische Bedeutung des Detektivromans".

Schimmelpfenning, A. Beiträge zur Geschichte des Kriminalromans.

Schmidt-Henkel, G. "Kriminalroman und Trivialliteratur".

Schönhaar, R. Novelle und Kriminalschema.

Schulz-Buschaus, U. Formen und Ideologien des Kriminalromans.

Sehlbach, H. Untersuchungen über die Romankunst von Wilkie Collins.

Shrapnel, N. "Die Literatur der Gewalttatigkeit und der Verfolgung".

Skreb, Z. "Die neue Gattung".

Smuda, M. "Variation und Innovation".

Suerbaum, U.   "Der gefesselte Detektivromans".

Thalmann, M.   "E.T.A. Hoffmans 'Fraulein von Scuderi'".

Triviallitteratur.

Tschimmel, I.   Kriminalroman und Gesellschaftsdarstellung.

Van Selms, A.   "Aristotle en die speurverhaal".

Vogt, J.   Der Kriminalroman.

Wölcken, F.   Der literarische Mord.

Wulff, A.   "Beiträgen".

Würtenberger, T.   Die deutsche Kriminalerzählung.

Žmegač, V.   "Aspekte des Detektivromans".

Žmegač, V.   Der wohltemperierte Mord.

Zulliger, H.   "Der Abenteurer-Schundroman".

ITALIAN

Buono, O.D.   Il caso Bond.

Del Monte, A.   Breve storia del romanzo poliziesco.

Ercoli, E.   "Agatha Christie".

Ferri, E.   I delinquenti nell'arte.

Pensa, C.M.   "Sua maestà Agatha Christie".

JAPANESE

Gonda, M.   Shukumei no bigaku.

Ikushima, J.   Hangyaku no kokoro o torimodose.

Kosakai, F.   Kindai hanzai kenkyu.

Kuki, S.   Tantei shosetsu hyakka.

Kusumoto, K.   Ninkyō eiga no sekai.

Nakajima, K.   Nihon suiri shōsetsu shi.

Nakauchi, M.   Amerika fūbutsushi.

Tsuzuki, M.   Shitai o buji ni kesu made.

Uekusa, J. Amefuri dakara misuterí de mo benkyōshiyō.

Yamamura, M. Suiri bundem sengo shi.

NETHERLANDISH

Droom en onthulling.

Visser, A. Kaïn sloeg Abel.

Visser, A. Onder de gordel.

NORWEGIAN

Dahl, W. Blå briller og løsskjegg i Kristiania.

Degn, P. Blodige fotspur.

Kvam, L.N. Om norsk kriminallitteratur.

POLISH

Helman, A. Filmy kryminalne.

PORTUGESE

Albuquerque, P. de M. e. Os maiores detetives de todos os tempos.

Cascudo, L. da C. Flor de romances trágicos.

Lemos Britto, J.G. de O crime e os criminosos na literatura brasileira.

Lins, A. No mundo do romance policial.

Paiva, S.C. de. O ganster no cinema.

ROMANIAN

Cristea, V. "Voluptatea teroarei".

Popescu, C. "Arta simplă a romanului polițist".

RUSSIAN

Shishkina, T. "(Foreword)". (Sbornik rasskazov).

SERBO CROAT

Lasić, S. Poetika kriminalističkog romana.

SPANISH

Díaz, C.E. La novela policíaca.

Gubern, R. La novela criminal.

Mira, J.J. Biografía de la novela policíaca.

Ortiz Vidales, S. Los bandidos en la literatura mexicana.

Portuondo, J.A. En torno a la novela detectivesca.

Quintano Ripollés, A. La criminología en la literatura universal.

Rodríguez Joulia Saint-Cyr, C. La novela de intriga.

Ves Losada, A.E. En torno al género policial.

Zamorano, M. Crimen y literatura.

SWEDISH

Alexandersson, J. Leslie Charteris och Helgonet.

Broberg, J. "Lew Archer och hans värld".

Broberg, J. Meningar om mord.

Broberg, J. Mord för ro skull.

Broberg, J. Mord i minne.

Broberg, J. Mordisk familjebok.

Broberg, J. "Reverens för Rinehart".

Elgström, J. Mord i biblioteket.

Elgström, J. Svensk mordbok.

Hedman, I. Fyra decennier med Dennis Wheatley.

Hedman, I. Svensk deckare - & thrillerbibliografi.

la Cour, T. Mord i Biblioteket.

Lundin, B. "Den gamle Mästaren".

Lundin, B.   Mordets enkla konst.

Lundin, B.   "Poeten och deckaren".

Lundin, B.   "Den skarpsinnige snobben".

Lundin, B.   Sparhundarna.

Muhlenbock, K.   "Tung mans liv".

Ord om mord.

Queen, E.   Med hälsningar.

Richert, J.G.   Detektiven i romanen och i verkligheten.

Tullberg, S.   O och A.

ABOUT THE COMPILERS

DAVID SKENE MELVIN is the supervisor of publications in the Historical Planning and Research Branch of the Ontario (Canada) Ministry of Culture and Recreation. Earlier books he has edited include *How to Find Out About Canada* and *Collected Archaeological Papers*. He lectures on the spy and the detective novel at the University of Toronto.

ANN SKENE MELVIN is a former reference librarian and independent researcher, now a bookseller specializing in the mystery field.